## ALSO IN THE *FOLGER GUIDE* SERIES

The Folger Guide to Teaching *Hamlet*

The Folger Guide to Teaching *Macbeth*

**(2025)**

The Folger Guide to Teaching *Othello*

The Folger Guide to Teaching *A Midsummer Night's Dream*

# THE FOLGER GUIDE TO TEACHING ROMEO AND JULIET

The Folger Guides to Teaching Shakespeare Series
— Volume 3 —

Peggy O'Brien, Ph.D., General Editor

Folger Shakespeare Library
WASHINGTON, DC

Simon & Schuster Paperbacks

NEW YORK   LONDON   TORONTO   SYDNEY   NEW DELHI

100 YEARS
SIMON &
SCHUSTER
PAPERBACKS

1230 Avenue of the Americas
New York, NY 10020

First Simon & Schuster trade paperback edition November 2024

SIMON & SCHUSTER and colophon are registered trademarks of Simon & Schuster LLC

For information about special discounts for bulk purchases, please contact Simon & Schuster Special Sales at 1-866-506-1949 or business@simonandschuster.com.

The Simon & Schuster Speakers Bureau can bring authors to your live event. For more information or to book an event, contact the Simon & Schuster Speakers Bureau at 1-866-248-3049 or visit our website at www.simonspeakers.com.

Manufactured in the United States of America

1   3   5   7   9   10   8   6   4   2

Library of Congress Cataloging-in-Publication Data is available upon request.

ISBN 978-1-9821-0568-6
ISBN 978-1-6680-1763-0 (ebook)

# THE FOLGER SHAKESPEARE LIBRARY

The Folger Shakespeare Library makes Shakespeare's stories and the world in which he lived accessible. Anchored by the world's largest Shakespeare collection, the Folger is a place where curiosity and creativity are embraced and conversation is always encouraged. Visitors to the Folger can choose how they want to experience the arts and humanities, from interactive exhibitions to captivating performances, and from pathbreaking research to transformative educational programming.

The Folger seeks to be a catalyst for:

**Discovery.** The Folger's collection is meant to be used, and it is made accessible in the Folger's Reading Room to anyone who is researching Shakespeare or the Early Modern world. The Folger collection has flourished since founders Henry and Emily Folger made their first rare book purchase in 1889, and today contains more than 300,000 objects. The Folger Institute facilitates scholarly and artistic collections-based research, providing research opportunities, lectures, conversations, and other programs to an international community of scholars.

**Curiosity.** The Folger designs learning opportunities for inquisitive minds at every stage of life, from tours to virtual and in-person workshops. Teachers working with the Folger are trained in the Folger Method, a way of teaching complex texts like Shakespeare that enables students to own and enjoy the process of close-reading, interrogating texts, discovering language with peers, and contributing to the ongoing human conversation about words and ideas.

**Participation.** The Folger evolves with each member and visitor interaction. Our exhibition halls, learning lab, gardens, theater, and historic spaces are open to be explored and to provide entry points for connecting with Shakespeare and the Folger's collection, as well as forming new pathways to experiencing and understanding the arts.

**Creativity.** The Folger invites everyone to tell their story and experience the stories of and inspired by Shakespeare. Folger Theatre, Music, and Poetry are programmed in conversation with Folger audiences, exploring our collective past, present, and future. Shakespeare's imagination resonates across centuries, and his works are a wellspring for the creativity that imbues the Folger's stage and all its programmatic offerings.

The Folger welcomes everyone—from communities throughout Washington, DC, to communities across the globe—to connect in their own way. Learn more at folger.edu.

All Shakespeare used in this book is taken from the Folger
Shakespeare editions of the text. Available in paperback and for free at
folger.edu/folgershakespeare.

# IMAGE CREDITS

Morocco: Abd el-Ouahed ben Messaoud ben Mohammed Anoun, Moorish Ambassador to Queen Elizabeth I (1600).
©RESEARCH AND CULTURAL COLLECTIONS, UNIVERSITY OF BIRMINGHAM.

Smith, John. The generall historie of Virginia, New-England, and the Summer Isles . . . (1631) map of Virginia after page 168.
CALL # STC 22790C.2. USED BY PERMISSION OF THE FOLGER SHAKESPEARE LIBRARY.

Hollar, Wenceslaus. Head of a Black woman with a lace kerchief hat (1645) no. 46, plate opposite page 88.
CALL # ART VOL. B35 NO.46. USED BY PERMISSION OF THE FOLGER SHAKESPEARE LIBRARY.

Hollar, Wenceslaus. Head of a Black woman in profile to left (1645).
CALL # ART 237212. USED BY PERMISSION OF THE FOLGER SHAKESPEARE LIBRARY.

Hollar, Wenceslaus. Head of a young Black boy in profile to right (17th century).
CALL # ART 236023. USED BY PERMISSION OF THE FOLGER SHAKESPEARE LIBRARY.

Ira Aldridge's first appearance at Covent Garden in the role of Othello—a play bill dated 1833 plus 2 small engraved portraits and an article in German, mounted together (early to mid-19th century).
CALL # ART FILE A365.5 NO.5. USED BY PERMISSION OF THE FOLGER SHAKESPEARE LIBRARY.

Romeo y Julieta. Traducción de Pablo Neruda.
PEHUÉN EDITORES, SANTIAGO DE CHILE, 1984.

Shakespeare, William. Romeo and Juliet: a tragedy . . . accurately printed from the text of Mr. Steevens's last edition.
PROMPT ROM. 31, P.16–17; 52–53. USED BY PERMISSION OF THE FSL.
LONDON: PUBLISHED BY E. HARDING, J. WRIGHT, G. SAEL, AND VERNOR AND HOOD, 1798.

Wright, John Massey. Drawings for or after engravings designed by J.M. Wright (late 18th century or 19th century).
CALL # ART BOX W951 NO.10 (SIZE S). USED BY PERMISSION OF THE FOLGER SHAKESPEARE LIBRARY.

*If you are a teacher,*
*you are doing the world's most important work.*
*This book is for you.*

# CONTENTS

# THE FOLGER GUIDE
# TO TEACHING
# *ROMEO AND JULIET*

# PART ONE

# Shakespeare for a Changing World

# Why Shakespeare?

## Michael Witmore

You have more in common with the person seated next to you on a bus, a sporting event, or a concert than you will ever have with William Shakespeare. The England he grew up in nearly 400 years ago had some of the features of our world today, but modern developments such as industry, mass communication, global networks, and democracy did not exist. His country was ruled by a monarch, and his days were divided into hours by church bells rather than a watch or a phone. The religion practiced around him was chosen by the state, as were the colors he could wear when he went out in public.

When Shakespeare thought of our planet, there were no satellites to show him a green and blue ball. The Northern European island where he grew up was, by our standards, racially homogeneous, although we do know that there were Africans, Asians, Native Americans, Muslims, Jews, and others living in London in the early 1600s—and that Shakespeare likely saw or knew about them. The very idea that people of different backgrounds could live in a democracy would probably have struck him as absurd. What could an English playwright living centuries ago possibly say about our changed and changing world? Would he understand the conflicts that dominate our politics, the "isms" that shape reception of his work? What would he make of debates about freedom, the fairness of our economies, or the fragility of our planet?

The conversation about Shakespeare over the last 250 years has created other obstacles and distance. Starting around that time, artists and promoters put Shakespeare on a pedestal so high that he became almost divine. One such promoter was an English actor named David Garrick, who erected a classical temple to Shakespeare in 1756 and filled it with "relics" from Shakespeare's life. Garrick praised Shakespeare as "the God of our idolatry," and in his temple included a throne-like chair made of wood from a tree that Shakespeare may have planted. Today, that chair sits in a nook at the Folger Shakespeare Library. The chair's existence reminds us that the impulse to put Shakespeare in a temple has been at times overwhelming. But temples can exclude as well as elevate, which is why the Folger Shakespeare Library—itself a monument to Shakespeare built in 1932—needs to celebrate a writer whose audience is contemporary, diverse, and growing.

While Shakespeare was and is truly an amazing writer, the "worship" of his talent becomes problematic as soon as it is expected. If Shakespeare's stories and poetry continue to be enjoyed and passed along, it should be because we see their value, not because we have been told that they are great. Today, if someone tells you that Shake-

3

speare's appeal is "universal," you might take away the idea that his works represent the experience of everyone, or that someone can only be fully human if they appreciate and enjoy his work. Can that possibly be true? How can one appreciate or enjoy the things in his work that are offensive and degrading—for example, the racism and sexism that come so easily to several of his characters? What about such plays as *The Merchant of Venice*, *Othello*, or *The Taming of the Shrew*, where the outcomes suggest that certain kinds of characters—a Jew, an African, a woman—deserve to suffer?

When we talk about Shakespeare, we have to confront these facts and appreciate the blind spots in his plays, blind spots that are still real and reach beyond his specific culture. In acknowledging such facts, we are actually in a better position to appreciate Shakespeare's incredible talent as a writer and creator of stories. Yes, he wrote from a dated perspective of a Northern European man who was a frequent flatterer of kings and queens. Within those limits, he is nevertheless able to dazzle with his poetry and offer insights into human motivations. We are not *required* to appreciate the language or dramatic arcs of his characters, but we can appreciate both with the help of talented teachers or moving performances. Memorable phrases such as Hamlet's "To be or not to be" are worth understanding because they capture a situation perfectly—the moment when someone asks, "Why go on?" By pausing on this question, we learn something at a distance, without having to suffer through everything that prompts Hamlet to say these famous words.

Had Shakespeare's plays not been published and reanimated in performance over several centuries, these stories would no longer be remembered. Yet the tales of Lady Macbeth or Richard III still populate the stories we tell today. They survive in the phrases that such characters use and the archetypal situations in which these characters appear—"out, out damned spot" or "my kingdom for a horse?" Marvel characters and professional politicians regularly channel Shakespeare. When a supervillain turns to the camera to brag about their evil deeds, we are hearing echoes of King Richard III. When the media criticizes a leader for being power-hungry, some version of Lady Macbeth is often implied, especially if that leader is a woman.

While they are from another time, Shakespeare's characters and situations remain exciting because they view life from a perspective that is both familiar and distant. The better able we are to recognize the experiences described in Shakespeare's plays in our lives, the broader our vocabulary becomes for understanding ourselves. We see and hear more when the plays dramatize important questions, such as:

- What does a child owe a parent and what does a parent owe their child? Why must children sometimes teach their parents to grow up? *King Lear*, *Hamlet*, and *Henry IV, Part 1* all ask some version of these questions.

- Are we born ready to love or is the capacity to love another something that is learned? Shakespeare's comedies—*Twelfth Night*, *As You Like It*, *Much Ado About Nothing*—are filled with characters whose entire stories are about learning to accept and give love.

- How does one deal with an awful memory or the knowledge of a brutal crime? Hamlet is burdened with both, just as many are today who are haunted by trauma.

These questions get at situations that anyone might experience at some point in their life. If you are a teenager whose mad crush is turning into love, you will have to go out on that balcony, just like Juliet. Will you be confident or afraid? If a "friend" who knows you well is feeding you lies, you will be challenged to resist them—as Othello is when faced with Iago. Will you be able to think for yourself? These questions come up in any life, and the answers are not predetermined. A goal in any humanities classroom is to improve the questions we ask ourselves by engaging our specific experiences, something very different from looking for "timeless truths" in the past.

Do not believe that you must master Shakespeare in order to appreciate literature, language, or the human condition. Do, however, be confident that the time you and your students spend with these plays will result in insight, new skills, and pleasure. Shakespeare was a deeply creative person in a deeply polarized world, one where religious and economic conflicts regularly led to violence. He used that creativity to illustrate the many ways human beings need to be saved from themselves, even if they sometimes resist what they need most. He also understood that stories can change minds even when the facts cannot. If there was ever a time to appreciate these insights, it is now.

The Folger Teaching Guides are the product of decades of experience and conversation with talented educators and students. The Folger continues to offer teachers the best and most effective techniques for cultivating students' abilities in the classroom, starting with Shakespeare but opening out on the great range of writers and experiences your students can explore. We invite you to visit the Folger in person in Washington, DC, where our exhibitions, performances, and programs put into practice the methods and insights you will find here. And we extend our gratitude to you for doing the most important work in the world, which deserves the dedicated support we are providing in these guides.

# Good Books, Great Books, Monumental Texts—Shakespeare, Relevance, and New Audiences: GenZ and Beyond

## Jocelyn A. Chadwick

"People can find small parts of themselves in each character and learn what it may be like to let the hidden parts of themselves out. Regardless of personal background, everyone can relate to the humanity and vulnerability that is revealed in Shakespeare's works." (Student, 2023)

" 'To me, there is no such thing as black or yellow Shakespeare,' Mr. Earle Hyman, a celebrated African-American actor said. 'There is good Shakespeare or bad Shakespeare. It's simply a matter of good training and opportunity.' " ("Papp Starts a Shakespeare Repertory Troupe Made Up Entirely of Black and Hispanic Actors," *New York Times*, January 21, 1979)

"The question for us now is to be or not to be. Oh no, this Shakespearean question. For 13 days this question could have been asked but now I can give you a definitive answer. It's definitely yes, to be." (President Volodymyr Zelenskyy's speech to UK Parliament, March 8, 2022)

"I, at least, do not intend to live without Aeschylus or William Shakespeare, or James, or Twain, or Hawthorne, or Melville, etc., etc., etc." (Toni Morrison, "Unspeakable Things Unspoken: The Afro-American Presence in Literature," *The Source of Self-Regard*, 2019)

How have William Shakespeare's brilliant and probing plays about the human condition come to *an either/or* to some contemporary audiences? The preceding quotes reveal appreciation, understanding, and metaphorical applications along with definitions of the playwright's depth and breadth. And yet, a misunderstanding *and* sometimes *conscious cancellation* of the man, his work, and his impact have undergone substantial *misunderstanding and misinterpretation*.

For as long as any of us can or will remember, William Shakespeare has continued to be with us and our students. True, this is a bold and assertive declarative statement; however, in the 21st century, is it and will it continue to be accurate and still *valid*?

In 1621, playwright Robert Greene, a contemporary of William Shakespeare, did not think much of Shakespeare's work or his talent:

> There is an upstart Crow, beautified with our feathers that with his Tygers hart wrapt in a Players hyde, supposes he is as well able to bombast out a blank verse as the best of you: and being an absolute Johannes factotum is in his owne conceit the onely Shake-scene in a country. (Robert Greene, *Greene's Groats-Worth of Wit*, 1621)

Clearly, Greene was jealous of Shakespeare's popularity and talent.

Interestingly, what Greene objects to parallels some 21st-century perspectives that at this writing recommend removal of Shakespeare's plays and poetry from curricula throughout the country—*just because*. For Greene, the objection was Shakespeare's talent, his appeal to his contemporary audience, his rising popularity, and cross-cultural exposure—not only angering Greene but also resulting in his undeniable jealousy.

Today, however, the primary argument is that Shakespeare's texts are old and dated; he is white and male—all of which from this perspective identify him, his time, and his work as disconnected from the realities of 21st-century students: antiquated, anachronistic, even racially tinged. These arguments persist, even though without doubt, Shakespeare's London was metropolitan, multicultural, and influenced by the city's international trade—imports as well as exports.

And further, to be clear, as Toni Morrison and so many other scholars, writers, *and* readers have asserted, the *durability of* a text lies with its present *and* future audiences. I should add here that Morrison was engaging with, and "talking back to," Shakespeare's play *Othello* when she wrote her play *Desdemona* in 2011.

At this writing, there are a number of contemporary catalysts pointing out the necessity of rethinking, reflection, and consubstantiation of such texts that have long been a part of the canon. We are experiencing not only that resurgence but also a book-banning tsunami in schools and public libraries. The result of such movements and actions indeed causes us to rethink; they have also compelled educators at all levels, parents, librarians, writers, and GenZ students to speak up and out.

To illustrate concretely students' responses, this introduction necessarily includes the perspectives and voices from some high school students (grades 9–12), who attend Commonwealth Governors School (CGS) in Virginia. I asked a number of them what they thought about Shakespeare, and they told me. Their statements are in *their own words*; I did no editing. In addition, the students within the CGS system represent the panoply of inclusion and diversity.

> It's the big ideas that make Shakespeare relevant to myself and other students. Everyone loves, and everyone feels pain, so while we each might experience these feelings at different points in our lives, in different degrees, and for different reasons than others, I think Shakespeare's work is enough out of our times so that all students can connect to his themes and imagine themselves in the positions of his characters. (Student, May 2023)

And . . .

> I feel his general influence; I feel like he created a lot of literary words, and musicians like Taylor Swift draw from the works of earlier people, and Shakespeare continues to be relevant. (Student, 2023)

Interestingly, students *tapestry* what they read and experience in Shakespeare's works into their contemporary world, concomitantly, reflecting Umberto Eco's assertion about the import, impact, and protean qualities of a text's life: students create their own meaning and connections—building onto and extending Shakespeare's words, expression, characters, and challenges, ultimately scaffolding into their present realities, experiences, and challenges.

With all of these developments and conversations in mind, this Folger series of teaching guides provides that crossroad and intersection of analysis and rethinking. The central question that joins both those who see at present limited or no redeemable value in Shakespeare and those who view these texts as windows of the past, present, and, yes, the future is *"Do William Shakespeare's plays resonate, connect, and speak to 21st-century readers of all ages, and especially to our new generations of students?"*

Let us consider Eco's assertion: each time playwrights, directors, and artists reinterpret, every text undergoes a disruption, thereby reflecting new audiences. To *re-see* a character or setting when producing Shakespeare's plays is with each iteration a kind of disruption—a disruption designed to bring Shakespeare's 16th-century texts to audiences from multiple perspectives and epochs. The term *disruption* here takes on a more modern definition, a more protean and productive definition: Every time a reader enters into a text—one of Shakespeare's plays, to be specific—that reader can meld, align, interweave experiences, memories, thoughts, aspirations, and fears, and yes, as the first student quote alludes, empower the reader to *identify* which characters, and moments and consequences. This reading and/or viewing is indeed a positive kind of disruption—*not to harm or destroy*; on the contrary, a positive disruption that expands and interrelates both reader and viewer with Shakespeare and each play. Past *and* present intersect for each generation of readers. In this positive disruption texts remain relevant, alive, and *speak verisimilitude*.

Similarly, we ask 21st-century students studying Shakespeare to bring their *whole selves* to the work, and to come up with their own interpretations. Allowing and privileging 21st-century students to compare and contrast and then examine, inquire, and express their own perspectives and voices remains the primary goal of English language arts: independent thinking, developed voice, and ability to think and discern critically for oneself. Both primary text and adaptations are reflections *and* extended lenses:

> *The man i' th' moon's too slow—till new-born chins*
> *Be rough and razorable; she that from whom*
> *We all were sea-swallowed, though some cast again,*
> *And by that destiny to perform an act*
> *Whereof what's past is prologue, what to come*
> *In your and my discharge.* (The Tempest 2.1, 285–89)

Just as the past continuously informs and reminds the present, the present—each new generation—brings new eyes, new thoughts, new perspectives. Of course, each generation sees itself as unique and completely different; however, the echoes of the past are and will always be ever-present.

In so many *unexpected* ways, the 21st-century Shakespeare audience in school—students, teachers, and others—share far more with William Shakespeare and his time than we may initially recognize and acknowledge. From his infancy to his death, Shakespeare and his world closely paralleled and reflects ours: upheavals and substantial shifts culturally, sociopolitically, scientifically, and religiously, as well as the always-evolving human condition. Each of the plays represented in this series—*Hamlet*, *Macbeth*, *Othello*, *Romeo and Juliet*, and *A Midsummer Night's Dream*—illustrates just how much William Shakespeare not only observed and lived with and among tragedy, comedy, cultural diversity, challenges, and new explorations, but also, from childhood, honed his perspective of both past and present and—as Toni Morrison expresses—*rememoried* it in his plays and poems. Tragedy and Comedy is rooted in the antiquities of Greek, Roman, and Greco-Roman literature and history. William Shakespeare uniquely crafts these genres to reflect and inform his own time; more importantly, the plays he left us foreshadow past and future connections for audiences to come—audiences who would encounter cross-cultures, ethnicities, genders, geography, even time itself.

More than at any other time in our collective history experienced through literature, the past's ability to inform, advise, and even "cushion" challenges our students' experience today. It will continue to experience into the foreseeable future and will continue to support and inform, and yes, even protect them. Protecting, meaning that what we and our students can read and experience from the safe distance literature provides, allows, even encourages, readers to process, reflect, and think about how we respond, engage, inquire, and learn.

> The play . . . *Macbeth* . . . is about pride; there are lots of common human themes. He's the basis for a lot of literature like *Hamlet* is just the *Lion King*; it is just *Hamlet,* but it's lions. (Student, May 2023)

One fascinating trait of GenZ readers I find so important is *the how* of their processing and relating canonical texts with other contemporary texts and other genres around them: TV, movies, songs, even advertisements. What I so admire and respect about *students' processing* is their critical thinking and their ability to create and different comprehension-pathways that relate to their own here and now. In this new instructional paradigm, we *all* are exploring, discovering, and learning together, with William Shakespeare as our reading-nucleus.

Although many writers and playwrights preceded William Shakespeare, his scope and depth far exceeded that of his predecessors and even his peers. His constant depiction and examinations of the human condition writ large and illustrated from a myriad of perspectives, times, cultures, and worlds set Shakespeare decidedly apart. The result of his depth and scope not only previewed the immediate future following his death, but more profoundly, his thematic threads, characters, settings, and cross-cultural inclusions continue to illustrate *us to us*.

The pivotal and critical point here is GenZ's continued reading and experiencing of William Shakespeare's plays. As they experience this playwright, they take bits and pieces of what they have read and experienced directly into other texts they read and experience in classes and daily living. In fact, in the "tidbits" they experience initially through Shakespeare, students will connect and interpret *and make their own meaning and connections*, even *outside* of textual reading. Malcolm X, in fact, provides us with an example of how that works:

> I read once, passingly, about a man named Shakespeare. I only read about him passingly, but I remember one thing he wrote that kind of moved me. He put it in the mouth of Hamlet, I think, it was, who said, 'To be or not to be.' He was in doubt about something—whether it was nobler in the mind of man to suffer the slings and arrows of outrageous fortune—moderation—or to take up arms against a sea of troubles and by opposing end them. And I go for that. If you take up arms, you'll end it, but if you sit around and wait for the one who's in power to make up his mind that he should end it, you'll be waiting a long time. And in my opinion the young generation of whites, blacks, browns, whatever else there is, you're living at a time of extremism, a time of revolution, and now there has to be a change and a better world has to be built, and the only way it's going to be built—is with extreme methods. And I, for one, will join with anyone—I don't care what color you are—as long as you want to change this miserable condition that exists on this earth. (Oxford Union Queen and Country Debate, Oxford University, December 3, 1964)

Like Malcolm X, GenZ students turn toward the wind, staring directly and earnestly into their present and future, determined to exert their voices and perspectives. Their exposure to past and present literature, sciences, histories, and humanities allows, even empowers, this unique generation to say, "I choose my destiny." And the myriad of texts to which we expose them informs, challenges, and compels them to always push back and move toward a truth and empowerment *they* seek. Some of us who are older may very well find such empowerment disconcerting—not of the "old ways." But then, just what is a comprehensive education for lifelong literacy supposed to do, if not expose, awaken, engage, even challenge and open new, prescient doors of inquiry, exploration, and discovery? This is the broad scope of not just education for education's sake but of reading and experiencing for oneself *devoid of outside agendas—whatever they may be or from wherever they may emanate.*

A student put this succinctly:

> Elements of his writing are still relevant in today's films and books, like his strong emotional themes, tropes, and character archetypes. Shakespeare's works are quoted often by common people [everyday people] and even by more influential individuals, including civil rights leader Martin Luther King Jr., who was known to quote Shakespeare often. I believe the beautiful and unique work by William Shakespeare is still greatly relevant and appreciated now and will go on to remain relevant for centuries more. (Student, May 2023)

The plays comprising this series represent curricula inclusion around the country and also represent the angst some parents, activists, and politicians, even some fearful teachers, have about our continuing to include Shakespeare's works. That said, there are many, many teachers who continue to teach William Shakespeare's plays, not only allowing students from all walks of life to experience the man, his time, and the sheer scope of his thematic and powerful reach, but also privileging the voices and perspectives GenZ brings to the texts:

> We can see in Shakespeare our contemporary and sometimes frightening range of humanity today—I am specifically thinking of our current political turmoil—is not unique, and that just like the evil monarchs such as Richard III appear in Shakespeare's plays, they are always counterbalanced by bright rays of hope: in *Romeo and Juliet*, the union between the Montagues and Capulets at play's end restoring peace and civility, . . . It is impossible for me to watch any performance or read any Shakespeare play—especially the tragedies—without leaving the theatre buoyed up by hope and respect for humankind, a deeper appreciation of the uses of the English language, and a feeling that I have been on a cathartic journey which leaves my students and me enriched, strengthened, and hopeful. (Winona Siegmund, Teacher, CGS)

> I'm going to be honest, I'm not very knowledgeable on the subject of Shakespeare . . . I never really went out of my way to understand and retain it. All I know is that I can't escape him. No matter how hard I try, and trust me, I try, he will always be somewhere, running through the media with his "art thous" and biting of thumbs. Perhaps people see themselves in the plays of Shakespeare. Maybe Shakespeare is a dramatization of the hardships we experience every day . . . Shakespeare has stained my life. One of those annoying stains that you can't get out. A bright, colorful stain that's easy to notice. But who cares? It was an ugly shirt anyway; might as well add some color. (Student, May 2023)

> Taylor Swift's "Love Story." I LOVE the STORY of *Romeo and Juliet*. See what I did there? But in all honesty, there are so many Shakespeare inspired works (*Rotten Tomatoes, West Side Story, Twelfth Grade Night,* etc.) that I liked and remained relevant to me, and prove that Shakespeare will always be relevant. The first Shakespeare play I read was *Macbeth* when I was twelve and going to school in Azerbaijan. And even as a preteen studying in a foreign country, I loved the story and found it morbid, funny, and wise all at the same time. My Azerbaijani classmates liked it, too. Due to this unique experience, I think that anyone can enjoy and identify with Shakespeare's works, no matter their age or country of origin. (Student, May 2023)

The five plays in this Folger series represent the universal and social depth and breadth of all Shakespeare's poetry and plays—verisimilitude, relevance, *our* human condition—all writ large in the 21st century and beyond. Through characters, locations, time periods, challenges, and *difference*, William Shakespeare takes us all into real-life moments and decisions and actions—even into our *not yet known or experienced*—to illustrate the human thread joining and holding us all as one. Despite being several hundred years old, Shakespeare's works have yet to Become antiquated. There are several reasons for this long-lasting relevance—namely the enduring themes. Shakespeare's themes on humanity, morality, loss, and love remain relatable for people across all walks of life. (Student, May 2023)

In sum, a colleague asked me quite recently, "Jocelyn, why do you think students just don't want to read?" To add to this query, at this writing, I have tracked an increasing, and to be honest, disturbing sentiment expressed on social media: some teachers positing, essentially, the same perspective. My response to both is the same: our students—elementary through graduate school—*do* read and write every day. They will also read what we assign in our classes. However, this generation of students first think or ask outright—*Why? What do I get* if I invest the time and effort? Most assuredly direct inquiries with which many veteran teachers *and* professors are unfamiliar—perhaps even resentful. But let's be honest. Our students of a now patinated past most likely felt the same way. Remember the plethora of *Cliffs Notes* and *Monarch Notes*? I know I threw my share of students' copies in the trash—wanting them to read for themselves.

Just like adults, our students, especially today, have a right to ask us *Why? What do* they *get* if they invest their time in reading assigned texts? Umberto Eco brilliantly answers why our students *must* continue reading and experiencing texts—for this series, William Shakespeare's plays—and learning through performance:

Now a text, once it is written, no longer has anyone behind it; it has, on the contrary, when it survives, and for as long as it survives, thousands of interpreters ahead of it. Their reading of it generates other texts, which can be paraphrase, commentary, carefree exploitation, translation into other signs, words, images, even into music. ("Waiting for the millennium," *FMR* No. 2, July 1981, 66)

To illustrate Eco's assertion, I will leave it to one student and two people with whom all teachers and many students are familiar:

Shakespeare's work is relevant because his legacy allows people from all walks of life to understand that they can make a difference. Although people from all walks of life may not always relate to his works, the impact that he made on modern literature and theater is undeniable. The lasting dreams that his works have provided for young people lay the groundwork for our future. Shakespeare's living works are proof that one small man with one small pen can change the future of everything around him. (Student, May 2023)

I met and fell in love with Shakespeare . . . It was a state with which I felt myself most familiar. I pacified myself about his whiteness by saying after all he had been dead so long it couldn't matter to anyone anymore. (Maya

Angelou on her childhood introduction to and love of Shakespeare in *I Know Why the Caged Bird Sings*, 1969)

and, as Malcolm X proclaimed:

I go for that. (Oxford Union Queen and Country Debate, Oxford University, December 3, 1964)

# Why This Book?

## Peggy O'Brien

First, let's start with YOU: If you are a schoolteacher, know that you are the most precious resource in the world. In every school, town, city, state, country, civilization, solar system or universe, there is none more valuable than you. It is hard, hard work and yet . . . you are doing the most important work on earth. Period.

At the Folger Shakespeare Library, we know this well and deeply, and that's why you are a clear focus of our work. If you teach Shakespeare and other complex literature—and particularly if you are a middle or high school teacher—it is our mission, passion, and honor to serve you. Therefore . . . welcome to *The Folger Guides to Teaching Shakespeare* and our five volumes on teaching *Hamlet, Macbeth, Othello, Romeo and Juliet,* and *A Midsummer Night's Dream.*

**Here's why this book: our overall purpose.** We know that many of you find yourselves teaching plays that you don't know well, or that you've taught so often that they are beginning to bore you to death. (You talk to us, and we listen.) So, these books give you fresh information and hopefully meaningful new ideas about the plays you teach most frequently, along with a very specific way to teach them to *all* students—highfliers, slow readers, the gamut. We see the Shakespeare content and the teaching methodology as one whole.

We often get these questions from y'all. You may recognize some or all of them:

- How on earth do I even begin to think about teaching a Shakespeare play? No one has really ever taught me how to teach Shakespeare and my own experience with Shakespeare as a high school student was . . . not great.

- How can Shakespeare possibly make sense in this day and age? In this changing world? Old dead white guy?

- Shakespeare can't possibly be engaging to *all* my students, right? I mean, it's true that really only the brightest kids will "get" Shakespeare, right?

- SO . . . what's the Folger Method and how does it fit into all of this?

- I have to teach the "10th-grade Shakespeare play"—whatever it is—and I haven't read it since high school, or maybe I have never read it.

- I'm a schoolteacher and don't have extra time to spend studying up before I teach this stuff.

- Doesn't using those watered-down, "modernized" Shakespeare texts make it easier? Aren't they the most obvious way to go?

- Can learning and teaching Shakespeare really be a great experience for my kids and for me too?

Our *Folger Guides to Teaching Shakespeare* are hopefully an answer to these questions too.

**Here's why this book: the Folger Method.** At the Folger, not only are we home to the largest Shakespeare collection in the world but we have developed, over the last four decades or so, a way of teaching Shakespeare and other complex texts that is effective for *all* students. We're talking well-developed content and methodology from the same source, and in your case, *in the same book.* Imagine!

The Folger Method is language-based, student-centered, interactive, and rigorous, and provides all students with ways into the language and therefore into the plays. Our focus is words, because the words are where Shakespeare started, and where scholars, actors, directors, and editors start. Shakespeare's language turns out to be not a barrier but *the way in.* The lessons in this book are sequenced carefully, scaffolding your students' path. They will find themselves close-reading, figuring out and understanding language, characters, and the questions that the play is asking. All of this when they may have started out with "Why doesn't he write in English?" It's pretty delicious. If you want to know more about the Folger Method right this minute, go to the chapter that starts on page 39.

A couple of things I want you to know right off the bat:

- Because the Folger Method involves lots of classroom work that is interactive and exciting (and even joyful), sometimes teachers are tempted to pull a few lessons out of this book and use them to spruce up whatever they usually do. Oh resist, please. Take the whole path and see what your students learn and what you learn.

- There is no "right" interpretation of any play (or work of literature, for that matter).
  In working with the Folger Method principles and essentials, your students come up with their own sense of what's going on in *Romeo and Juliet.* Their own interpretation. Not yours, or the interpretation of famous literary critics, but their own. And then they bring it to life. Exciting! That's what we're after, because the skills that they'll develop in doing this—close-reading, analysis, collaboration, research—they will use forever.

- The Folger Method may call on you to teach differently than you have before. Be brave! You are not the explainer or the translator or the connector between your students and Shakespeare. You're the architect who sets up the ways in which Shakespeare and your students discover each other . . . and we'll show you very explicitly how to do that.

**Here's why this book: parts of the whole.** Each of these guides is organized in the same way:

- **Part One is the big picture:** Folger director Michael Witmore and Jocelyn Chadwick both take on the "Why Shakespeare?" question from very different angles. And Jocelyn brings students into the conversation too. Delicious!

- **Part Two is** *YOU* **and** *Romeo and Juliet.* Through a set of short takes and one delicious long take, you'll get a stronger sense of the play. The shorts are some speedy and pretty painless ways to learn both the basics and a few surprises about both *Romeo and Juliet* and Shakespeare.

  The long take is "What Happens to Verona when the Torches Burn Bright," an essay written for you by Ellen MacKay, an accomplished and celebrated Shakespeare scholar. We know that you have no "extra" time ever, but we also know that schoolteachers find connecting with new scholarship to be enlivening and compelling. New ways to look at old plays—new ways most often sparked by the changing world in which we live—continue to open up many new ways to look at Shakespeare. What you take away from MacKay's essay may show up in your teaching soon, or maybe at some point, or maybe never—and all of those are good. You may agree with or grasp her perspective on *Romeo and Juliet,* or you may not; she will get you thinking, though—as she gets us thinking all the time—and that's what we're about.

- **Part Three is you,** *Romeo and Juliet,* **your students, and what happens in your classroom.**

  - The Folger Method is laid out clearly—and bonus: with the kind of energy that it produces in classrooms—so that you can get a sense of the foundational principles and practices before you all get into those lessons, and your own classroom starts buzzing.

  - A five-week *Romeo and Juliet* unit, day-by-day lessons for your classes, with accompanying resources and/or handouts for each. We know that the people who are the smartest and most talented and creative about the "how" of teaching are those who are working in middle and high school classrooms every day. So, working schoolteachers created all of the "What Happens in Your Classroom" section of this book. They do what you do every day. While these writers were writing, testing, and revising for you and your classroom, they were teaching their own middle and high school kids in their own. And I am not mentioning their family obligations or even whispering the word *pandemic.* At the Folger, we are in awe of them, and for many of the same reasons, are in awe of all of you.

  - Two essays full of practical advice about two groups of students whom teachers ask us about often. The first details and demonstrates the affinity that English Learners and Shakespeare and *Romeo and Juliet* have for one another. The second focuses on the deep connections that can flourish between students with intellectual and emotional disabilities and Shakespeare and *Romeo and Juliet.* No barriers to Shakespeare anywhere here.

  - The last essay is packed with information and examples on pairing texts— how we make sure that students are exposed to the broad sweep of literature while at the same time are busy taking Shakespeare right off that pedestal and into conversations with authors of other centuries, races, genders, ethnicities, and cultures. This is where magic starts to happen!

This is Why You, and Why This Book, and now **. . . back to YOU!** Get busy! And as Juliet says to Romeo in Act 3 (and, OK, in a completely different context), "Hie hence . . . away!"! Get into this play! A joyful and energized journey of mutual discovery is at hand—for you and your students. Get it all going in Verona! And tell us how it all goes. As always, we want to know *everything*. Get online with us! Follow us at folger.edu! Come visit our newly expanded building and new programs right near the Capitol in Washington, DC. You belong here! We will always leave the light on for you.

# PART TWO

# Getting Up to Speed, or Reviving Your Spirit, with *Romeo and Juliet*

# Ten Amazing Things You May Not Know About Shakespeare

## Catherine Loomis and Michael LoMonico

The basics: Shakespeare was a playwright, poet, and actor who grew up in the market town of Stratford-upon-Avon, England, spent his professional life in London, and returned to Stratford a wealthy landowner. He was born in 1564—the same year Galileo was born and Michelangelo died. Shakespeare died in 1616, and Cervantes did too.

1. In the summer of 1564, an outbreak of bubonic plague killed one out of every seven people in Stratford, but the newborn William Shakespeare survived.

2. In Shakespeare's family, the women were made of sterner stuff: Shakespeare's mother, his sister Joan, his wife, Anne Hathaway, their daughters, and granddaughter all outlived their husbands. And Joan lived longer than all four of her brothers. The sad exception is Shakespeare's younger sister, Anne. She died when she was seven and Shakespeare was fifteen.

3. Shakespeare appears in public records up until 1585, when he was a 21-year-old father of three, and then not until 1592, when he turns up in London as a playwright. During those lost years, he may have been a schoolmaster or tutor, and one legend has him fleeing to London to escape prosecution for deer poaching. No one has any idea really, but maybe there is a theatrical possibility: An acting company called the Queen's Men was on tour in the summer of 1587, and, since one of their actors had been killed in a duel in Oxford, the town just down the road, the company arrived in Stratford minus an actor. At age 23, did Shakespeare leave his family and join them on tour?

4. Shakespeare wrote globally: in addition to all over Britain, his plays take you to Italy, Greece, Egypt, Turkey, Spain, France, Austria, Cyprus, Denmark and, in the case of *The Tempest*, pretty close to what was to become America.

5. Shakespeare died of a killer hangover. The Reverend John Ward, a Stratford vicar, wrote about Shakespeare's death on April 23, 1616, this way: "Shakespeare, [Michael] Drayton, and Ben Jonson had a merry meeting, and it seems drank too hard, for Shakespeare died of a fever there contracted."

**6.** On Shakespeare's gravestone in Stratford's Holy Trinity Church is a fierce curse on anyone who "moves my bones." In 2016, archeologists used ground-penetrating radar to examine the grave, and . . . Shakespeare's skull is missing.

**7.** Frederick Douglass escaped slavery and as a free man became a celebrated orator, statesman, and leader of the American abolitionist movement—and he was a student and lover of Shakespeare. Visitors to Cedar Hill, his home in DC's Anacostia neighborhood, can see Douglass's volumes of Shakespeare's complete works still on his library shelves and a framed print of Othello and Desdemona on the parlor wall. In addition to studying and often referencing Shakespeare in his speeches, Douglass was an active member of his local Anacostia community theater group, the Uniontown Shakespeare Club.

**8.** Shakespeare is the most frequently produced playwright in the U.S. Despite this, *American Theatre* magazine has never crowned him America's "Most Produced Playwright," an honor bestowed annually based on data from nearly 400 theaters. He always wins by such a large margin—usually there are about five times more Shakespeare productions than plays by the second-place finisher—that the magazine decided to just set him aside so that other playwrights could have a chance to win.

**9.** While Nelson Mandela was incarcerated on South Africa's Robben Island, one of the other political prisoners retained a copy of Shakespeare's complete works, and secretly circulated it through the group. At his request, many of the other prisoners—including Mandela—signed their names next to their favorite passages.

> *Cowards die many times before their deaths;*
> *The valiant only taste of death but once.*
> *Of all the wonders that I yet have heard,*
> *It seems to me most strange that men should fear,*
> *Seeing that death, a necessary end,*
> *Will come when it will come.*

These lines from *Julius Caesar* were marked "N. R. Mandela, December 16, 1977." Nelson Mandela was released from prison in 1990.

**10.** The Folger Shakespeare Library is in Washington, DC, and houses the largest Shakespeare collection in the world, just a block from the U.S. Capitol. We are Shakespeare's home in America! We are abuzz with visitors and audience members from our own DC neighborhoods, from across the country and around the world: teachers and students, researchers and scholars, lovers of the performing arts, all kinds of learners, and the curious of all ages and stages. Find us online at folger.edu/teach—and do come visit our beautiful new spaces. Be a part of our lively and accessible exhibitions and programs, explore rare books and other artifacts, join a teaching workshop, and enjoy the magic of theatre, poetry, and music. We're waiting for you, your classes, and your families!

# Ten Amazing Things You May Not Know About *Romeo and Juliet*

## Catherine Loomis and Michael LoMonico

**1.** As he did with most of his plays, Shakespeare based *Romeo and Juliet* on a story already known to his audiences. Arthur Brooke's 3,000-line poem, "The Tragicall History of Romeus and Juliet," was first published in 1562 and was frequently reprinted after that. Shakespeare probably wrote *Romeo and Juliet* sometime between 1591 and 1595 and, per usual, he changed or improved upon his source. In Brooke's poem, after the deaths of Romeus and Juliet, the Nurse is banished, the Apothecary is hanged, and Friar Lawrence becomes a hermit.

**2.** Perhaps more than any other Shakespeare play, the story of the love between Romeo and Juliet, the disapproving Capulets, and the rivalry between the Montagues and the Capulets and more has been retold, adapted, translated, and referenced for hundreds of years—in thousands of plays and films, in opera and ballet, in rap, rock and roll, jazz, hip-hop, and symphonic music, in television episodes and comic books, in cartoons and board books for babies, in online nuggets and in many, many other elements of popular culture.

**3.** Pablo Neruda—celebrated internationally and considered the national poet of Chile—published *Romeo y Julieta* in 1964. This was his own translated version of *Romeo and Juliet*. Neruda's version is read routinely by students in Cuba and has become part of their study of Spanish-language literature.

**4.** "But soft, what light through yonder window breaks?" and "O Romeo, Romeo, wherefore art thou, Romeo?" are two of the most famous lines in all of Shakespeare. They appear in what most people call "the balcony scene"—Act 2, scene 2—even though Shakespeare doesn't use the word *balcony* anywhere in the play. The Oxford English Dictionary tells us that the English word *balcone*—as it was spelled then—was first used in 1618 . . . and Shakespeare's play was old news by then.

**5.** In the play, Shakespeare sets Juliet's age at 13, and Romeo's age is not specified. In 16th-century real life, though, the average marriage age for women was 24, and for men it was 27.

**6.** Lady Montague is Romeo's mother, and she appears only in the play's first scene. She has only three lines, all in Act 1, scene 1. Scholars believe that her part was probably played by the same boy actor who played Juliet. Since Shakespeare's plays routinely had more characters than his acting company had actors, the actors were used to "doubling," or playing more than one part.

**7.** *Folger Shakespeare* (folger.edu/shakespeares-works) tells us that in the play, Romeo speaks 4,673 words and Juliet has 4,265 words. In his play, Hamlet speaks 11,613 words, far more than both of the star-crossed lovers put together.

**8.** *Romeo and Juliet* was printed and sold at bookstalls only after it was a success onstage. Its first two printings were in quartos—small books that today might look to us like cheap paperbacks: the first in 1597 (called Quarto 1 or Q1), and the second in 1599 (Q2). These quartos are different from each other in several ways. Juliet as written in Q1 is a girl who is very eager to get married! She says to Friar Lawrence, "Make hast(e), make hast(e), this lingring doth us wrong." The Q2 Juliet is much less excited and more polite. This difference is an example of a textual variant. Often Shakespeare's quartos give us versions of the same play that are different from one another, but no one is entirely sure how they came to differ.

**9.** Hands down, *Romeo and Juliet* is the most popular Shakespeare play in U.S. high schools. A ninth-grade favorite!

**10.** At the Folger Shakespeare Library, we have lots of *Romeo and Juliets*—395 different stand-alone editions of the play, for starters, and in 33 different languages: Arabic, Armenian, Bulgarian, Catalan, Chinese, Croatian, Czech, Danish, Dutch, English, Esperanto, French, German, Greek, Hebrew, Hindi, Hungarian, Icelandic, Italian, Japanese, Kannada, Polish, Portuguese, Romanian, Russian, Serbian, Spanish, Swedish, Thai, Tibetan, Turkish, Turkmen, and Ukrainian. *Romeo and Juliet* for all! We have promptbooks and playbills from many productions of the play, and in our Reading Room, you can have a look at the single largest item in our collection—a quite huge painting of the Capulets' burial monument depicting the dead Romeo and Paris with Juliet and Friar Lawrence alive and perhaps trying to make sense of it all (Act 5, scene 3). Since its beginnings in 1971, the Folger Theatre has performed *Romeo and Juliet* seven times, and on that same stage in our Elizabethan Theatre, hundreds and hundreds of students have performed scenes from *Romeo and Juliet* during our Shakespeare Festivals, while hundreds more have staged the balcony scene in the theater flash mob–style: all balcony dwellers are Juliets and all clustered below onstage are Romeos!

# What Happens in This Play Anyway?

## A Plot Summary of *Romeo and Juliet*

The prologue of *Romeo and Juliet* calls the title characters "star-crossed lovers"—and the stars do seem to conspire against these young lovers.

Romeo is a Montague, and Juliet a Capulet. Their families are enmeshed in a feud, but the moment they meet—when Romeo and his friends attend a party at Juliet's house in disguise—the two fall in love and quickly decide that they want to be married.

A friar secretly marries them, hoping to end the feud. Romeo and his companions almost immediately encounter Juliet's cousin Tybalt, who challenges Romeo. When Romeo refuses to fight, his friend Mercutio accepts the challenge and is killed. Romeo then kills Tybalt and is banished. He spends that night with Juliet and then leaves for Mantua.

Juliet's father forces her into a marriage with Count Paris. To avoid this marriage, Juliet takes a potion, given her by the friar, that makes her appear dead. The friar will send Romeo word to be at her family tomb when she awakes. The plan goes awry, and Romeo learns instead that she is dead. In the tomb, Romeo kills himself. Juliet wakes, sees his body, and commits suicide. Their deaths appear finally to end the feud.

# What Happens in This Play Anyway?

## A PLAY MAP OF *ROMEO AND JULIET*

### Mya Gosling and Peggy O'Brien

## What happens in ***ROMEO & JULIET*** ?

**WHY, when two families are at war...**

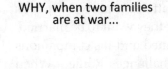

**...and their teenagers fall in love with each other...**

**...does everything end in violence and death?**

### Who's Who in Verona

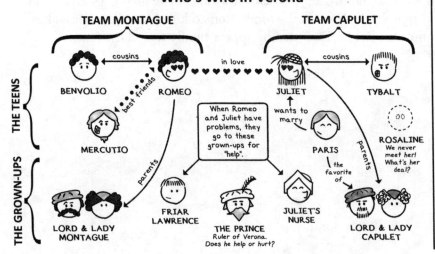

**TEAM MONTAGUE**

**TEAM CAPULET**

THE TEENS

THE GROWN-UPS

cousins

BENVOLIO

ROMEO

best friends

MERCUTIO

in love

When Romeo and Juliet have problems, they go to these grown-ups for "help".

parents

LORD & LADY MONTAGUE

FRIAR LAWRENCE

THE PRINCE
Ruler of Verona.
Does he help or hurt?

JULIET'S NURSE

JULIET

cousins

TYBALT

wants to marry

PARIS
the favorite of

parents

ROSALINE
We never meet her!
What's her deal?

LORD & LADY CAPULET

## What is this play about?

What's love?
What's lust?

How scary is it for a girl to disobey her father?
Her mother?

Who dies, and why?
Who lives, and why?

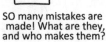

SO many mistakes are made! What are they, and who makes them?

Art by Mya Lixian Gosling of goodticklebrain.com
Concept by Peggy O'Brien

# What Happens to Verona when the Torches Burn Bright

## Ellen MacKay

No play of Shakespeare's is as strongly associated with adolescence as *Romeo and Juliet*. Famously, it is a work *about* teenagers. The tragedy is unusual for its specification of Juliet's age as not quite fourteen, and "young Romeo," who starts the play shut away in his bedroom, "so secret and so close," seems not much above that (2.4.121; 1.1.152). It is also a work *for* teenagers. Because it is common for the play to be the first work of Shakespeare's that students are taught, *Romeo and Juliet* is well established as a high school rite of passage. Like the quadratic formula or parallel parking, it is a step on the ladder to informed maturity. Of course, its status as a curricular mainstay doesn't ensure that the play is remembered in any particular way. Like the quadradic formula or parallel parking, its specifics are as likely to be forgotten as remembered. But what is assured by the fact that teachers keep teaching *Romeo and Juliet* to teenagers is the prominence that Anglo-American culture accords the work in the construction of a shared reality. If education is the key site for a nation to make its truths evident, *Romeo and Juliet* is teenaged in the sense that for decades it has been chosen to help realize the transition from child to citizen. Served up to a population on the brink of legal majority, and about to enjoy all the rights that come with that change in status (among them, the right to vote, the right to serve in the military, the right to consent to marriage, the right to control their own bodies and to administer their own property, etc.), the play shows something that the culture wants its budding members to know.

What is that something, though? Oddly for a work that is such a fixture of high school reading lists, this is a question without a clear answer. Editors of Shakespeare from the 18th and 19th centuries would be surprised to learn that *Romeo and Juliet* has become the most school-identified of Shakespeare's works. In their time too, the play was considered adolescent, but not because of its content or its audience. (Nor was it because Shakespeare wrote the play in his youth—so far as we know, Shakespeare left behind no juvenilia; *Romeo and Juliet* likely dates from 1596, when the playwright was in his early thirties.) Rather, the play was classified as an immature work because it was seen as a less developed version of a genre that Shakespeare would go on to master. Judged in comparison with *Hamlet* (1600), *Othello* (1604), *Macbeth* (1606), and *King Lear* (1606), the four plays widely considered to be Shakespeare's "great" tragedies, *Romeo and Juliet* has long been viewed as a less enlightening, less exemplary precursor.

This judgment has a lot to do with the narrow outlook of the leading couple. Tragedy in its classic Shakespearean form tends to end in an expanded view, with the fall of the protagonist shown in relation to the grand scheme of things. A guiding example is King Lear's cry of self-reproach when the storm brings him face-to-face with his kingdom's "houseless" and "unfed": "O, I have ta'en / Too little care of this" (3.4.34, 36–37). The same pattern of ethical reckoning applies to Macbeth, Othello, and Claudius (Hamlet's villainous uncle), whose crimes take on the scope of failures of the state. But *Romeo and Juliet* takes the opposite course. As the play hurtles toward its back-to-back suicides, the protagonists pull away from their social environments. By the fifth act, parents, the Prince, Nurse, Page, and Friar have all dropped out of the picture, leaving the lovers utterly alone. This depopulation of the stage is striking in light of the crowded scenes that have preceded it—the street brawl at the play's start and the Capulets' feast at the culmination of Act 1. *Romeo and Juliet* is a play that teems with life from all social levels, yet among its crowd of attendants, servants, gentlemen, ladies, citizens, and clergy, no one is on hand to correct the false reality in which the lovers ultimately find themselves. They die ignorant of the events that they have unleashed; even worse, they die ignorant of the needlessness of their own suicides.

By leaving its lovers in the dark, the tragedy has provoked a divided response. The view of early editors was that *Romeo and Juliet* fell short of tragic excellence by failing to expose and chastise its young heroes' disobedience. The more recent consensus is that the play is great because it breaks free from old-fashioned literary conventions. Richard Wagner composed his opera *Tristan and Isolde* as a testament to this view (1859). He called the final aria, in which Isolde dies enraptured by her lover's "shining" corpse, a Liebestod (meaning "love death"), a term that critics have used to describe the paradigm of self-immolating transcendence that *Romeo and Juliet* has made famous. One of the most quoted musical compositions in the 20th century—Leonard Bernstein draws from its shimmering chromatic ascension in the final notes of *West Side Story*—the Liebestod was the theme of youthful rebellion before rock-and-roll anthems entered the scene.

This pendulum swing from critical disappointment to exaltation tracks with modern art's preference for rebellion over convention, and modern readers are correct to detect a willful irreverence at work in the play. In ways that seem designed to shake up the story's received understanding, Shakespeare deviated from his sources when he composed *Romeo and Juliet*. Because there were multiple, well-known versions circulating in the 16th century, his flouting of tradition would have been highly visible to a Renaissance audience. He drew especially strongly on Arthur Brooke's popular poem "The Tragicall Historye of Romeus and Juliet" (1562), which begins by announcing that the role of good literature is to give out "rules of chaste and honest life." Brooke goes on to explain that Romeus and Juliet's history is "tragical" because the lovers break several of those rules. First and worst of all, they fail to respect the "authority and advice of parents," and second, they fail to shun the bad influence of "drunken gossips" (the Nurse) and "superstitious friars." Quite pointedly, Shakespeare does not follow Brooke's lead. When the Prologue promises a "fearful" tale of "star-crossed lovers" and "death-marked love," he announces a play that is poised to jump the track of its own well-known, didactic precedents.

Yet *Romeo and Juliet* doesn't exactly take the side of its teenagers either, given its merciless tour of the damage caused by their secret marriage. A searing example is Romeo's murder of County Paris at the door to the Capulet crypt. When Romeo pauses over Paris's body to lament a fellow victim of "sour misfortune," it's hard not to notice his total failure to hold himself accountable for his innocent rival's death (5.3.83). If, as Juliet tells the Nurse, you can't be too tired to talk if you have the breath to say so (2.5.31–32), then surely you can't be too "desperate" to keep from killing a man if you have the presence of mind to warn him of your desperation (5.3.59). Here especially, but elsewhere too, the play cuts a jagged line between the fateful cruelty of a world that fails to accommodate the lovers' desires and the seemingly inadvertent cruelty of Romeo and Juliet, whose belief that they are star-crossed gives license to devastating recklessness. If there is heroic transcendence to be found in the couple's "death-marked love," the couple's disregard for the lives of others tugs hard against it.

It is this mingled construction that makes *Romeo and Juliet* a teenage play in the best sense. Uprooted from the hectoring tone of the story's earlier versions, and unversed in the tragic form that will bring Shakespeare future glory, the play's condition recalls Malvolio's description of the youth Cesario in *Twelfth Night*: "Tis with him in standing water, between boy and man" (1.5.157). The middle space of adolescence, in which skepticism and alienation mix with moments of profound self- and social recognition, aptly describes the play's turbulent vision, which lurches from the violent disorder in Verona's streets, to the merry hospitality of the Capulets' feast, to the electric jolt of love at first sight, to the occult experiments of the Friar's cell, to the "grubs and eyeless skulls" of the grave (5.3.126). It also describes the unsettled state in which it concludes. The Prince's rushed inquest, which merely recaps incidents that have already been witnessed, seems designed to show that *Romeo and Juliet*'s tragic "ambiguities" won't be "clear[ed]" judicially (5.3.225). With the lovers dead, it lies with the audience to figure out what went wrong—the closing lines of the play demand as much with their instruction to "Go hence to have more talk of these sad things" (5.3.318). Such "talk" promises to be difficult work, since the lovers' failure to make better choices is hopelessly entangled with the culture's failure to envision better possibilities, beyond self-sacrificing obedience (the option that Brooke backed) and self-sacrificing resistance (the option that Wagner glorified in his opera). But it is also *teenage* work, since the capacity to set aside the given conditions of the world to ask what else might be possible is a quintessential virtue of youth. This invitation to notice and judge its construction of events is what makes the play ideal for educational use. Left to take up the unfinished business of pardoning and punishment, the audience is asked to participate in an ethical reckoning no less weighty than what *King Lear, Macbeth, Othello,* or *Hamlet* represent. Since achieving this expanded view means raising in conversation the "sad things" that the play's theatrical action cannot resolve, one might even say that the classroom is the designated location of *Romeo and Juliet*'s last act. The archetypal domain of inquiry and debate, it provides a space to draw conclusions by the clear light of day.

Since the plot's events are distorted by each character's limited point of view, selecting the evidence for this postmortem is bound to be a challenge. A good place to start would seem to be the sonnet at the play's opening, which summarizes the action from an impersonal distance:

> Two households, both alike in dignity
> (In fair Verona, where we lay our scene),
> From ancient grudge break to new mutiny,

Where civil blood makes civil hands unclean.
From forth the fatal loins of these two foes
A pair of star-crossed lovers take their life;
Whose misadventured piteous overthrows
Doth with their death bury their parents' strife.
The fearful passage of their death-marked love
And the continuance of their parents' rage,
Which, but their children's end, naught could remove,
Is now the two hours' traffic of our stage;
The which, if you with patient ears attend,
What here shall miss, our toil shall strive to mend.

Yet anyone who has "with patient ears attend[ed]" the play will recognize that the Chorus's neutral appearance is deceptive. What this sonnet tells the audience isn't strictly wrong—as promised, the overthrow and suicide of "a pair of star-crossed lovers" will dispel the "ancient grudge" that divides "two households" (Prol. 6, 3, 1). Omitted from this account, however, is the destruction the lovers' misadventures leaves in its wake. Beyond the protagonist "pair," a heap of corpses will pile up by the play's end, and several more characters will hover on death's brink. A complete list of lives taken or put in peril would include Mercutio, Tybalt, and County Paris, who are killed while performing roles or asserting rights they do not know have been materially changed by the couple's secret marriage; Lady Montague, who perishes offstage from her sorrow at Romeo's exile, ignorant of his return; Lady Capulet, who says she cannot recover from the sight of her ostensibly dead daughter's second, actual death; and Friar Lawrence, the Nurse, and the "poor pothecary," who will end the play in jeopardy for the parts they played in the lovers' plots (in Brooke's version, the Friar is pardoned, the Nurse is banished, and the apothecary is hanged). Viewed in retrospect, the Chorus's reduction of the death count to a single "pair" is a very selective record of the play's human cost (Prol. 6).

Much like the assurance that *Romeo and Juliet* will speed by in a mere "two hours"—a running time that is far too short for a work of more than three thousand lines—the Chorus's claim that the couple's death "remove[s]" the city's "strife" is on several counts a miscalculation. It disregards the many casualties that the audience has witnessed to single out only one pair of lives, and only one pair of deaths, as important. It asserts a restored civility that the play doesn't show, since *Romeo and Juliet* ends in the mixed mood of a "glooming peace," with justice deferred, not restored ("some shall be pardoned, and some punishèd" ([5.3.319]). And it tilts the play into a realm of fateful inevitability with the dubious assertion that "naught" but the lovers' deaths "could remove" the feud between the families. That "naught" is especially galling in light of the alternative plan for peace-making that is raised only to be abandoned. Friar Lawrence consents to marry Romeo and Juliet out of the conviction that their "alliance" will "turn [their] households' rancor to pure love" (2.4.87, 88). Among the play's most painful possibilities is that this prediction might well have come true if the Friar had chosen to follow through on it, by alerting the families to their children's union.

Reading the Prologue in retrospect, after having already seen the incidents it foretells, exposes a gap between the play's course of events and its poetic expression. This is a foundational concern among those who study literature—it's the same problem

George Orwell raises when he warns that language corrupts thought. Orwell's point is that stale metaphors and pat phrases can do real damage by packaging people and actions in terms that constrain what they can mean. The tremendous popularity of sonnets in the late 16th century caused a similar difficulty for poets like Shakespeare. The public couldn't get enough of verses describing the beauty of the beloved or the anguish of the speaker who longs for her, but as these tropes flooded the literary marketplace, it became increasingly difficult to profess love in a way that felt personal or sincere. Shakespeare leans into this dilemma, first by having Mercutio make fun of Romeo for acting like a cliché ("Cry but 'Ay me,' pronounce but 'love' and 'dove'" [2.1.12–13]), and then by having Juliet abandon "form" and "compliment" when she is overheard confessing her "passion" in the balcony scene (2.2.93, 94, 109). Her utter sincerity sets the lovers apart from love poetry's well-rehearsed moves. Hence, the sonnet, a form so familiar that Mercutio will mock its "by-the-numbers" composition (1.4.40), is an ideal way for Shakespeare to introduce these two prospects at once: the love story's poetic formula, and the mishaps and "overthrows" that will single this couple out (321).

Shakespeare orchestrates this double vision by making heavy use of contrast—especially the opposition of dark to light. To make the lovers' the only lives that the Chorus counts, the play has to distinguish Romeo and Juliet from Verona's large and dynamic community. This is a hard task, since his own friends point out that Romeo enters the play as a bit of a dud. His reputation for moping in his darkened bedroom is the first thing the audience learns about him, and he remains a sad sack until Benvolio drags him to the Capulets' party to snap him out of it. Juliet is similarly unremarkable at her first appearance, but then the expectations governing a young girl's conduct are much more limiting. She is given barely 50 words before she meets Romeo, and they are almost all conventional expressions of deference, modesty, and duty (the one exception is her effort to stop the Nurse from repeating an embarrassing joke).

All this dullness at the outset helps to set off the brilliance of the lovers when love sparks between them. Shakespeare highlights this transformation by having Benvolio predict it:

> At this same ancient feast of Capulet's
> Sups the fair Rosaline whom thou so loves,
> With all the admirèd beauties of Verona.
> Go thither, and with unattainted eye
> Compare her face with some that I shall show,
> And I will make thee think thy swan a crow (1.2.89–94).

As promised, Juliet's appearance in his line of sight inspires Romeo to discard his dim outlook, or "attainted eye." Gone are his stiff couplets and trite expressions of self-pity ("She hath forsworn to love, and in that vow / Do I live dead, that live to tell it now" [1.1.231–32]). Struck by Juliet's radiance, Romeo speaks as if his powers of perception have suddenly switched on: "O, she doth teach the torches to burn bright" (1.5.51).

At least one director thought to literalize this transformation by electrifying it. During the heyday of theatrical experimentation in post–World War I Paris, Jean Cocteau directed a production of *Roméo et Juliette* in which he turned Verona into a shadowy backdrop where the lovers could shine. By applying iridescent paint to sets and

costumes that were coated in black, Cocteau created scenes that fluoresced under ul-
traviolet stage light. In this production, Romeo's imagery of a torch-surpassing Juliet,
and Juliet's conceit of a sun-surpassing Romeo, were transformed into a state-of-the-art
light show.

Cocteau's glow-in-the-dark production illustrates the extraordinary vibrancy the
play's interpreters tend to attach to its pattern of outshining. It must have offered a glorious environment for scenes like Juliet's serenade (or "night song"):

> Come, gentle night; come, loving black-browed night,
> Give me my Romeo, and when I shall die,
> Take him and cut him out in little stars,
> And he will make the face of heaven so fine
> That all the world will be in love with night
> And pay no worship to the garish sun (3.2.21–27).

Yet this antithesis of light and dark trails into the play a persistent and harmful way
of seeing the world. The racist depersonalization at the center of Romeo's famous sim-
ile, "It seems she hangs upon the cheek of night / As a rich jewel in an Ethiop's ear"
(1.5.52–53), brings out the problem with the (figurative) torch he carries for Juliet: she
can only dazzle if everyone else is thrown into the shade. Romeo spells out this zero-sum
relation as he elaborates his conceit: "So shows a snowy dove trooping with crows / As
yonder lady o'er her fellows shows" (1.5.55–56). Harking back to Benvolio's promise to
"show" Romeo that his "swan" (Rosaline) is really a "crow," the couplet elevates Juliet
by deprecating his first love, along with every other woman present. The image of a
snowy dove among crows is therefore not just a way of asserting who is fairest (a word
that indexes the equivalence of whiteness with beauty in the Renaissance), it's also a
way of dropping those who are left in the dark out of sight and out of mind. This use of
blackness as a cue for collective ignorance and neglect is a known feature of England's
colonial mindset. Applied here, it does the figurative work of cloaking all other persons
and relations with indifference.

Of course, Romeo doesn't exactly choose the form his declaration takes. Poets from
time immemorial have described how love dulls the surrounding world to spotlight a
particular person within it. Given that this high-contrast view is the convention used
to convey love at first sight, how else is Shakespeare to convince the audience that the
couple's sudden passion is the real thing, and not the minor and fleeting feeling that
Romeo felt for Rosaline? Without dimming and blurring all other claims on a person,
what would make true love seem true? This dilemma recalls the Prologue's under-
statement, in that it shows the imperfect fit of the play's unfolding events to the love
story's preexisting script. Except now it shows that even the way that the lovers break
from convention constrains them within a preexisting script. Like Shakespeare's rift
with previous versions of *Romeo and Juliet*, this tension between truth and form would
have been noticeable to a Renaissance audience, since the scene onstage would have
looked very different from the sight that Romeo describes. In 1596, the public theaters
were outdoor playhouses that depended on sunlight for their illumination. Though the
torches Romeo mentions were used to signal nighttime, there was no effective technique to turn up the lights on Juliet or fade the scene around her. Consequently, the
dark and empty space that Romeo says she shines in, and that he glibly likens to the

"ear" of an Ethiopian person, could not have looked the way he says it does, like the void between stars. Instead, the audience would have seen Juliet as one among many friends, neighbors, servants, and countrymen who populate the party.

The disparity between what Romeo sees and what the stage shows is in fact a feature of the scene's design, for Shakespeare opens up a surprisingly broad view of the Capulets' party. Beginning with a peek at its backstage preparations, the feast presents a series of intimate glimpses of Verona's community. There is the serving man who clears the table while chatting about his desire for a "marchpane" (a marzipan sweet) and a spin around the dance floor with Susan or Nell (1.5.9, 1.5.10–11). There is an unnamed guest, an elder cousin, who recalls a happy litany of family weddings, births, and holiday celebrations (1.5.36). There is the host, Capulet, whose disarming response to Tybalt's threat of violence reveals to the audience that he recognizes Romeo as a "virtuous and well-governed youth" (1.5.77). Finally, there is the little search party made up of Benvolio and Mercutio, who seek their friend and fear for his safety when Romeo gives them "the slip" (2.4.50). Their escalating concern when they find that he "came . . . not home tonight" expresses the deep affection that until then has been hidden beneath their teasing byplay (2.4.2). Before and after Romeo and Juliet catch sight of each other, the play puts before the audience a series of characters who express endearing forms of social connection—servant to servant, kinsman to kinsman, citizen to citizen, and friend to friend.

The fact that in the name of love, Romeo and Juliet will go on to cut their bonds to this community is a "sad thing," perhaps even *the* sad thing, at the center of their tragedy. If at first Romeo's starry-eyed perspective passes for proof of his devotion, his failure to recognize the life around him quickly proves disastrous. When he reunites with Juliet in the tomb, his dogged assertion that even in death she looks supernaturally radiant—"her beauty makes this vault a feasting presence full of light" (5.3.85–86)—prevents him from recognizing that she appears so well because she is not actually dead. He kills himself only moments before she fully regains the life that he witnesses but that his "attainted eye" cannot perceive.

Left to watch helplessly as Romeo mistakes his bride for a corpse, the audience absorbs the cost of his reliance on poetry's "well-seeming forms" (1.1.169). His high-contrast conceits generate the play's most immortal lines, including "what light through yonder window breaks? / It is the East, and Juliet is the sun (2.2.2–3). But as the Friar tells Romeo at their last encounter, his all-or-nothing paradigm turns out to be a catastrophic form of "ignorance": "Like powder in a skilless soldier's flask," it will burn everything to the ground (3.3.142).

The Chorus announces from the start that the Friar will not succeed in correcting the play's tragic course. Yet by urging Romeo to "take heed" of the "pack of blessings" that "light upon" his "back," he proposes an alternate way of paying attention to the world that could have averted disaster (3.3.144, 140, 128). By way of considering what this reversal of Romeo's outlook might involve, this essay ends by taking a closer look at two incidents in the play that are utterly removed from the dazzle of its love poetry. The first is the single scene featuring the play's waylaid messenger, Friar John. The audience learns from Friar Lawrence's greeting, "What says Romeo?" that Friar John must be the same brother who was sent "with speed / To Mantua" to inform Romeo of Juliet's faked death and guide him to the place and hour of her revival (5.2.3–4; 4.1.123–24). Friar John's reply reveals that Friar Lawrence's plan has been thwarted.

He explains that his progress was unexpectedly stopped when he was detained by "searchers" and "sealed up" in a house (5.2.8, 11). Searchers are the townspeople deputized in plague time to detect the spread of the disease and enforce isolation, and they do so in this case because a second brother who was required to join the mission to Mantua had recently been tending to the sick "in a house / Where the infectious pestilence did reign" (5.2.9–10). On suspicion of exposure, both men were required to quarantine, and they were prevented from recruiting someone else to deliver the letter when Mantua sealed its borders. Friar John ends his report by handing back the missive to its author, leaving a disastrous gap in the lovers' escape plan. By the time Friar Lawrence rushes off to intercept Juliet, Romeo is at her tomb, poison in hand, and his desperate course is set.

As the first editors and critics of *Romeo and Juliet* pointed out, the delivery of the mail is an oddly mundane business for the plot to snag on. Compared with the secret marriage, the bloody quarrel with Tybalt, the violation of the Prince's banishment decree, and the death-defying potion-taking of Juliet, this "return to sender" incident is the sort of run-of-the-mill inconvenience to which tragedy, in its grand design, pays no mind. To a modernizing fan of the play like Wagner (composer of *Tristan and Isolde*), the fact that civic rules get in the way of Romeo and Juliet's reunion makes the world to blame for the lovers' rash behavior. According to this view, the indifference of Verona to the couple's survival transforms the double suicide into a heroic escape from an unfree, unjust life. However, neither school of thought takes into account the narrowness of its view. Especially when looked at from the perspective of the wider public—which is the way Shakespeare's plays were designed to be shown—what hinders the lovers relieves the community of threats to the common good. The rule that the friars must travel in pairs secures the mail, as well as those who deliver it, from criminals and accidents. The rule that those exposed to the plague must quarantine protects the citizenry from a devastating pandemic, as does the policy of closing the city gates when the disease is spreading. It is easy to disregard these measures since they are so out of keeping with the flashy rhetoric that a love story trains audiences to embrace. A final example makes this point with disarming literalness. When Capulet stays up all night to assist with the preparations for Juliet's wedding to Paris, he notes that "the curfew bell hath rung" (4.4.4). In an open-air playhouse, his remark helps the audience track the darkening night. But as Shakespeare's audience knew, the curfew was not implemented to toll the hour; it was the signal used to tell the community to put out their lights before going to bed (the word derives from the French phrase *couvre-feu*, meaning "cover fire"). Like the searchers who restrict the movement of exposed citizens to prevent the spread of the infection, the bell is a civic system put in place to keep neighbors safe. As something like the antithesis to Romeo's lovestruck exclamation, "she doth teach the torches to burn bright," the curfew's reminder to extinguish torches emphasizes the lack of difference between the one and the many. The bell is a reminder that a single act of negligence can burn a whole city to the ground.

It is not likely that Shakespeare intended for the curfew bell to signal a world blacked out by the love story's high-contrast system of exclusion. After all, in every time and all places, teenagers have tended not to heed curfews. Still, the way that the play treats as minimally significant (in the case of the curfew) or even as inept or unjust (in the case of Friar John's setbacks) the civic infrastructure designed to care for the citizenry tracks nicely with *Romeo and Juliet*'s most serious fallacy, which is that the "star-crossed" lovers are innocent of the tragedy that befalls them. Looked at with an eye to the life of the community rather than the stars that overshine it, Romeo and Juliet do not "defy" their fate so much as they defy Verona's safety regulations (5.1.24). By doing so, they bring about far more than their own catastrophe. If they had followed the Prince's law prohibiting disturbances of the peace, Mercutio and Tybalt would not have been murdered, Romeo would not have been exiled for his part in the crime, and Lady Montague would not have died of grief at her son's exile. If Romeo had obeyed the judgment barring him from Verona, he would have spared his own life, as well as Juliet's and Paris's. If he had heeded the Mantuan ban on mortal poison, the Apothecary would not have faced the gallows. If he had complied with Paris's citizen arrest ("I . . . / apprehend thee for a felon here" [5.3.68–69]), Verona would have been spared the final trio of corpses—a sight that kills Lady Capulet. While Romeo and Juliet do not intend the casualties that ensue from their choices, their consistent indifference to the rules designed to protect the citizenry has the result of escalating their private desires into a public disaster.

The bigger issue, though, is that it will seem ridiculous to expect that a love-at-first-sight story will show any regard for the maintenance of everyday life. It has become a truth universally acknowledged that no speaker of a sonnet can care that the curfew bell tolls for him. It is well within the scope of tragedy, however, to confront the cost of this convention. With its aptitude for reckoning, tragedy is built to address the corruption of thought set loose by the antithesis of dark and light. Juliet, the play's iconic teenager, comes tantalizingly close to doing just that during the balcony scene:

> Although I joy in thee,
> I have no joy of this contract tonight.
> It is too rash, too unadvised, too sudden,
> Too like the lightning (2.2.123–26).

Freed in her cloister to speak frankly of what she wants, Juliet tries to shift the poetic terms of the "contract" between herself and Romeo from a "lightning" flash to a slow-"ripening" "flower" (2.2.128, 129). The fact that she fails only makes the quest seem all the more necessary. For poetry to do justice to its subjects, there must be language that can convey the transformative feeling of love without constraining that feeling in a pattern of ignorance and neglect. Both sets of parents and the Prince engage in the "post-show talk" provoked by the play's pile-up of preventable deaths; this is an opportunity for students to imagine what it might sound like to express a love that does not extinguish social bonds but keeps the wide world in plain sight (224).

# PART THREE

*Romeo and Juliet* in *Your* Classroom with *Your* Students

# The Folger Method:
# You Will Never Teach Literature
# the Same Way Again

## Corinne Viglietta and Peggy O'Brien

Imagine a classroom where every student is so immersed in reading that they don't want to stop. A place that is buzzing with the energy of student-driven learning. Where students shout, whisper, and play with lines from Shakespeare and other authors. Where small groups discuss, with textual evidence and passion, which parts of a text are the most compelling and how to perform them effectively. Where all students bring their identities and customs, their whole selves, to fresh performances of juicy scenes. Where every student experiences firsthand that literary language is *their* language, demanding to be interpreted and reinterpreted, questioned, and yes, even resisted sometimes. Where students are doing the lion's share of the work, and the teacher, who has thoughtfully set up this zone of discovery, is observing from the side. Where joy and rigor work hand in hand. Where everyone is engaged in something that feels important and adventurous. Where every student realizes they can do hard things on their own.

This is a real place. This is *your* classroom as you try the lessons in this book. Yes, *you*.

Will it be perfect all the time? Heck no. Will it be messy, especially at first? Almost certainly. Will you have to take risks? Yes.

Does this way of teaching really work? You bet.

Don't take our word for it, though. For four decades, the Folger has been working with teachers on what has become known as the Folger Method, and here's a small sample of what teachers—mostly middle and high school teachers—have had to say:

- *"With the Folger Method, my students are reading more deeply than they ever have before. They are breaking down language and really understanding it."*

- *"I was unsure of myself and my ability to tackle Shakespeare, but this has been empowering."*

- *"Students complain when it's time to leave. I have gleefully stepped back so they can create scenes, shout words and lines, and cut speeches. They volunteer to read aloud even when reading aloud is hard for them. We dive in and focus on the words. It's working."*

- *"Over the course of this Folger unit, I've seen amazing things in my special education students. This one student has had an entire transformation—like, fellow teachers are asking me what happened. Before, he always had great pronunciation and sounded fluent, but he could never really understand what it was he was saying. And then all of a sudden in the middle of this play, something clicked. I think it's because he has all these strategies for understanding the words on the page now."*

- *"The Folger Method didn't just transform how I teach Shakespeare—it's changed how I teach everything."*

Great, but what *is* the Folger Method, exactly?

It is a transformative way of approaching complex texts. (And not just Shakespeare, but any complex text.) Consisting of both principles and practices, it provides a framework for everything that goes into great teaching: designing, planning, assessing, reflecting, revising, communicating, guiding, growing, listening, laughing, learning—all of it.

Behind it all is a precise, tried-and-true philosophy that we've broken down into 8 parts.

# 8 Foundational Principles

The more you practice this way of teaching, the more you'll see these **8 foundational principles** in action, and the clearer it all becomes. Watching your students move through the lessons in this book will give you (and them) a profound, almost visceral, understanding of these principles. They will become part of the fabric of your classroom. Teaching this way—even if it's completely new to you—will feel intuitive in no time.

**1. Shakespeare's language is not a barrier but a portal.** The language is what enables students to discover amazing things in the texts, the world, and themselves.

**2. All students and teachers deserve the real thing**—whether it's Shakespeare's original language, primary source materials, new information that expands our understanding of history, or honest conversations about tough issues that the plays present.

**3. Give up Shakespeare worship.** If your Shakespeare lives on a pedestal, take him down and move him to a space where he can talk to everyday people and great writers like Toni Morrison and Julia Alvarez, Frederick Douglass and Joy Harjo, F. Scott Fitzgerald and Azar Nafisi, Amy Tan and George Moses Horton, Jane Austen and Pablo Neruda, James Baldwin and Homer.

**4. Throw out themes, tidy explanations, and the idea of a single right interpretation.** Resist the urge to wrap up a text with a neat bow, or, as Billy Collins puts it, to tie it to a chair and "torture a confession out of it." With ambiguity comes possibility. Alongside your students, embrace the questions. How liberating!

**5. The teacher is not the explainer but rather the architect.** Set up the interactions through which your students and Shakespeare discover each other. This might be hard to hear (it was for Corinne at first!), but the helpful teacher is not the one who explains what the text means or who "translates" Shakespeare's words for students. The truly helpful teacher is the one who crafts opportunities for students to be successful at figuring things out for themselves. It's about getting out of the way so students can do things on their own.

**6. Set students on fire with excitement about literature.** When reading brings mysteries, delights, and surprises, students are motivated to read closely and cite evidence. And they gain confidence in their ability to tackle the next challenge.

**7. Amplify the voice of every single student.** Shakespeare has something to say to everybody, and everybody has something to say back to Shakespeare. Student voices, both literal and figurative, create the most vibrant and inclusive learning communities. The future of the humanities—and our world—depends on the insights and contributions of *all* students.

As tempting as it may be to impose our own interpretation of the text on students, or to ask students to imitate the brilliant arguments of seasoned scholars, we beg you to resist that urge. Students need to dive into a play and shape and reshape their own interpretations in order to become independent thinkers. Teaching literature is about the sparks that fly when readers of an infinite variety of perspectives engage directly and personally with the text.

**8. The Folger Method is a radical engine for equity.** Every student can learn this way, and every teacher can teach this way. The goal is to help all students read closely, interrogate actively, and make meaning from texts.

Now let's put these ideas into practice.

# The Arc of Learning

The first step to applying these principles in class is understanding the journey, what we call **the arc of learning**, that your students will experience.

The activities in this book are not isolated, interchangeable exercises. They are a complete set of practices that work together to bring the 8 principles to life. Sequencing, scaffolding, pacing, differentiating—it's all here.

And because each of your students is unique, each journey will be unique too. If you teach AP or IB classes, this book will help each of your students navigate their own path and reach rigorous course outcomes, starting right where scholars, editors, directors, and actors start—with the words. If you teach students who have the ability and desire to dive deep—and we mean *deep*, luxuriating in the mysteries and puzzles of complex literature—the Folger Method will enable them to do just that. Alongside these students you probably also have students who need some extra support before diving deep, and these lessons are just as much for them (more on differentiation later). By its very design, this way of teaching is flexible and roomy enough to challenge and support every single learner. Use this book to meet *all* students where they are, give them space to stretch, and be amazed at what they do.

What happens over the course of a Folger unit often astonishes teachers, administrators, families, and students themselves. Remember that spirited classroom from the first paragraph? Pass by and hear students shouting lines from Romeo and Juliet's soliloquies in a cacophony. (*What in the world?*) Poke your head in and watch them mark up their scripts with notes on which words ought to be stressed or cut out entirely, which tone to use when. (*Hmmm . . . this is interesting.*) Walk into the classroom, take a seat, and observe different student performances of the same scene—and a robust whole-class discussion about the textual evidence and knowledge that led to each group's interpretive decisions. Listen to students question and teach one another. (*Whoa! Every single student just totally owned Shakespeare.*)

What at the start might appear simply as a "fun" way to meet Shakespeare's words reveals itself to be a wild and daring, deep and demanding, meaty and memorable learning experience. Behind this magic is a very deliberate design.

From day one, your students will engage directly with the language of the text(s). That's right: There's no "I do, we do, you do" teacher modeling here. Students are always doing, doing, doing. Beginning with single words and lines, your students will learn to read closely and critically and eventually tackle longer pieces of text such as speeches, scenes, text sets, and whole texts. (Real talk: Yes, scaffolding learning by increasing the length and complexity of the language means doing some prep work. It's part of being the architect. Good news: This book has already selected and chunked most of the text for you!) Like other teachers using this method, you will likely notice that pre-reading *is* reading, just in small bites. You'll also notice your students using and reusing strategies. Sometimes you'll revisit a strategy from Week One later in the unit, with a new piece of text or an added layer of complexity. For example, Choral Reading and Cutting a Scene are favorite classroom routines that teachers use multiple times not just in a Shakespeare unit but throughout the school year. Over time, as you progress through the lessons, you will observe your students doing literacy tasks that are increasingly demanding and sophisticated, and you'll all have gained a method to help you tackle any complex text.

The process of speaking lines, interrogating and editing text, negotiating meaning, deciding how language should be embodied and performed, and owning literature—and doing it all without much teacher explanation—is what matters most. Simply put, the process is more important than the product. Don't fret if the final product is not perfect (what human endeavor is "perfect," anyway?). Did the students collaborate to analyze language and create something new? Do they know what they're saying? Have they made Shakespeare's language their own? So what if a group's performance has some awkward pauses or someone mispronounces a word? If your students have been reading actively, asking and answering good questions, and reaching their own evidence-based conclusions, it's all good. The real work happens along the arc, not at the end.

# 9 Essential Practices

This is the moment in our live workshops when teachers typically tell us how simultaneously *excited* and *nervous* they are about trying the Folger Method.

*Excited* because the Principles, the Arc, the whole philosophy of turning the learning over to the students, speaks to their own deeply held conviction that all students can do much more than is often asked of them. As one high school English teacher put it, "These Principles express something I know deep down and want to act on."

*Nervous* because this Folger thing is really different from how most of us were taught in school. Exactly how does a teacher "act on" the 8 Foundational Principles? What happens in class? What does the teacher do and not do? What does the student do and learn? What do teachers and students have to "unlearn" or let go of in order to try this approach?

The answers to these questions lie in the nine core practices of the Folger Method—the 9 Essentials. Within the lessons that follow this chapter, you will find step-by-step instructions for these Essentials right when you need them. For now, we will provide you with a brief overview of each one.

**1. Tone and Stress** boosts students' confidence in speaking text aloud and explores how a text's meanings are revealed through vocal expression. Students experience firsthand how variations in tone of voice and word stress influence a listener's understanding of subtext. They see and hear that there's no single right way to interpret a text. Longtime teacher and Teaching Shakespeare Institute faculty member Mike Lo-Monico spent a lot of time and expertise developing this!

**2. Tossing Words and Lines** puts text into students' hands and mouths and gets them up on their feet reading, speaking, and analyzing the language together. Bonus: Students are able to make inferences about the text based on the words they encounter.

**3. Two-line Scenes** get all students up on their feet, creating and performing two-person mini-scenes. They discover how making collaborative decisions to enact text is exciting and reveals new understandings. They also realize they can encounter a text "cold" and make meaning from it all on their own—dispelling the myth that Shakespeare's language is too dense to understand.

**4. Twenty-minute Plays** involve the whole class in performing lines of text that becomes an express tour through the play. Early on, students learn and own the story and the language of the play and are motivated to keep reading. Folger Director of Education Peggy O'Brien originated this Essential and has perfected the art of finding the most fun-to-say lines in a play!

**5. Choral Reading** asks all students to read and reread a text aloud together. By changing what the "chorus" does in each rereading, this exercise gives students multiple opportunities to refine their understanding of the text. Students discover how the simple acts of speaking and rereading strengthen comprehension and analysis—all without any teacher explanation. In the chorus, there's an anonymity that's freeing, especially for English Learners and shy readers. Choral Reading is immersive, low-stakes, and really, really powerful.

**6. 3D Lit** enables a class or group of students to work together, figuring out (a) what is going on in a scene they have never before read with no explanation and very little help from you, and (b) how to informally act it out, making decisions as they go. This process enables them to refine their understanding as they transform the text from the page to a 3D "stage" in class. Michael Tolaydo, an actor, director, and faculty member of the Teaching Shakespeare Institute, created this groundbreaking Essential.

**7. Cutting a Scene** gets students close reading with a purpose by challenging groups to eliminate half the lines from a piece of text while retaining its meaning. Since editors, scholars, directors, actors, and students have been cutting Shakespeare *forever*, yours are in good company. In fulfilling their mission as editors, students will naturally have to examine what the text says and implies, how the scene works, who's who, how language functions, and what's at stake. The fun part? Listening to your students debating which lines should stay or go and what the scene's "meaning" is anyway.

**8. Promptbooks** engage students in a process of text-based decision-making and collaborative annotation that reflects how they would stage a text. Many teachers and students call promptbooks "annotating with a real purpose." As with other Essentials, promptbooks are useful for students grappling with an unfamiliar text.

**9. Group Scenes** enable students to put all the pieces together. Students collaborate to select, cut, rehearse, memorize, and perform a scene for their classmates. Sometimes group scenes consist entirely of the original language of the text; other times they might include mashups or adaptations that incorporate home languages, pop culture, and/or the wide world of literature. Students make their own Shakespeares, demonstrating how they have used textual evidence and background knowledge not only to understand but also reinvent complex dramatic language.

# A Note on Differentiation

You know better than anyone else that inside every single one of your students is a whole lot of talent and a whole lot of room to improve. Therefore, when we talk about "differentiation," we are not talking about "struggling readers" or "remediation." We are talking about the rich diversity of what everyone brings to—and takes from—the learning. And everyone—*everyone*—has a great deal to bring and take!

So, are we talking about students in your AP or IB classes? Neurodiverse students? Students with IEPs? Nontraditional students? English Learners? So-called high-fliers? Yes. All of the above. In other words, differentiation is about hearing, seeing, challenging, supporting, and inspiring each unique learner.

When teachers experience the Folger Method for themselves, they often point out how differentiation is woven right into the Essentials. Because this mode of teaching relies so heavily on student voice, it is inherently personalized.

Beyond this general fact, though, there are several specific ways in which the Folger Method accounts for the variety of learners in your classroom. Allow us to zoom in on just two of them.

Example #1: The Essential called "Two-Line Scenes" provides opportunities for students of all reading abilities to be successful. Each student works with a partner to make a "mini-play" from just two lines of Shakespeare. If, in one pair, Student A knows just two words in their assigned line, they can base their performance on those two words, or they can collaborate with their scene partner, Student B, to work out the meaning of the rest of their line. And if Student B knows not only the literal but also the figurative meaning of both lines, they can share their understanding with Student A and work together to take on the additional challenge of expressing subtext with their voices and bodies. Differentiation is happening on two fronts here: first, through the "wiggle room" that allows each student to bring their own knowledge and creativity to the final product (sometimes called "variable outcomes" by learning experts); second, through peer collaboration. Throughout this book, you will see that students are supporting and stretching each other, and developing their own independent thinking skills, thanks to all kinds of grouping configurations.

Example #2: Since much of the Folger Method relies on selecting and chunking text for our students, there is a ready-made structure for matching students with passages that meet them where they are and stretch them to the next level. In this book you will find that a relentless focus on language is one of the best tools you have for differentiating learning. In other words, don't change the task, water anything down, or make it overly complicated—just chunk the text into appropriately challenging parts. (If you teach English Learners and multilingual students—who are used to attending very carefully to language, its sound, its sense, its nuance—all this will strike you as familiar. For more on the unique power of the Folger Method with English Learners, turn to Dr. Christina Porter's excellent essay in this book.)

# 7 Touchstone Questions

As you jump into this book and these lessons, try using the following "Touchstone Questions" as your guide to reflecting on your own teaching. Think of them as a kind of checklist for student-driven, language-focused learning. Like everything else in this book, they are grounded in the 8 Foundational Principles.

If you can answer "yes" to each Touchstone Question, there must be some serious sparks flying in your classroom!

**1.** Did I, the teacher, get out of the way and let students own their learning?

**2.** Is the language of the text(s) front and center?

**3.** Are the words of the text in ALL students' mouths?

**4.** Are students collaborating to develop their own interpretations?

**5.** Are students daring to grapple with complex language and issues in the text?

**6.** Has every voice been included and honored?

**7.** Am I always giving students the real thing, whether it's Shakespeare's language, or primary sources, or supporting tough conversations as prompted by the text?

## You've Got This

The Folger Method is proof of what's possible when we as teachers step back and let students own their learning. When we teachers realize we don't need to have all the answers. When students are invited to question and grapple. When they approach language with curiosity and care. When they tackle the real thing. When everyone tries new challenges, takes big risks, and supports one another along the way. When all students realize they can do hard things on their own.

You have everything you need to make this happen. We believe in you and can't wait to hear how it goes.

# *Romeo and Juliet* Day-by-Day: The Five-Week Unit Plan

### TEACHER-TO-TEACHER THOUGHTS AND THE GAME PLAN FOR THIS *ROMEO AND JULIET*

## Amber Phelps and Deborah Gascon

## Teacher-to-Teacher Thoughts

It's like a rite of passage to read *Romeo and Juliet* in any middle school or high school English Language Arts classroom. There is so much cultural significance attached to this play that in spite of its tragic ending, many of our students have consumed some sort of facsimile of this old tale—and particularly the delightfully sappy romance embedded in the balcony scene.

But what happens when we jettison that sort of weight connected to this iconic text and look to see what else the play has to teach? Students find lots of the questions and mindsets that *Romeo and Juliet* presents highly compelling, both when considering them within the confines of the play and more broadly with respect to their own lives. What are the dangers of drifting through the world without solid support systems? What do we owe our parents and, in turn, what do they owe their children? The play—as do many of Shakespeare's—presents a binary view of beauty: "fair," "pale," "snowy," and in general, whiteness describes the beautiful, while "black," "sooty," and "dusty" is never beautiful—Shakespeare uses those words to describe ugliness. Diving into *Romeo and Juliet* through the language serves as a way to connect students with the plot, the characters, and these questions. It also offers them chances to bring their full selves—their own knowledge, experience, and lives—to the text and to talk back to Shakespeare. Excellent!

So HOW do we do that? How do we connect our students with *Romeo and Juliet* while bringing new life and welcome joy into our classrooms? We want your students to come to their own interpretation of the play! These lessons will get your students out of their seats to collaborate on their learning, add their own to the chorus of "words, words, words" in your room, and respond to these questions that Shakespeare raises in this play.

In the lessons ahead, we'll show you how to teach *Romeo and Juliet* in a way that ensures your students dive deep and build confidence with the language through careful scaffolding that is "wisely and slow" so that they, unlike Romeo and Juliet, won't "stumble" by "running fast" through the text. Let's take the Bard off the pedestal, and have some fun living in the language and the world of this play. You may be surprised to see what fresh ideas your students will add to your classroom community.

## FROM DEBORAH GASCON

I felt so fortunate to teach *Romeo and Juliet* when I student-taught my last semester of college. I was especially thrilled because it was the year of the textbook caravan and I had five different box sets from the publishers of ninth-grade textbooks and ancillary materials to use however I wanted. This was the first time I was fully in charge of the lesson planning and I spent hours upon hours in the teachers' lounge reading every word the publisher had printed in the side notes of *Romeo and Juliet*. I cut and pasted the worksheets and question banks, and I pieced together what I thought was the best summative assessment. I worked so hard. Then I taught the lesson and I worked even harder. I had the answer to every question they asked (How could I not? The answers were in the side notes!), I translated every word they didn't understand, and I felt confident and successful. We read the play in its entirety and they aced the final assessment. In my mind it was a success and for the first time, I felt like a real teacher. Even a great teacher. Because in my mind (and training), this is what great teachers did—they used the materials, they made copies, they followed the textbook, they taught the students what the words on the page meant, they celebrated all As in the gradebook. And now I know that in that moment, the feeling of success and pride in my work was important. Teaching in this traditional way gave me the confidence to try something else, something new, something more active, something student-centered.

After a few years of teaching, I looked back on that first *Romeo and Juliet* unit and realized I did all the work (and realized a lot of other problems as well). I explained. I pronounced. I defined. I gave insight. I stood in front of them and basically did ALL of the work. And what did they do? Nothing. They passively sat at their desks and obediently listened to me do all the explaining, waiting for the "right" answer—then they regurgitated it all on the final assessment. I was just so excited to TEACH. I was thrilled to be sharing all I had studied. But they didn't LEARN. I was missing the most important piece. I doubt they learned a single thing—except maybe that I loved worksheets. I am confident if you tracked those students down they wouldn't remember a single thing about *Romeo and Juliet*. They didn't own any part of that play; I owned it all and doled it out to them on my terms.

Fast-forward a few years to my reading Shakespeare Set Free, then a few years later to attending the 2012 Teaching Shakespeare Institute at the Folger. After that summer, just like when I was student-teaching, I took notes, I organized, and I planned a new *Romeo and Juliet* unit. But this time the teaching experience was so, so different. There were no worksheets, but rather scripts with Shakespeare's words on them. Instead of me, THEY read. They performed. They analyzed. They asked questions. And then they answered each other's questions. They made connections. And what did I do? Nothing. Granted, I set up the lessons and managed the students with directions, but the onus to understand and interpret was all on them and to my surprise, they could do most of it without me. They didn't need me as much as I thought they did (what a revelation!). It took us longer to move through the play, and wow, it was really messy and noisy and I struggled at first getting out of the way and allowing the mess and noise to happen, but they LEARNED. And I'm confident if you tracked any of them down, they would still remember reading *Romeo and Juliet*. They owned it and they carried the experience and skills with them to their next complex reading experience. What more could a teacher possibly want?

I'm still tweaking my Shakespeare units—I am always searching for ways to include diversity, analyze current issues connected to Shakespeare's words, have characters from other texts we read talk to Shakespeare's characters. Its revision is iterative and it never stands still. Very much like my students reading *Romeo and Juliet*.

## FROM AMBER PHELPS

Like many of us, I learned early on in my teacher preparation courses that a "good" lesson plan includes a slow release of control of the lesson. We all know the "I do, we do, you do" section of our lesson plan that is the north star for scaffolding our daily plans.

And that's how the planning of my lesson plans went during my first year of teaching *Romeo and Juliet*: showing my comfort with the language of the text was absolutely going to lead to students' owning the language and finding fun with the Bard, right? Wrong. I wanted to tie my unit plan with neat and tidy thematic bows, teach them a long list of literary devices, and fill out a bunch of boxes on handouts. All these efforts led to my students speaking "an infinite deal of nothing" about what I wanted them to know about the play and Shakespeare.

I really lost sight of what was really important: my students deserved to have the freedom to grapple with the language and find their own entry point into the world of the play. But as Shakespeare would say, "the past is prologue," and after a wonderful summer in 2012 at the Folger's Teaching Shakespeare Institute—an experience that changed my personal and professional life—I discovered ways to structure my class that transformed my planning into "you do, you do, you do."

For the first time in my classroom, and for ALL of my units, my students were at the helm of their learning, my students were drawing their own interpretations of the texts, my students were analyzing how authors from all kinds of backgrounds talk back to the ideas about the human condition that Shakespeare explores in his plays and whose voices are left out of these conversations. They were LEARNING, and most importantly, they were learning about themselves.

# The Game Plan for This *Romeo and Juliet*

This chart plans out the unit of the five weeks of lessons shared in this book. These lessons don't cover all of the scenes in the play, but they lead to the final project: a student-created scene performance and written defense of the choices evident in the scene performed.

These lessons can be completed without assigning much homework in between and could be used in isolation from one another (most of the time). But you, of course, know your students. Scenes studied in class one day could be read the night before; scenes skipped by these lessons could become fun class warm-ups as pantomimes or mini versions of a 20-Minute Play. Or maybe students will perform those missing scenes for their final projects.

The procedure for each lesson is called **"What Students Hear (From You) and (Then What They'll) Do."** In that section of each lesson, we've written instructions for what you will say (thus, what students hear) and what you will see students do as the lesson proceeds. It's as close as we can get to inviting you into our classrooms to watch and listen as a lesson unfolds. In some places, we have shared any additional "teacher thoughts" that should factor into the work in a **TEACHER NOTE**. The lessons close with **"Here's What Just Happened in Class,"** so you can get a sense of what students learned and what skills they practiced over the course of the lesson.

| DAY BY DAY | | |
|---|---|---|
| **Week/Act** | **Questions guiding exploration of the play** | **Lessons** |
| **1**<br><br>Act 1 | What world was Willie Shakes in?<br><br>What is this play?<br><br>How do I read it? | **1.** Shakespeare in His Own Context<br><br>**2.** Getting Into Lines!<br><br>**3.** Sampling the Language and the Play!<br><br>**4.** What's Going On in the Beginning of *Romeo and Juliet* (1.1)?<br><br>**5.** "Too Soon Marr'd": Parenting in 1.3 |

| 2 Acts 1 & 2 | Who are these characters?<br><br>How do they define beauty?<br><br>Do they help or hurt each other? | **6.** "We Die Soon": Beginning to Understand Mercutio Through Cutting and Comparing<br><br>**7.** "You kiss by the book!": Creating Prompt-books!<br><br>**8.** All of 1.5 in Motion, *and* Defining Beauty Across Time and Culture: "I'll make thee think thy swan a crow"<br><br>**9.** On the Balcony: *Romeo and Juliet*, 2.2<br><br>**10.** "I'll thy assistant be": Evaluating the Friar's Advice in 2.3 & 2.6 |
|---|---|---|
| 3 Act 3 | How does the text lead us to action and interpretation?<br><br>What do parents owe their children?<br><br>What do children owe their parents? | **11.** "We Shall Not 'Scape a Brawl": Creating and Analyzing Action in 3.1<br><br>**12.** Performing 3.1 with a Mystery Guest from 3.2!<br><br>**13.** Advice to Teenagers Through Time and Space<br><br>**14.** "Hear me with patience": Revisiting Parenting in 3.5<br><br>**15.** "Let them gaze . . .": Visualizing Acts 1, 2, and 3 |
| 4 Acts 4 & 5 | What is everyone feeling?<br><br>The Acts 4 and 5 speed-through! | **16.** Intermission and Review: Ten-Minute Character Plays<br><br>**17.** Juliet, Friar Lawrence, and Paris: Multiple Perspectives in 4.1<br><br>**18.** "I Drink to Thee": Breaking Up Juliet's Soliloquy in 4.3<br><br>**19.** "Then I'll be brief": Creating a Five-Minute Act 5 in *Romeo and Juliet*<br><br>**20.** "See what a scourge is laid upon your hate": Resounding Words in *Romeo and Juliet* and Contemporary Poetry |
| 5 Acts 1–5 | How will WE tell the rest of this story together?<br><br>How does the text guide your decisions, your interpretations, your performances? | **21.** YOUR FINAL PROJECTS!<br><br>**22–24.** YOUR FINAL PROJECT: MAKING *ROMEO AND JULIET* YOUR OWN<br><br>**25.** THE FINAL PROJECT: YOUR OWN *ROMEO AND JULIET*, PERFORMED! |

# Shakespeare in Context

## Here's What We're Doing Today and Why

Today you'll take a minute to allow your students to discover that the universe of Shakespeare is bigger, more diverse, and more interesting than they may realize. This lesson is all about giving everyone a taste of context—a brief glimpse into some of the most expansive, exciting, and surprising aspects of studying Shakespeare, his words, and his world. It zooms out way beyond *Romeo and Juliet* for a moment!

By the end of this lesson, students will have examined their own ideas about Shakespeare's world. They will have enlarged their sense of history by studying 4 primary-source documents and a single 21st-century one, spanning the 1600s to the 1900s. They will have reflected on the wide world of Shakespeare and their place in it.

## What Will I Need?

- Portrait of Abd el-Ouahed ben Messaoud ben Mohammed Anoun, Moroccan Ambassador to Queen Elizabeth I, ca. 1600 – **RESOURCE #1.1A**

- John Smith's Map of Virginia and the Chesapeake, a 1631 copy of the 1612 original – **RESOURCE #1.1B**

- Portraits by Wenceslaus Hollar, 1645 – **RESOURCE #1.1C**

- Broadside publicizing Ira Aldridge's first appearance at Covent Garden as Othello, 1833 – **RESOURCE #1.1D**

- *Romeo y Julieta*, "Prologo," Pablo Neruda, written in 1964, published in 2001 – **RESOURCE #1.1E**

- 6 Mind-blowing Facts about Shakespeare and History – **RESOURCE #1.1F**

- Large paper, markers, and/or Post-it Notes for the gallery walk we're calling "Document Speed Dating"

## How Should I Prepare?

- Set up your classroom for "Document Speed Dating":
  - Post the 5 documents at various stations around the room.
  - Make sure the images are big and clear enough for everyone to see details and there's enough space around each document for students to respond in writing. You can use whiteboards, butcher paper, or Post-it Notes—just make sure that there's room for everyone to "talk back" to each image.
  - Organize your students into 5 groups, each one starting at a different station.

## Agenda (~ 45-minute class)

- ❏ Prior Knowledge Free Write: 7 minutes
- ❏ Speed Dating Instructions: 3 minutes
- ❏ Speed Dating Exercise: 21 minutes
- ❏ The List: 6 minutes
- ❏ Reflection Round: 8 minutes

## Here's What Students Hear (From You) and (Then What They'll) Do

### Part One: Prior Knowledge Free Write

1. Jot down your thoughts on any of the following questions. When you imagine the world of Shakespeare, what do you see? What images come to your mind? Who are the people? What do they look and sound like? What are the places and objects? What's the vibe?

2. Turn to a classmate and discuss what each of you wrote.

3. As a class, we'll share the images and ideas that arose in the paired conversations.

[**TEACHER NOTE:** Record student responses on the board in a broad way—no need to be exhaustive here. The point is to capture things like "people in ruffs and crowns" or "outdoor theaters" or "white Europeans" or "candlelight and quills" or "street fighting" or "plague" or "boring" or "lively" or "smelly clothes" or "harp music"—whatever comes to your students' minds. **Welcome all responses without editorializing.**]

### Part Two: Document Speed Dating

1. Now you are going to meet actual historical documents from the world of Shakespeare. Your job is to:

   a. look very closely at what you see

   b. write down your observations right alongside the document

   c. Keeping in mind your earlier impressions of Shakespeare's world, what in each image jumps out at you? What do you wonder about?

[**TEACHER NOTE:** You can keep the "What in the image jumps out at you?" prompt posted for students to see throughout this exercise.]

   d. Get into your groups and begin at your assigned station. Each group should be at a different station.

   e. You will have roughly 3 minutes at each station. As a group, move to the next station when you hear "Next!" Continue until every group has studied and written observations about all 5 documents.

   f. Now that everyone has gone on a "speed date" with each document, return to your seat and find a partner.

g. With this partner, discuss the main things that jumped out at you in these documents. Did anything surprise you? Did you learn anything new about the world of Shakespeare? We'll share more as a whole class in a few moments . . .

### Part Three: The List

1. Let's look at the list of "6 Mind-blowing Facts about Shakespeare and History" – **RESOURCE #1.1F**.

[**TEACHER NOTE:** Call for 6 volunteers to read each fact aloud. Save discussion for the reflection round below.]

### Part Four: Reflection Round

1. Now it's time for each of you to share your reflections on today's learning. We'll do 2 rounds. Remember, just one sentence from each student and not more at this point. We want to hear from EVERY voice!

2. First, finish the sentence, "Something that changed my original mental picture of Shakespeare's world was . . ."

3. Second, finish the sentence, "I am still wondering . . ."

4. In closing, can you summarize the main ways in which these documents have enlarged or transformed your understanding of Shakespeare's world? Individually? As a class?

## Here's What Just Happened in Class

- Students have identified and interrogated their prior knowledge—and assumptions—of Shakespeare's world.

- Students have examined 5 different documents spanning 4 centuries in order to enlarge their understanding of Shakespeare and history. They have seen for themselves that Shakespeare's Britain was multicultural and very much connected to the Americas.

- Students know important and surprising facts about the wide world of Shakespeare.

## RESOURCE #1.1A

# Abd el-Ouahed ben Messaoud ben Mohammed Anoun, Ambassador from Morocco to the court of Queen Elizabeth I, beginning in 1600

**RESOURCE #1.1B**

# John Smith's Map of Virginia and the Chesapeake, a 1631 copy of the 1612 original

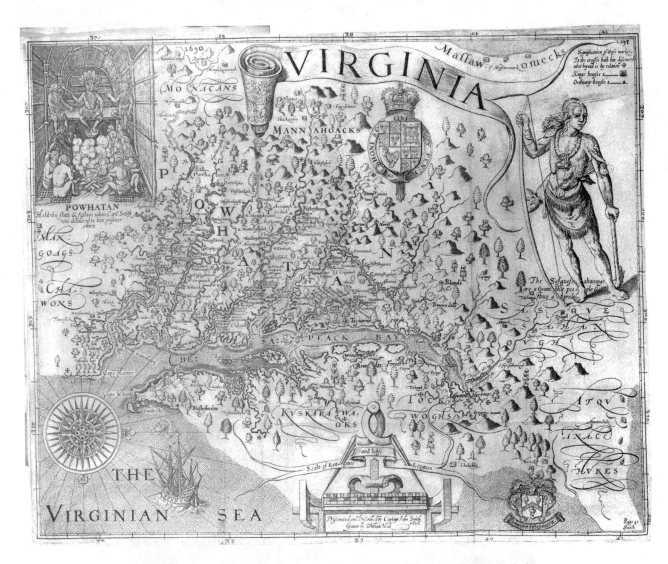

John Smith's Map of Virginia, the original published first in 1612, then included in
the first edition of his book that was published in 1624. His book was popular—
this image map is copied from the second edition, published in 1631.

**RESOURCE #1.1C**

# Portraits by Wenceslaus Hollar, made in and around 1645

**RESOURCE #1.1D**

# Ira Aldridge's First Appearance at Covent Garden as Othello

## RESOURCE #1.1E

# *Romeo y Julieta*, "Prologo," Pablo Neruda, written in 1964, published in 2001

### PRÓLOGO

*ENTRA EL CORO*

CORO
    En la bella Verona esto sucede:
    dos casas ambas en nobleza iguales
    con odio antiguo hacen discordia nueva.
    La sangre tiñe sus civiles manos.

*Dos horas durará en nuestro escenario esta historia: escuchadla con paciencia, suplirá nuestro esfuerzo lo que falte.*

# 6 Mind-blowing Facts about Shakespeare and History

**1.** There were many people of different ethnicities and religions in Shakespeare's Britain. An important facet of this history: Africans participated in life at many social levels. Many were baptized—Protestant parishes retain the records. Black citizens included merchants, silk weavers, seamstresses, shoemakers, a circumnavigator who sailed with Sir Francis Drake, and a royal musician.

**2.** During her coronation festivities in 1600, Queen Elizabeth I entertained a large delegation of Muslim African officials, including Moroccan ambassador Abd el-Ouahed ben Messaoud ben Mohammed Anoun. He returned to court often and served as her advisor. Some think that Shakespeare might have seen him and African diplomats at court and drawn inspiration from them.

**3.** William Shakespeare was writing plays as English settlers colonized Jamestown, Virginia, in 1607. He is even thought to have based his play *The Tempest* on accounts of the wreck of a ship called the *Sea Venture*, which was on its way to Jamestown.

**4.** Ira Aldridge was the first African American actor to play the role of Othello at a professional theater: the Theatre Royal, Covent Garden, London, in 1833. Born in New York City, Aldridge performed all over Europe and was one of the first international stars of the Shakespeare stage. Paul Robeson was the first African American actor to play Othello in the United States—more than 100 years later, in 1943.

**5.** It was not until 1660 that the first woman performed Shakespeare onstage. Until then, men and boys had played all the parts. After this point, though, women took on not just female characters but also male characters.

**6.** Shakespeare's works have been adapted and performed around the globe for centuries, and they have been translated into over 100 languages.

# Getting Into Lines!

## Here's What We're Doing and Why

Starting with a single line is one of the least intimidating ways to begin grappling with the language of a complex text. It's especially freeing to try out new words with a familiar physical action: throwing and catching!

This lesson uses one of the nine essential practices of the Folger Method: Tossing Words and Lines, which gets students owning the language from the minute they enter the room. You, the teacher, will get pieces of text into students' hands and mouths, and students will get quickly on their feet reading, speaking and analyzing the language together. Along the way, they will realize that this low-stakes learning experience is not about getting the right answer, but rather about grappling with text and discovering new things about words, texts, the world, and themselves.

We recommend starting any literature unit with Tossing Words and Lines and revisiting this essential practice—with different words and lines of your or your students' choosing, of course—at various points throughout the unit.

[**TEACHER NOTE:** In this lesson—and in many lessons that follow—please avoid correcting pronunciation and/or supplying definitions of words! Your job is to let students own the words and the process, and to discover for themselves. When it comes to Shakespeare, we have no audio of how anybody pronounced words then, so . . . there's no such thing as an absolutely "correct" pronunciation, anyway. At this stage, what matters most is comfort and confidence with the words. If students are saying the words and enjoying their sounds, they're on target! Students can determine and clarify pronunciation and meanings later.]

## What Will I Need?

- Lines about unrest:
    - Printed lines for tossing from *Romeo and Juliet* that paint a picture of the world that readers of this play are entering, pulled from the free online Folger Shakespeare (**RESOURCE #1.2A**)
    - Lines from poems that will be revisited after reading Act 5: "I Look at the World" by Langston Hughes, "Boy Breaking Glass" by Gwendolyn Brooks, "Watts Bleeds" by Luis J. Rodríguez, and "Haiku and Tanka for Harriet Tubman" by Sonia Sanchez (These lines, along with ones from *Romeo and Juliet*, are all included in **RESOURCE #1.2A**; complete poems are available in Week Four, Lesson 5, **RESOURCE #4.5A**.)
    - The separate set of lines entirely from *Romeo and Juliet* (**RESOURCE #1.2B**) that your students will use to create two-line scenes from the play

## How Should I Prepare?

- Set up your classroom so that there is space for active movement. If you can, try desks in a circle around the room with an open space in the middle.

- Have beanbags or rolled-up socks for tossing the lines in action—one for each group. Groups can have 6–7 students each.

- Have a basket or a can full of the individual lines cut into slips of paper. Make sure to read the list of lines and be mindful about how they are distributed. A few of the lines might be inappropriate or awkward for some students to deliver. You know your students; use your discretion. **(RESOURCE #1.2A)**

- Cut the *R + J* lines in **RESOURCE #1.2B** into square "cards" and have them ready to distribute to students.

## Agenda

- ❏ Tossing Lines: 15 minutes
- ❏ Discussion: 10 minutes
- ❏ Two-Line Scenes: 10 minutes
- ❏ Reflection: 10 minutes

## Here's What Students Hear (From You) and (Then What They'll) Do

**Part One: Tossing Lines**

[**TEACHER NOTE:** Have students complete the following steps in a joyful, respectful, language-centered environment with a low barrier to success. Don't over-explain or over-introduce the activity. Let students dive right in. To save time, you could also hand each student their slip of paper as they enter the room and ask everyone to group up right away.]

1. Let's get into circular groups of 6–7. I'm going to walk around with this can of lines, and each of you will take a strip of paper out of the can and read the line printed on it silently to yourself. I am also going to give a beanbag (or sock ball) to one person in the group.

2. In each circle, the student with the beanbag will toss it to another student in the circle while saying their line. The student receiving the beanbag catches it, tosses it, and says their line or phrase to yet another student, and so on. Keep the language and the beanbags going for 5 minutes or so and keep tossing and repeating your line. Play around with different ways of saying the line: change your volume, change the emotion, or change which word you emphasize.

3. Great! Now, let's add a gesture to accompany our lines. Whenever you catch the beanbag, you will say your line and make a movement that helps to communicate what you think your line says or means. Take a few seconds to come up with your movement and then begin tossing the beanbag and tossing your lines. Make sure everyone in the circle delivers their line at least three times.

4. Let's reconvene as a whole class and talk about what you just did. First, let's go around the room one more time to hear everyone read their line aloud. How did it feel to say the lines out loud? What do you think your line might mean? What

is its tone? What did the physical movement add? Why? What did you notice about the lines you said/heard?

5. Now let's make some inferences and predictions. What kind of text do you think we are about to read? What kind of world do you think we're about to enter? What makes you say that? What information about the setting, conflicts, characters, mood, story, and big ideas can we glean from these lines?

[**TEACHER NOTE:** For deeper reflection, post all the lines on the board and invite students to write their responses to some or all of the post-activity questions. Some of the questions ask students to reflect on their own learning (metacognition), and others invite students to draw conclusions about *Romeo and Juliet* based on the language they encountered today (cognition).]

**Part Two: Two-Line Scenes**

1. Now we will play with lines again. This time, we'll use a new set of lines. Once you have pulled your new line, read it to yourself and play around with tone, stress, and movement.

2. Next, we will count off to make partners. Each pair of partners is responsible for creating a scene using just the two lines you have. You can add movement to help communicate where or when your scene is happening and who your characters are, but the only words you speak will be the words on your paper strips. You and your partner can decide who speaks first and who speaks second.

3. Take 5 minutes to practice your scene. Then, all pairs will perform their scenes, one after another. Once they have all finished, they will take a bow! During the bow, your classmates and I will applaud wildly!

4. BRAVO! Those scenes were a lot of fun! Let's talk about what you noticed about your or your classmates' scenes: How did you make decisions about who spoke first and who spoke second? What surprised you about some scenes? Which words or phrases helped you figure out how to deliver your line? These lines are all from *Romeo and Juliet*. What sort of world do these lines lead us into?

## Here's What Just Happened in Class

- The room filled with energy and the sounds of ALL of your students speaking Shakespeare and other authors' words.

- You resisted defining or explaining words and stepped back to let students own the experience and the language.

- Students felt empowered to speak up and bring their unique voices, knowledge, and perspectives to the text they encountered today.

- Students made observations and inferences based on the text they spoke and heard.

- Students realized the impressive thing they just did: made meaning from the original language of Shakespeare and other authors without any teacher explanation.

# Line Tossing on Unrest for *Romeo and Juliet*

## Authors: Shakespeare, Hughes, Brooks, Rodríguez, Sanchez

1. The quarrel is between our masters and us their men.

2. Our beautiful flaw and terrible ornament.

3. Clubs, bills, and partisans! Strike! Beat them down!

4. Watts bleeds leaving stained reminders on dusty sidewalks.

5. Come alive as once you tried to do from the ashes.

6. Throw your mistempered weapons to the ground.

7. Your lives shall pay the forfeit of the peace.

8. Picture her saying *no.*

9. Each to his grief, each to his loneliness and fidgety revenge.

10. It was you, it was you who threw away my name!
And this is everything I have for me.

11. Temples desolated by a people's rage.

12. For now, these hot days, is the mad blood stirring.

13. Make it a word and a blow.

14. Picture this woman freedom bound.

15. Picture her words: *There's two things I got a right to: death or liberty*

16. I look at the world from awakening eyes in a black face

17. Then, dreadful trumpet, sound the general doom

18. Unable to stop the flow from this swollen and festering sore.

19. Proud can I never be of what I hate.

20. In the warmth of a summer night, gunshots echo their deadly song

21. Accursed, unhappy, wretched, hateful day!

22. Watts bleeds on vacant lots and burned-out buildings

23. See what a scourge is laid upon your hate.

24. That all these walls oppression builds will have to go!

25. Broken window is a cry of art

**26.** *Every great dream begins with a dreamer.*

**27.** Picture her leaning into the eyes of our birth clouds

**28.** Picture her kissing our spines saying *no* to the eyes of slavery

**29.** Picture a woman jumping rivers her legs inhaling moons

## RESOURCE #1.2B

[Thou art] the very butcher of a silk button.

[Thou] candle-holder.
[Thou] scurvy knave!

Thou wilt quarrel with a man that hath a hair more, or a hair less, in his beard, than thou hast.

Thy head is as full of quarrels as an egg is full of meat.

Thou wilt quarrel with a man for cracking nuts, having no other reason but because thou hast hazel eyes.

Thou hast quarreled with a man for coughing in the street, because he hath wakened thy dog that hath lain asleep in the sun.

Thou detestable maw, thou womb of death.

She speaks yet she says nothing.
Talk not to me, for I'll not speak a word.

Why he's a man of wax.

[Thou] small grey-coated gnat.
Out, you baggage!

You kiss by the book.

I will dry-beat you with an iron wit.

You ratcatcher.

My naked weapon is out.

You tallow-face!

I will bite thee by the ear for that jest.

I am the very pink of courtesy.

He is not the flower of courtesy.

He heareth not, he stirreth not, he moveth not, the ape is dead

Hang, beg, starve, die in the streets!

[Thou] disobedient wretch!

Hang thee, young baggage!

Go thy ways, wench.

[You're] not so big as a round little worm. A plague on both your houses.

The hate I bear thee can afford no better term than this thou art a villain.

## WEEK ONE: LESSON 3

# Sampling the Language and the Play!

### Here's What We're Doing and Why

Yesterday, students made predictions about the plot of the play that were prompted by lines from Shakespeare and other poets. Today, we are going to build more anticipation about the world of *Romeo and Juliet* and explore the basic plot of the play, once again using Shakespeare's language as our "way in" to the play.

The Folger essential practice Choral Reading focuses students on Shakespeare's language and how choices with the language create meaning. In addition, the 20-Minute version of *Romeo and Juliet* helps give students a road map of the play so that instruction can focus on language and students' own interpretations rather than plot. During Shakespeare's time, in fact, most of the audience would have known the plots of his plays before seeing the performance, at least in broad strokes; today, students will get a brief, fun way of knowing the basic plot structure of *Romeo and Juliet* while also being introduced to some of its most intriguing lines.

Performing a choral reading of the Prologue is a great introduction to the world of the play and to a tool for understanding that students will use throughout the unit.

In this lesson—and often in lessons that follow—we use Reflection Rounds to close the lesson because we've learned that oral reflection is a good way for students to synthesize what they just experienced. It also builds community to uplift and affirm student-driven thoughts, ideas, predictions, and all the fun they had during that process. In addition, rounds are a good way for you to learn more about your students' journey toward developing confidence with the content and the language. At the end of this lesson, we detail how these rounds work in class.

### What Will I Need?

- Copies of the Prologue for each student – **RESOURCE #1.3A**

- Strips with one line from *Romeo and Juliet* on each strip – **RESOURCE #1.3B**

- 20-Minute *Romeo and Juliet* (Narration), one copy for you – **RESOURCE #1.3C**

### How Should I Prepare?

- Make copies of the Prologue in 1.1 – **RESOURCE #1.3A**

- Make one copy of the 20-Minute *Romeo and Juliet* numbered lines – **RESOURCE #1.3B** – and cut them into 25 separate strips—one line per strip.

- Have your own copy of the Narration on paper – **RESOURCE #1.3C**

### Agenda (~ 45-minute class period)

- ❏ Choral Reading of the Prologue: 15 minutes
- ❏ 20-Minute *Romeo and Juliet*: 20 minutes
- ❏ Reflection Rounds: 10 minutes

## Here's What Students Hear (From You) and (Then What They'll) Do

### Part One: Choral Reading

Here, we follow the steps for Choral Reading, a Folger Essential.

1. We're going to read through the Prologue to *Romeo and Juliet* – **RESOURCE #1.3A** – using a technique called "choral reading." We will read through this passage together a few times, and at some points, I will stop to ask questions about what you understand in the passage.

2. Everyone, gather and stand (if you are able) in a circle.

3. The first time through, let's read the script as loud and fast as you can while still staying together with the rest of the class.

4. Great! Read the speech again, loud and fast. This time through, imagine that you are a narrator, beginning to tell a grand story.

5. By a show of fingers (5 fingers means "I've totally got this" and 1 finger means "You speak an infinite deal of nothing and I might need some more rereads"), indicate your understanding of the speech.

6. Now, let's divide our circle into 2 halves. Then, let's read again, this time with each side alternating lines ("Side A" reads lines 1, 3, 5, etc.; "Side B" reads lines 2, 4, 6, etc.).

7. By a show of fingers, indicate your understanding.

8. After these first three reads, what did you notice?

[TEACHER NOTE: Leave the question open; students might mention something about the contrasting language, the foreshadowing of the end of the play, etc. Be sure to keep the activity moving, though. Some may not have anything to share. Hang on! The real discussion comes later!]

9. By a show of fingers, indicate your understanding.

10. What do you notice about this passage? What do you hear? If a prologue is an introduction, what sort of story does this passage introduce? How do you know? Can you find some text to support your thinking?

[TEACHER NOTE: "How do you know?" is THE magic question!]

11. Now we are going to read the whole prologue chorally 2 more times. This first time we are going to start with a whisper and end with a shout.

12. Again, and now this time we are going to start with a shout and end with a whisper.

13. What have we learned about the play from reading this chunk of text, and from reading it like this? Which style (whisper to shout/shout to whisper) felt more appropriate for reading this passage? Why? What are some juicy words from the Prologue that you noticed? Share your observations, and then tell us what makes you say that . . . what words in the text give you that idea.

[**TEACHER NOTE:** Typically, students share that they understand why we had so many images of unrest and violence in yesterday's lesson and bridge it to the language of the Prologue.]

## Part Two: 20-Minute *Romeo and Juliet*

1. Now, we're going to move into the whole play! During our study, we will focus more on the language and ideas of *Romeo and Juliet* and not as much on the plot. Indeed, Shakespeare's own audience also would have been mostly familiar with the stories his plays were telling. The Prologue you just read gives you an idea about what happens in the play, and this "20-Minute *Romeo and Juliet*" will give you more of a road map to the whole story while we get Shakespeare's language in our mouths.

2. Form small groups and receive your lines. You'll notice that there is a number on the paper with each of your lines.

3. In your groups, practice dramatic enactments of each of your lines, making sure that for each enactment . . .

   All group members are involved in each enactment

   All group members read each line

   All enactments involve some kind of movement before, during, or after the line

4. You have 7 minutes to practice.

5. It's time for our 20-Minute *Romeo and Juliet*. I'm going to read a narrative of the plot – **RESOURCE #1.3C**. When I call your number, your group should stand up and share your line—be expressive!

[**TEACHER NOTE:** If there is time, perform the play a second time.]

6. Bravo! Everybody, take a bow! Let's form a circle for some Reflection Rounds.

## Part Three: Reflection Rounds—reflect on the entire class

[**TEACHER NOTE:** To conclude today's lesson, we'll do a "round" that includes all voices and helps students reflect on what they've just experienced. Teaching Shakespeare Institute faculty member Michael Tolaydo brought these to the Folger. When he starts rounds, he puts to use a range of verbs that include *observed, discovered, noticed, resented, learned, saw, wished,* and *wondered*. Use any of these that you like. Resist the urge to provide feedback during reflection rounds.]

1. We're going to wrap up by doing a Reflection Round. Rounds are about students sharing their immediate reactions to what has happened in the classroom without fear of judgment. During rounds, everyone contributes by responding to the same prompt by completing the sentence briefly. One of you will begin by the prompt and your response, and then we'll continue sharing responses one by one around the class.

2. Finish the sentence begun by the prompt. Your answers should be just one sentence—and no judgment or interruption, please. We'll talk together after everyone has shared their reflection.

3. Thinking about what we did in class today, let's have everyone respond to:
   - I noticed . . .
   - I was surprised that . . .
   - I learned that . . .

## Here's What Just Happened in Class

- Students spoke Shakespeare's words to gain confidence with the language in nonthreatening ways, in both whole groups and individually with a single line.

- Students learned how repetitive reading can improve understanding through their choral reading of the Prologue.

- Students familiarized themselves with the plot of *Romeo and Juliet* by reading and discussing the Prologue and performing a 20-minute version of the play.

- Students collaborated with Shakespeare and each other to perform their 20-minute play.

- Students processed their own learning in reflection rounds.

**RESOURCE #1.3A**

# *The Prologue*

Two households, both alike in dignity
(In fair Verona, where we lay our scene),
From ancient grudge break to new mutiny,
Where civil blood makes civil hands unclean.
From forth the fatal loins of these two foes
A pair of star-crossed lovers take their life;
Whose misadventured piteous overthrows
Doth with their death bury their parents' strife.
The fearful passage of their death-marked love
And the continuance of their parents' rage,
Which, but their children's end, naught could remove,
Is now the two hours' traffic of our stage;
The which, if you with patient ears attend,
What here shall miss, our toil shall strive to mend.

**RESOURCE #1.3B**

# 20-Minute *Romeo and Juliet* Lines

1. Down with the Capulets!

2. Down with the Montagues!

3. If ever you disturb our streets again, your lives shall pay the forfeit.

4. Examine other beauties.

5. You are welcome, gentlemen! Come, musicians, play!

6. O, she doth teach the torches to burn bright!

7. You kiss by the book.

8. But soft, what light through yonder window breaks?

9. O Romeo, Romeo, wherefore art thou Romeo?

10. Wilt thou leave me so unsatisfied?

11. If that thy bent of love be honorable, Thy purpose marriage, send me word tomorrow.

12. Tybalt, you ratcatcher, will you walk?

13. I am for you.

14. Here comes the furious Tybalt back again!

15. O, I am Fortune's Fool!

16. Then, window, let day in, and let life out.

17. I'll not marry yet.

18. Hang thee, young baggage, Disobedient wretch!

19. Romeo! Here's drink—I drink to thee.

20. Alack the day, she's dead, she's dead, she's dead!

21. O, I am slain!

22. Here's to my love . . . thus with a kiss I die.

23. I'll dispose of thee among a sisterhood of holy nuns.

24. O, happy dagger, this is thy sheath.

25. Never was a story of more woe Than this of Juliet and her Romeo.

## RESOURCE #1.3C

# 20-Minute *Romeo and Juliet*

### Narrator's Script for the 20-Minute *Romeo and Juliet*

In Verona there are two families that have hated each other for a long time. They yell in the streets, (**1. Down with the Capulets!**) and (**2. Down with the Montagues!**). There is a fight in the street that is so disruptive that the Prince, tired of this violence, lays down the law: (**3. If ever you disturb our streets again, your lives shall pay the forfeit.**)

Meanwhile, Romeo has been staying out all night and sleeping all day because he is in love with Rosaline, who doesn't love him back. His friends Benvolio and Mercutio are headed to a party at the Capulets' house. It's a masked ball, so they all can sneak in undetected and no one will know who they are. Benvolio is excited because the ball will give Romeo a chance to get over Rosaline. (**4. Examine other beauties.**) Juliet's father doesn't know that Romeo and his friends are Montagues, and he welcomes them. (**5. You are welcome, gentlemen! Come, musicians, play!**)

There, at this party, is where Romeo first sees Juliet. (**6. O, she doth teach the torches to burn bright!**) They dance. They kiss. She says, (**7. You kiss by the book.**) Only at the end of the party do they learn that the other is from their own family's hated enemy. It's too late; they are in love with each other. Romeo sneaks away from his friends, climbs the wall into the Capulets' orchard, and sees Juliet at her window. (**8. But soft, what light through yonder window breaks?**) Juliet, not knowing Romeo is nearby, says, (**9. O Romeo, Romeo, wherefore art thou Romeo?**) They confess their love to each other, but Juliet is called inside. Romeo says, (**10. Wilt thou leave me so unsatisfied?**) Juliet says, (**11. If that thy bent of love be honorable, Thy purpose marriage, send me word tomorrow.**) They enlist the help of Juliet's nurse to send messages and Friar Lawrence to marry them.

Even so, the feud continues. In the town square, Tybalt, Juliet's cousin, comes looking for Romeo. Mercutio takes the bait. (**12. Tybalt, you ratcatcher, will you walk?**) Tybalt angrily answers, (**13. I am for you.**) They fight. Romeo tries to peacefully break them up, but only gets in Mercutio's way, allowing Tybalt to stab Mercutio. Mercutio dies, and Tybalt runs away. A few minutes later, (**14. Here comes the furious Tybalt back again!**) In a fury, Romeo kills Tybalt. He immediately realizes his horrible mistake and says, (**15. O, I am Fortune's Fool!**) The Prince banishes Romeo to Mantua for killing Tybalt.

Before Romeo leaves Verona, he spends the night with Juliet. As he climbs out her window the next morning, she says, (**16. Then, window, let day in, and let life out.**) Juliet's parents burst in to inform her that they have arranged for her to marry the County Paris. She says, (**17. I'll not marry yet.**) Her father, angry that Juliet is refusing him, says, (**18. Hang thee, young baggage, Disobedient wretch!**) and tells her that if she won't marry Paris he will cast her into the streets to beg.

Juliet and the Friar come up with a plan. Juliet will take a potion in order to appear dead so her parents will put her body in their funeral monument. Then Friar Lawrence will fetch her and take her to Mantua. Juliet takes the potion. (**19. Romeo! Here's** drink—**I drink to thee.**) It works. Her nurse and her mother find her in the morning. (**20. Alack the day, she's dead, she's dead, she's dead!**) They put her body in the tomb.

In Mantua, Romeo gets the news that Juliet is dead. He buys some poison and heads to the tomb to join Juliet in death. Friar Lawrence is on his way to the tomb as well, to get Juliet and take her to Mantua. Paris is also heading to the tomb to mourn his almost-wife. Paris gets there first and tries to defend the tomb from Romeo. Romeo kills him. (**21. O, I am slain!**) Then Romeo drinks his poison and bids Juliet a final farewell. (**22. Here's to my love . . . thus with a kiss I die.**)

Friar Lawrence arrives to find Romeo dead, Juliet waking up, and the city of Verona on its way to see what the commotion was. He tries to console Juliet and hurry her away (**23. I'll dispose of thee among a sisterhood of holy nuns**), but Juliet refuses to leave. Friar Lawrence runs away, and Juliet decides to join Romeo in death. (**24. O, happy dagger, this is thy sheath.**) They are discovered by their families, who finally see that their quarrels have gone too far. They vow to make peace, for (**25. Never was a story of more woe Than this of Juliet and her Romeo.**)

WEEK ONE: LESSON 4

# What's Going On in the Beginning of *Romeo and Juliet* (1.1)?

## Here's What We're Doing and Why

This lesson is an example of 3D Lit, one of the nine essential practices of the Folger Method. 3D Lit is genius because it gets students not only understanding a scene they have never read before but seeing it as an active play and not just words on paper. 3D also prompts students to *make decisions about how to stage this scene*—all on their own. Performance becomes the means through which students build comprehension and ownership of the language. In other words, this is another Folger "sneaky" close reading experience.

This lesson isn't about arriving at an answer. Nor is it about creating a polished product. It's about letting your students discover for themselves the power of Shakespeare's language and the power of their own brains—something they will do repeatedly throughout this unit and will fine-tune for the final project. Act as a facilitator. Let your kids lead this one. And make space for every single student to contribute.

## What Will I Need?

- *Romeo and Juliet* 1.1, edited – **RESOURCE #1.4**

- Stick-on name tags with the names of characters in this scene

## How Should I Prepare?

- Make one copy of *Romeo and Juliet* 1.1, edited – **RESOURCE #1.4** – for each student and one for yourself.

- Set up the classroom in a circle with a big empty space in the middle of the room for movement and motion.

## Agenda (~ 45-minute period, and a little longer if you have it)

❑ Introduction: 5 minutes

❑ Read through the scene multiple times: 15 minutes

❑ Students perform with director suggestions: 20 minutes

❑ Reflection: 5 minutes

## Here's What Students Hear (From You) and (Then What They'll) Do

### INTRODUCTION:

1. We're about to tackle a scene you've never read, and first we're going to read it out loud in a few different ways.

2. When we finish reading in many different ways, we're going to perform it—it's the opening scene of *Romeo and Juliet*.

**Part One: First Reading of the Scene**

1. Pass out the copies of 1.1 – **RESOURCE #1.4**

2. The first time, we will read the scene around the circle. One person will start and read to the first end-punctuation mark (periods, semicolons, question marks, exclamation points). Read through a comma. Then, the next person will continue reading to the next end-punctuation mark, and so on. We'll start here with you and go around until we have read through the whole text . . . And, if you aren't sure how to pronounce a word, just give it a try. Any way you say it is fine. Let's begin.

[**TEACHER NOTE:** If a student reads past an end-punctuation mark, let it go. Do not correct any mispronunciation of any names or other words. If a reader hesitates and asks you how to say a word, tell them to just take a stab at it. If a fellow student offers to help or correct the perplexed student, don't let them do it.]

3. Now that we've read it once, even though we're not really interested in comprehension on this first reading, how much do you think you understand—on a scale from 1 to 5, with 1 being "I have no idea what's going on" to 5 being "I understand everything." Put your fingers in the air to show your number.

[**TEACHER NOTE:** Student responses can be anywhere after a first read; usually they range between 1 and 3.]

4. Why do you think we're reading it this way?

[**TEACHER NOTE:** Their responses can be perceptive, with comments like "not making anyone read too much" and "to get us to just say the words out loud."]

5. But let's check in about what we might know . . .
   – Who is talking?
   – What else did you notice? And where does that show up in the text?

**Part Two: Second Reading of the Scene**

1. The second time we read, you will read around the circle again. We will read end-mark to end-mark one more time. Have a pen or pencil at hand—as we go and if you can, mark any words or phrases you are unsure about.

2. Now that we've read this a second time, what's your level of understanding? Show me your fingers.

[**TEACHER NOTE:** The numbers will go up significantly.]
   So . . .
   – Who are these people? How do you know? Show us in the text.
   – What is going on here? How do you know? Show us in the text.
   – Do they know each other? How do you know? Show us in the text.

- Can you tell anything else about each of the characters from the text? How do you know? Show us in the text.

3. Let's share any words that you didn't understand. Let's see if we can work out the meanings together. Guesses based on what's going on in the scene are perfect.

[**TEACHER NOTE:** Students getting the basic gist of a word or phrase on their own is far better than having the teacher give a precise definition.]

We're going to see if we can puzzle these out together, and we'll resist the urge to look up words in a glossary or dictionary. You will be able to figure many of these out as a class!

4. Instead of reading to end-punctuation, for our third reading, each person will read a character's lines. Each time a new character speaks, the next person will read.

- Can you tell anything else about the characters or plot of the scene? How do you know? Show us in the text.

5. If another reading is needed, assign parts and read character by character rather than around the circle.

**Part Two: Performing the Scene**

1. I'm going to give each of you a stick-on name tag with the name of the character you are portraying.

2. To those of you who are not playing parts, you are the key people now—you are the directors! The actors have nothing to say or do except read their lines and do what the directors tell them to do.

3. I'm going to start by asking the directors some basic questions, and we'll discuss some of the possibilities after each one:

- Where do you want to set the scene?
- Who should enter first? Last?
- What do they do when they get there?
- What tone should certain lines be read with?

[**TEACHER NOTE:** If you see a shy student who is not offering any suggestions, ask them some simple A/B questions such as "Do you want Character A to enter from the left side or the right side? Do you want Character B sitting or standing at this point?" If we see the actors follow that decision, the shy student now feels ownership of that choice.]

[**TEACHER NOTE:** If you have an especially large class, or you need to take an extra step to engage every "director," you can divide the class into "directing groups": one group for every character. This optional strategy gives students who need it a little more focus.]

4. Directors or directing groups, you can sit together and decide what you want your assigned character to do in the scene.

5. Don't worry if you don't finish the scene. Remember, it's the process that is important here.

**Part Three: Reflection**

Let's take a few minutes at the end of the class so that we can go around the room, and each of you can complete the following sentences: "I noticed . . ." and "I learned . . ."

## Here's What Just Happened in Class

- Students owned the process of discovering Shakespeare's language.

- Students' comprehension of the scene increased through rereading.

- Every student's voice was heard (literally and figuratively).

- Students supported close reading with textual evidence.

- Students realized that they can understand Shakespeare without teacher explanation.

- Students made decisions about performance based on textual evidence.

- Students collaborated to perform a scene from Shakespeare—in week one of their *Romeo and Juliet* study!

**RESOURCE #1.4**

# 3D Literature: *Romeo and Juliet* 1.1 (edited)

GREGORY

Draw thy tool! Here comes two of the house of the Montagues.

SAMPSON

My naked weapon is out: quarrel, I will back thee.

GREGORY

How! turn thy back and run?

SAMPSON

I will bite my thumb at them;
which is a disgrace to them, if they bear it.

ABRAM

Do you bite your thumb at us, sir?

SAMPSON

I do bite my thumb, sir.

ABRAM

Do you bite your thumb at us, sir?

GREGORY

Do you quarrel, sir?

ABRAM

Quarrel sir! no, sir.

SAMPSON

If you do, sir, I am for you: I serve as good a man as you.

ABRAM

No better.

SAMPSON

Well, sir.

GREGORY

Say "better"; here comes one of my master's kinsmen.

SAMPSON

> Yes, better, sir.

ABRAM

> You lie.

SAMPSON

> Draw, if you be men. Gregory, remember thy washing blow.

BENVOLIO

> Part, fools!
> Put up your swords; you know not what you do.

TYBALT

> What, art thou drawn among these heartless hinds?
> Turn thee, Benvolio, look upon thy death.

BENVOLIO

> I do but keep the peace. Put up thy sword,
> Or manage it to part these men with me.

TYBALT

> What, drawn, and talk of peace! I hate the word,
> As I hate hell, all Montagues, and thee:
> Have at thee, coward!

FIRST CITIZEN

> Clubs, bills, and partisans! Strike! Beat them down!
> Down with the Capulets! Down with the Montagues!

CAPULET

> What noise is this? Give me my long sword, ho!

LADY CAPULET

> A crutch, a crutch! Why call you for a sword?

CAPULET

> My sword, I say! Old Montague is come,
> And flourishes his blade in spite of me.

MONTAGUE

> Thou villain Capulet!—Hold me not; let me go.

LADY MONTAGUE

> Thou shalt not stir a foot to seek a foe.

PRINCE

Rebellious subjects, enemies to peace,
What, ho! You men, you beasts,
That quench the fire of your pernicious rage
With purple fountains issuing from your veins,
On pain of torture, from those bloody hands
Throw your mistemper'd weapons to the ground,
Once more, on pain of death, all men depart.

## WEEK ONE: LESSON 5

# "Too Soon Marr'd": Parenting in 1.3

### Here's What We're Doing and Why

Today, we are examining the pre-party scene in which Juliet and Lady Capulet discuss Juliet's desire—or lack thereof—to pursue a marriage with the County Paris. Students will have a chance to discover the intentions, possibilities, and limitations of Lady Capulet's advice to Juliet. After students do a deep dive into Lady Capulet's advice, they will compare hers to parental advice from another time and place—via a close read of part of Clint Smith's "My Hopes, Dreams, Fears for My Future Black Son." In this piece, Smith shares deeply personal advice for how his Black son should navigate this world.

Getting students inside of a smaller piece of a larger scene can lead to all kinds of deep reading and surprising discoveries about the words, characters, and big questions of a play. Pairing texts—taking in Shakespeare along with authors of other centuries, cultures, and genders—allows students to consider the sweep of literature . . . how writers who differ in time period, geography, gender, and race can collide and/or complement as they consider many of the same life situations. These juxtapositions put students in a position to deeply explore the world of the texts—and their own worlds—with vigor, excitement, and joy.

Students are also going to cut Shakespeare! When students are asked to cut lines from any text, they must do all kinds of close reading in order to make their decisions about what stays and what goes. All along the way, students are experimenting with and owning the language.

Because the act of cutting a text is a catalyst for collaborative and close reading, it's important, especially for you, the teacher, to remember that the process matters far more than the product. When your students are engaged and discussing which lines to include or cut and why—no matter which lines they're advocating for—they are learning deeply and gaining confidence. Please feel wildly successful about this!

### What Will I Need?

- Act 1, scene 3, edited – **RESOURCE #1.5A**

- Clint Smith's "My Hopes, Dreams, Fears for My Future Black Son," edited – **RESOURCE #1.5B**

### How Should I Prepare?

- Set up your classroom for choral reading and also for working together in groups.

- Make available physical or digital copies of **RESOURCE #1.5A.**

- Make available physical or digital copies of **RESOURCE #1.5B.**

## Agenda (~ 45-minute class period)

❑ Choral Reading of Act 1, scene 3: 20 minutes

❑ Considering and cutting 21st-century parental advice: 15 minutes

❑ Discussion: 10 minutes

## Here's What Students Hear (From You) and (Then What They'll) Do

### Part One: Zeroing in on Act 1, scene 3

1. We're going to do a reading like we did earlier this week. We are not going to worry about pronunciation or knowing the meaning of every word. Every time we reread, we will focus on trying to build our collective understanding of the passage. So after each reading, I'm going to ask you to show your comprehension of the passage.

2. Let's circle up and read the passage—it's a conversation—all together. Read the passage out loud and fast.

3. For our second reading, we are going to read around the circle. Each of you is going to read to an end-punctuation and then the next student will pick up . . . as we did earlier.

[TEACHER NOTE: The group now reads sequentially—singly, one speaker after another, switching readers when they meet end-punctuation: period, semicolon, colon, question mark, or exclamation point.]

4. On a scale of 1 to 5 (with 1 meaning "I'm lost" and 5 meaning "I've got this!"), hold up the number of fingers that represents how well you understand the passage.

5. What can you tell us about the passage? What's going on? How do characters feel about that?

[TEACHER NOTE: Leave the question open: they might mention something about the two contrasting characters of Lady Capulet and Juliet, ideas about gender and parenting being explored, characterization, etc. Be sure to keep the activity moving.]

6. Can I have two volunteers come into the center of the circle and, while facing each other, read as the characters of Lady Capulet and Juliet?

[TEACHER NOTE: After the reading, do the quick self-assessment and keep it all moving.]

7. What do you notice about the passage now? What do you hear?

8. What advice is Lady Capulet giving to Juliet? How do you know?

9. Do you think Juliet will take her mother's advice? Why or why not?

10. What are some juicy words from this conversation that jump out at you? [Juicy words are words that feel good to say, have high connotative value.]

[**TEACHER NOTE:** Possible extension for homework or to turn this single-day lesson into a two-day plan: Divide students into groups of 3 or 4. Have each group rewrite the passage as a text message thread between Lady Capulet and Juliet. Ask each group to read aloud, or post online, the thread. What do students notice about the different messages? What was cut? What was saved? Why would an author have used so much more language than what is in this text exchange? There's no right or wrong answer—as long as students are talking about the words, it's all good!]

### Part Two: Lady Capulet Meets Clint Smith

1. Now, we are going to read some thoughts on parenting from Clint Smith, an American writer, teacher, scholar, and parent who is Black and living in the 21st century (more than 400 years after Shakespeare).

2. Take a few minutes to read this piece silently at your desk.

[**TEACHER NOTE:** Why aren't we reading this piece out loud? First, the length of the text and some paragraphs would make it difficult to perform a reading in unison. Second, the content of Smith's letter is sensitive; it speaks to the risks and discrimination that students of color, particularly young Black men, face. For these reasons, some students may find it difficult to read some passages aloud, and others might feel uncomfortable speaking in Smith's voice. Share this reasoning with your students.Clint Smith read this letter on the June 5, 2020, episode of *The TED Radio Hour*.]

3. Find a partner and cut Smith's essay down to what you think are the ten most important pieces of parental wisdom or advice that Smith shares. We'll do more cutting—including cutting lots of Shakespeare—in some later lessons.

4. Look at your cutting of Smith's essay and your copies of Juliet and Lady Capulet's conversation:

   a. Are the relationships between parent and child portrayed differently in these two pieces? If so, how?

   b. How do Lady Capulet's or Clint Smith's words share their values and societal structures?

   c. How is Smith's world different from the world of *Romeo and Juliet*? What concerns in the *Romeo and Juliet* world are still very real and present for us today?

   d. Are Lady Capulet and Clint Smith similar in their roles as parents? If so, how? How are they different?

## Here's What Just Happened in Class

- All students spoke Shakespeare's words aloud and experienced how repetitive reading can strengthen understanding of a complex text.

- Students collaborated to cut a text and, in doing so, close read the text.

- Students put Shakespeare in conversation with another great writer.

- Students made connections between their lives and the lives of characters in *Romeo and Juliet*.

# Cutting of Act 1, scene 3 of *Romeo and Juliet*

LADY CAPULET

    Marry, that "marry" is the very theme
    I came to talk of.—Tell me, daughter Juliet,
    How stands your disposition to be married?

JULIET

    It is an honor that I dream not of.

LADY CAPULET

    Well, think of marriage now. Younger than you
    Here in Verona, ladies of esteem,
    Are made already mothers. By my count
    I was your mother much upon these years
    That you are now a maid. Thus, then, in brief:
    The valiant Paris seeks you for his love.
    Verona's summer hath not such a flower.
    What say you? Can you love the gentleman?
    This night you shall behold him at our feast.
    Read o'er the volume of young Paris' face,
    And find delight writ there with beauty's pen.
    Examine every married lineament
    And see how one another lends content,
    And what obscured in this fair volume lies
    Find written in the margent of his eyes.
    This precious book of love, this unbound lover,
    To beautify him only lacks a cover.
    The fish lives in the sea, and 'tis much pride
    For fair without the fair within to hide.
    That book in many's eyes doth share the glory
    That in gold clasps locks in the golden story.
    So shall you share all that he doth possess
    By having him, making yourself no less.
    Speak briefly. Can you like of Paris' love?

JULIET

    I'll look to like, if looking liking move.
    But no more deep will I endart mine eye
    Than your consent gives strength to make it fly.

**RESOURCE #1.5B**

# Clint Smith's "My Hopes, Dreams, Fears for My Future Black Son"

Son,

I want to tell you how difficult it is to tell someone they are both beautiful and endangered. So worthy of life, yet so despised for living. I do not intend to scare you. My father, your grandfather, taught me to follow a certain set of rules before I even knew their purpose. He told me that these rules would not apply to everyone, that they would not even apply to all of my friends. But they were rules to abide by nonetheless. Too many black boys are killed for doing what others give no second thought. Playing our music too loud, wearing a sweatshirt with the hood up, playing with a toy in the park. My father knew these things. He knew that there was no room for error. He knew it was not fair. But he loved me too much not to teach me, to protect me.

I pray that you live in a radically different world from the one that my father and I have inherited.

I hope to teach you so much of what my father taught me, but I pray that you live in a radically different world from the one that he and I have inherited. I do not envy his task, one that might become my own. I tell you these things because I know how strong and resilient you will be. How you will take their fear and make a fort of this skin, and turn it into a bastion of love against unwarranted inhumanity.

You are not a mistake. You are not a deficit. You are not something to be eradicated or rendered obsolete.

I want you to realize that sometimes it will not be the things the world tells you, but the things it does not tell you. It will be the omissions, rather than the direct affronts that do the most damage. Your textbooks will likely not tell you how Thomas Jefferson thought that blacks were "inferior to the whites in the endowments both of body and mind"; how Franklin Delano Roosevelt's New Deal left a hole just wide enough for black families to fall through while lifting the rest of the country into the middle class; it will not tell you how the federal government actively prevented black families from purchasing homes in cities across this country; it will not tell you how police departments across this nation are incentivized to see you as a problem, something to be taken care of. They will not tell you these things, and because of that they will expect you to believe that the contemporary reality of our community is of our own doing, that we simply did not work hard enough, that things would be different if we would simply change our attitudes, the way we speak, the way we dress.

I hope the world you inherit is one in which you may love whomever you choose. I hope you read and write and laugh and sing and dance and build and cry and do all of the things a child should do.

I pray that you never have to stand on the other side of a fence and know that it is a world you cannot enter simply because of your skin.

# "We Die Soon": Beginning to Understand Mercutio Through Cutting and Comparing

## Here's What We're Doing and Why

Today students are going to look at how Shakespeare introduces us to the character of Mercutio in 1.4 and how he uses this intro to foreshadow—and also explain—Mercutio's actions during the upcoming fight scene with Tybalt in Act 3, scene 1. Through cutting the scene, students will preserve and draw attention to the language they feel is most interesting and most important in developing the character of Mercutio.

Students start by reading the scene out loud to put the words in their own mouths; they need to arrive at their own understanding of what is happening in the most basic sense:

- they need to identify words or lines that confuse them and proceed to make meaning from them,

- they need to deepen and refine their understanding of what is happening as well as their understanding of what every line says, and

- they need to think about how the passage works, as a whole and at the level of each line.

They will work in a group—or with at least one partner—because debating these points and reaching consensus is where massive amounts of learning happen. And of course, they need to evaluate Shakespeare's writing and edit it themselves. Talk about power!

Scholars, editors, directors, actors—all kinds of folks have been cutting Shakespeare for forever. We think that Shakespeare himself must have cut *Hamlet* for performance at the Globe because uncut, it would run more than 4 hours. So your students should have at it too!

Don't overcomplicate this lesson. **Give intentionally simple instructions and then step to the side.** Empower students to ask and answer their own questions, and to make good guesses and decisions based on textual evidence. Observe the cognitive and collaborative work your students do, and be amazed!

Students will then grow closer to Shakespeare's creation of Mercutio by putting him in conversation with the subjects of Gwendolyn Brooks's "We Real Cool" and the circumstances that allow one to accept death.

By the end of this exercise, ALL students will have spoken and read Shakespeare's original language multiple times, discovered the idea of foreshadowing, discussed their own various interpretations of the character of Mercutio, and, in a lively and authentic way, explored all those cool things going on with complex texts: tone, structure, characterization, and big ideas.

This lesson uses Choral Reading—a Folger Essential—because it enables students to build understanding of a new scene simply by rereading it together out loud.

## What Will I Need?

- Copies of Mercutio's Queen Mab conversation 1.4.53–121, edited – **RESOURCE #2.1A**

- Copies of Gwendolyn Brooks's "We Real Cool" – **RESOURCE #2.1B**

## How Should I Prepare?

- Set up your classroom for choral reading.

- Print copies of **RESOURCE #2.1A** and **RESOURCE #2.1B** for each student.

## Agenda (~ 45-minute class period)

- ❏ Cutting Act 1, scene 4, edited: 15 minutes

- ❏ Sharing, performing, and/or discussing cuts and character: 15 minutes

- ❏ Choral Reading of "We Real Cool": 8 minutes

- ❏ Discussion/Reflection on the pair: 7 minutes

## Here's What Students Hear (From You) and (Then What They'll) Do

### Part One: Cutting 1.4 in order to "see" Mercutio

1. Today, we are going to work through a challenging reality that directors face when directing a Shakespeare play, or any play: you're going to edit part of Act 1, scene 4.

2. Your job is to cut the scene in half, to shorten the scene without losing what is most important in it. That means you get to be very intentional about what you believe is most important.

[**TEACHER NOTE:** Remember, what matters far more than the final number of lines or the final cut scene is the learning process that occurs in getting there.]

3. The scene I'll give you is about 70 lines long. You are going to cut it down to roughly 33 lines. Imagine that you have to tell the story of this scene in just a few short minutes. And in each of your groups, you need to come to a consensus about what to cut.

4. In the play, we are just before Romeo and his friends crash the Capulet party, and Romeo and Mercutio exchange words about dreams—are they important, or not? And they're talking about whether we can control our fates. Do we have that ability, or not? Thinking about how we react in situations in which we can or cannot control our fate will be helpful in thinking about Romeo and Juliet's decision-making as we get further into the play.

   a. In groups of 3–4, read the scene out loud. You may assign parts or read around the group, changing readers when the speaker changes. You must read out loud. Don't worry about pronunciation!

    **b.** As a group, determine which lines to cut and which to keep, so that your scene ends up at around 33 lines. As you wrap up your cutting session, make sure that all of the scripts in your group reflect the cuts that you've decided to make.

[**TEACHER NOTE:** From time to time, walk around the room to hear the close reading and consensus-building going on! Get ready for some surprises—some groups might think that Mercutio's tirade about Queen Mab is more important than focusing on Romeo's reaction to his words, and that's totally fine. Others might want to save the lines that are musical and poetic, and might even notice the shared iambic pentameter between the two friends and want to preserve that too. That's fine as well. Let everyone come to their own decisions. Don't worry if students do not finish in the allotted time; this activity is about the process.]

    **c.** Before we share out with the class, each of you write an individual reflection on the back of your script.

        – What is the most important line you saved?

        – What makes this line so important to establishing the character of Mercutio? Of Romeo?

        – What is the most useless line you cut? Why was it useless in this scene?

        – Did you have any other reasons for cutting the lines you did?

    **d.** Groups share your scenes, either by reading them chorally or performing them.

    **e.** Wrap up this part of the work with a partner to discuss, and then we'll share our thoughts with the whole class:

        – What's going on in this scene?

        – What big questions is this scene asking?

        – How did it feel to cut Shakespeare's lines? What were some of the challenges?

        – Were there any words or lines that really stood out?

        – Were there any images that repeated or really stood out?

        – What did you learn (about yourself, about this text, about the world) through this process of making the text your own?

### Part Two: Pairing with Gwendolyn Brooks

**1.** Now that you've taken a closer look at Mercutio in 1.4, we are going to take a look at the poem by Gwendolyn Brooks. I'm not going to tell you much about her or the poem—you'll just dive in.

**2.** Like we have done before in class, we are going to read this poem in a bunch of different ways. During the first read, we are going to circle up and read the poem all together.

**3.** During the second read, let's go around in the circle, and each of you read to an end punctuation and then the next student will pick up.

4. Now we are going to read the whole poem chorally again, and this time we are going to start with a whisper and end with a shout. [After this, reverse it.] Now this time we are going to start with a shout and end with a whisper.

5. What's there to learn about the characters' situation?

   a. What do we know about the pool players? How do you know? Show us in the text.

   b. What do we know about how the pool players feel? How do you know? Show us in the text.

   c. What parallels do you see between Romeo and Mercutio's conversation and this poem? Text, please.

   d. How similarly or differently do these characters react to an inability to control their fate? How do you know? Text, please.

## Here's What Just Happened in Class

- Students collaborated to cut to the "heart" of a scene—a pretty complicated speech of Mercutio's—by reading closely.

- Students gained understanding of a Gwendolyn Brooks poem through repetitive choral reading.

- Students discussed the impact of tone and pitch on the mood of a passage.

- Students talked back to Shakespeare and his characters with the words of Gwendolyn Brooks.

- Students analyzed Mercutio's character by comparing him to Gwendolyn Brooks's pool players.

# Queen Mab Conversation, edited

## 1.4.53–100

**ROMEO**
I dreamt a dream tonight.

**MERCUTIO**
And so did I.

**ROMEO**
Well, what was yours?                                                55

**MERCUTIO**  That dreamers often lie.

**ROMEO**
In bed asleep while they do dream things true.

**MERCUTIO**
O, then I see Queen Mab hath been with you.
She is the fairies' midwife, and she comes
In shape no bigger than an agate stone                              60
On the forefinger of an alderman,
Drawn with a team of little atomi
Over men's noses as they lie asleep.
Her wagon spokes made of long spinners' legs,
The cover of the wings of grasshoppers,                            65
Her traces of the smallest spider web,
Her collars of the moonshine's wat'ry beams,
Her whip of cricket's bone, the lash of film,
Her wagoner a small gray-coated gnat,
Not half so big as a round little worm                             70
Pricked from the lazy finger of a maid.
Her chariot is an empty hazelnut,
Made by the joiner squirrel or old grub,
Time out o' mind the fairies' coachmakers.
And in this state she gallops night by night                       75
Through lovers' brains, and then they dream of love;
On courtiers' knees, that dream on cur'sies straight;
O'er lawyers' fingers, who straight dream on fees;
O'er ladies' lips, who straight on kisses dream,
Which oft the angry Mab with blisters plagues                      80
Because their breaths with sweetmeats tainted are.
Sometime she gallops o'er a courtier's nose,

And then dreams he of smelling out a suit.
And sometime comes she with a tithe-pig's tail,
Tickling a parson's nose as he lies asleep;                     85
Then he dreams of another benefice.
Sometime she driveth o'er a soldier's neck,
And then dreams he of cutting foreign throats,
Of breaches, ambuscadoes, Spanish blades,
Of healths five fathom deep, and then anon                       90
Drums in his ear, at which he starts and wakes
And, being thus frighted, swears a prayer or two
And sleeps again. This is that very Mab
That plats the manes of horses in the night
And bakes the elflocks in foul sluttish hairs,                   95
Which once untangled much misfortune bodes.
This is the hag, when maids lie on their backs,
That presses them and learns them first to bear,
Making them women of good carriage.
This is she—                                                     100

ROMEO  Peace, peace, Mercutio, peace.
  Thou talk'st of nothing.

MERCUTIO  True, I talk of dreams,
  Which are the children of an idle brain,
  Begot of nothing but vain fantasy,                             105
  Which is as thin of substance as the air
  And more inconstant than the wind, who woos
  Even now the frozen bosom of the north
  And, being angered, puffs away from thence,
  Turning his side to the dew-dropping south.                    110

BENVOLIO
  This wind you talk of blows us from ourselves.
  Supper is done, and we shall come too late.

ROMEO
  I fear too early, for my mind misgives
  Some consequence yet hanging in the stars
  Shall bitterly begin his fearful date                          115
  With this night's revels, and expire the term
  Of a despisèd life closed in my breast
  By some vile forfeit of untimely death.
  But he that hath the steerage of my course
  Direct my sail. On, lusty gentlemen.                           120

BENVOLIO  Strike, drum.

RESOURCE #2.1B

# Gwendolyn Brooks' "We Real Cool"

*THE POOL PLAYERS.*
*SEVEN AT THE GOLDEN SHOVEL.*

We real cool. We
Left school. We

Lurk late. We
Strike straight. We

Sing sin. We
Thin gin. We

Jazz June. We
Die soon.

# "You kiss by the book!": Creating Promptbooks!

## Here's What We're Doing and Why

In this lesson, we will be introducing the promptbook, a great Folger Essential that gets students to consider deeply—and record—all aspects of a scene. Creating a promptbook mirrors a practice that has been used in the world of theater for a long time—and we include some images of very early promptbooks from the Folger collection for you and your students to have a look at.

A promptbook is, at its core, a set of notes made directly on the text—in this case, the notes will be made by your students. These annotations give actors advice about how to convey meaning through the language, their vocalization, gestures, and movements onstage. They also record cuts to the text, entrances and exits of characters, and more. Because creating promptbooks brings students to consider all aspects of a scene deeply, we believe it is an important process in connecting our students to Shakespeare.

Creating our first promptbook is a logical step after working through 3D Lit in a previous lesson. Creating short promptbooks in small groups allows students to continue to take ownership over the language and the play, and this will also scaffold their work toward the final assessment.

We'll begin our work with promptbooks by examining digital images of two rare *Romeo and Juliet* promptbooks from the Folger collection.

## What Will I Need?

- Promptbook images from the Folger collection (from the 1846 London production) – **RESOURCE #2.2A**
- Print copies of *Romeo and Juliet* 1.5, divided into 6 separate sections – **RESOURCE #2.2B**
    - 1.5.1–47
    - 1.5.48–83
    - 1.5.84–103
    - 1.5.104–122
    - 1.5.123–141
    - 1.5.142–160

## How Should I Prepare?

- Set up your classroom in a large circle with space in the middle for action.
- Be ready to divide students into 6 groups. Each group will create a promptbook for their section of the scene.

## Agenda (~ 45-minute class period)

❏ Review of promptbook pages from the Folger collection and outlining the assignment: 5 minutes

❏ Reading of the scene as a whole class: 10 minutes

❏ Think/Pair/Share: 5 minutes

❏ Group work on the promptbook and rehearsal: 20 minutes

❏ Reflection rounds and discussion: 5 minutes

## Here's What Students Hear (From You) and (Then What They'll) Do

### Part One: Promptbooks in the Folger Collection

1. Today, we will create promptbooks for *Romeo and Juliet*, 1.5. Before we do, let's take a look at these images of rare promptbooks from the Folger collection – **RESOURCE #2.2A**

2. What do you notice, and what do you wonder, about these pages? On the board, let's gather some ideas about what else a promptbook might include.

[**TEACHER NOTE:** They may mention cut lines, tone, emotions, mood, pauses, whispers, exits, entrances, gestures, movements, laughter, lightning, hugs and handshakes, props, and more.]

### Part Two: Read the Scene

1. Pass out copies of *Romeo and Juliet* 1.5 – **RESOURCE #2.2B**

2. As a class, let's read this whole scene aloud together.

Mark on your script anything that stands out or is interesting to you.

3. After reading, turn to a partner and take 2 minutes to brainstorm your thoughts on what this scene is about—one of you share your thoughts for one minute and then the other person share for one minute. Then answer these two questions and write your responses:

    a. How would you summarize this scene in one sentence?

    b. What are some key lines and words that are essential to understanding the feelings and motives of the characters? Pick around 5 lines or words. Underline or circle them.

4. Now let's share with the whole class what we think is happening in this scene. Let's have volunteers share their thoughts on the scene.

### Part Three: Create Your Promptbooks

1. You are going to form six groups and I will assign each group a short section of the scene with which to create a promptbook. **RESOURCE #2.2B** is divided into six sections. Find the section assigned to your group and read through it as a group.

- Group One: 1.5.1–47
- Group Two: 1.5.48–83
- Group Three: 1.5.84–103
- Group Four: 1.5.104–122
- Group Five: 1.5.123–141
- Group Six: 1.5.142–160

2. In your groups, collaborate to make some annotations that show how your group would stage the text. All your choices must be supported by your understanding of the text. Write clear, detailed notes in the margins and on the text, marking specific words and lines. Note your group decisions about these elements:

    - **Mood/Tone**
        - Overall
        - Key moments
    - **Acting:** Describe what each character is doing.
        - Movement (gestures, exits, entrances, facial expressions)
        - Voice (tone of voice, stress, volume)
        - Emotion (nervous, angry, curious, elated, etc.)
        - Nonverbal human sound (laughter, sigh, cry, scream, etc.)

3. Once you make decisions about your scene, choose group members to perform and run through your short scene a few times to practice your mood, tone, and acting. Your performance does not have to be perfect and you can read your lines from your script. Those of you without speaking parts, direct the scene like we did with 3D Lit.

4. Let's close out with reflection rounds. I want each of you to complete this sentence:

    - "I noticed . . . "
    - Let's do another round. Complete this sentence: "I learned about myself . . ."

## Here's What Just Happened in Class

- Students had a chance to examine digitized versions of rare materials.

- Students pulled together meaning, movement, vocal inflection, and more into a full treatment of the scene.

- Students made collaborative decisions about staging the play without your help.

- Students reflected on how their staging choices impacted the audience's interpretation of the scene.

# From a Promptbook in the Folger Collection

Several pages from a promptbook created for an 1846 London production of *Romeo and Juliet*. The printed book was published in 1798, based on Steevens's text. This 1846 production used that text and marked up this copy to memorialize where cuts to the text were made.

16          ROMEO AND JULIET.          *Act* 1.

the pantry, and every thing in extremity. I must hence
to wait; I beseech you, follow straight.
   *La. Cap.* We follow thee.—Juliet, the county stays.
   *Nurse.* Go, girl, seek happy nights to happy days.
                               [*Exeunt.*

SCENE IV.

*A Street.*

Enter ROMEO, MERCUTIO, BENVOLIO, *with five or six
Maskers, Torch-bearers, and Others.*

   *Rom.* What, shall this speech be spoke for our excuse?
Or shall we on without apology?
   *Ben.* The date is out of such prolixity:
We'll have no Cupid hood-wink'd with a scarf,
Bearing a Tartar's painted bow of lath,
Scaring the ladies like a crow-keeper;
Nor no without-book prologue, faintly spoke
After the prompter, for our entrance:
But, let them measure us by what they will,
We'll measure them a measure, and be gone.
   *Rom.* Give me a torch,—I am not for this ambling;
Being but heavy, I will bear the light.
   *Mer.* Nay, gentle Romeo, we must have you dance.
   *Rom.* Not I, believe me: you have dancing shoes,
With nimble soles: I have a soul of lead,
So stakes me to the ground, I cannot move.
   *Mer.* You are a lover; borrow Cupid's wings,
And soar with them above a common bound.
   *Rom.* I am too sore enpierced with his shaft,
To soar with his light feathers; and so bound,
I cannot bound a pitch above dull woe:
Under love's heavy burden do I sink.
                              *Mer.*

*Act* 1.          ROMEO AND JULIET.          17

   *Mer.* And, to sink in it, should you burden love;
Too great oppression for a tender thing.
   *Rom.* Is love a tender thing? it is too rough,
Too rude, too boist'rous; and it pricks like thorn.
   *Mer.* If love be rough with you, be rough with love;
Prick love for pricking, and you beat love down.—
Give me a case to put my visage in: [*Putting on a mask.*
A visor for a visor!—what care I,
What curious eye doth quote deformities?
Here are the beetle-brows, shall blush for me.
   *Ben.* Come, knock, and enter; and no sooner in,
But every man betake him to his legs.
   *Rom.* A torch for me: let wantons, light of heart,
Tickle the senseless rushes with their heels;
For I am proverb'd with a grandsire phrase,—
I'll be a candle-holder, and look on,—
The game was ne'er so fair, and I am done.
   *Mer.* Tut! dun's the mouse, the constable's own word:
If thou art dun, we'll draw thee from the mire
Of this (save reverence) love, wherein thou stick'st
Up to the ears.—Come, we burn day-light, ho.
   *Rom.* Nay, that's not so.
   *Mer.*                  I mean, sir, in delay
We waste our lights in vain, like lamps by day.
Take our good meaning; for our judgement sits
Five times in that, ere once in our five wits.
   *Rom.* And we mean well, in going to this mask;
But 'tis no wit to go.
   *Mer.*              Why, may one ask?
   *Rom.* I dreamt a dream to-night.
   *Mer.*                 And so did I.
   *Rom.* Well, what was yours?
   *Mer.*              That dreamers often lie.
   *Rom.* In bed, asleep, while they do dream things true.
               C              *Mer.*

52 ROMEO AND JULIET. *Act* III.

~~Rom. This day's black fate on more days doth depend;~~
~~This but begins the woe, others must end.~~

*Re-enter* TYBALT.

*Ben.* Here comes the furious Tybalt back again.
*Rom.* Alive! in triumph! and Mercutio slain!
Away to heaven, respective lenity,
And fire-ey'd fury be my conduct now!
Now, Tybalt, take the *villain* back again,
That late thou gav'st me; for Mercutio's soul
Is but a little way above our heads,
Staying for thine to keep him company;
~~Either thou, or I, or both, must go with him.~~
~~Tyb. Thou, wretched boy, that didst consort him here,~~
~~Shalt with him hence.~~
~~Rom.~~ ~~This shall determine that.~~
[*They fight;* TYBALT *falls.*
*Ben.* Romeo, away, be gone!
The citizens are up, and Tybalt slain:—
Stand not amaz'd:—the prince will doom thee death,
If thou art taken:—hence!—be gone!—away!
*Rom.* O! I am fortune's fool!
~~Ben.~~ ~~Why dost thou stay?~~
[*Exit* ROMEO.

*Enter* Citizens, *&c.*

1. *Cit.* Which way ran he, that kill'd Mercutio?
Tybalt, that murderer, which way ran he?
*Ben.* There lies that Tybalt.
1. *Cit.* Up, sir, go with me;
I charge thee in the prince's name, obey.

*Enter*

*Act* III. ROMEO AND JULIET. 53

*Enter* Prince, *attended;* MONTAGUE, CAPULET, *their Wives, and Others.*

*Prince.* Where are the vile beginners of this fray?
*Ben.* O noble prince, I can discover all
The unlucky manage of this fatal brawl:
There lies the man, slain by young Romeo,
That slew thy kinsman, brave Mercutio.
*La. Cap.* Tybalt, my cousin!—O my brother's child!
Unhappy sight! ah me, the blood is spill'd
Of my dear kinsman!—Prince, as thou art true,
For blood of ours, shed blood of Montague.—
O cousin, cousin!
*Prin.* Benvolio, who began this bloody fray?
*Ben.* Tybalt, here slain, whom Romeo's hand did slay;
Romeo that spoke him fair, bade him bethink
How nice the quarrel was, and urg'd withal
Your high displeasure:—All this—uttered
With gentle breath, calm look, knees humbly bow'd,—
Could not take truce with the unruly spleen
Of Tybalt deaf to peace, but that he tilts
With piercing steel at bold Mercutio's breast;
Who, all as hot, turns deadly point to point,
And with a martial scorn, with one hand beats
Cold death aside, and with the other sends
It back to Tybalt, whose dexterity
Retorts it: Romeo he cries aloud,
*Hold, friends! friends, part!* and, swifter than his tongue,
His agile arm beats down their fatal points,
And 'twixt them rushes; underneath whose arm
An envious thrust from Tybalt hit the life
Of stout Mercutio, and then Tybalt fled:
But by and by comes back to Romeo,
Who had but newly entertain'd revenge,

E 3 And

From the collection of the Folger Shakespeare Library in Washington, DC.
Shakespeare, William. *Romeo and Juliet: a tragedy . . . accurately printed from the text of Mr. Steevens's last edition.* (London: Published by E. Harding, J. Wright, G. Sael, and Vernor and Hood, 1798.)

## RESOURCE #2.2B

## 1.5.1–160

**(GROUP ONE—2 ROLES)**

CAPULET
    Welcome, gentlemen. Ladies that have their toes
    Unplagued with corns will walk a bout with
      you.—                                        20
    Ah, my mistresses, which of you all
    Will now deny to dance? She that makes dainty,
    She, I'll swear, hath corns. Am I come near you
      now?—
    Welcome, gentlemen. I have seen the day           25
    That I have worn a visor and could tell
    A whispering tale in a fair lady's ear,
    Such as would please. 'Tis gone, 'tis gone, 'tis gone.
    You are welcome, gentlemen.—Come, musicians,
      play.                     *Music plays and they dance.*    30
    A hall, a hall, give room!—And foot it, girls.—
    More light, you knaves, and turn the tables up,
    And quench the fire; the room is grown too hot.—
    Ah, sirrah, this unlooked-for sport comes well.—
    Nay, sit, nay, sit, good cousin Capulet,        35
    For you and I are past our dancing days.
    How long is 't now since last yourself and I
    Were in a mask?

CAPULET'S COUSIN  By 'r Lady, thirty years.

CAPULET
    What, man, 'tis not so much, 'tis not so much.    40
    'Tis since the nuptial of Lucentio,
    Come Pentecost as quickly as it will,
    Some five and twenty years, and then we masked.

CAPULET'S COUSIN
    'Tis more, 'tis more. His son is elder, sir.
    His son is thirty.                         45

CAPULET  Will you tell me that?
    His son was but a ward two years ago.

**(GROUP TWO—4 ROLES)**

ROMEO, *to a Servingman*
   What lady's that which doth enrich the hand
   Of yonder knight?

SERVINGMAN  I know not, sir.                                                    50

ROMEO
   O, she doth teach the torches to burn bright!
   It seems she hangs upon the cheek of night
   As a rich jewel in an Ethiop's ear—
   Beauty too rich for use, for Earth too dear.
   So shows a snowy dove trooping with crows                                    55
   As yonder lady o'er her fellows shows.
   The measure done, I'll watch her place of stand
   And, touching hers, make blessèd my rude hand.
   Did my heart love till now? Forswear it, sight,
   For I ne'er saw true beauty till this night.                                 60

TYBALT
   This, by his voice, should be a Montague.—
   Fetch me my rapier, boy.          *Page exits.*
   What, dares the slave
   Come hither covered with an antic face
   To fleer and scorn at our solemnity?                                         65
   Now, by the stock and honor of my kin,
   To strike him dead I hold it not a sin.

CAPULET
   Why, how now, kinsman? Wherefore storm you so?

TYBALT
   Uncle, this is a Montague, our foe,
   A villain that is hither come in spite                                       70
   To scorn at our solemnity this night.

CAPULET
   Young Romeo is it?

TYBALT  'Tis he, that villain Romeo.

CAPULET
   Content thee, gentle coz. Let him alone.
   He bears him like a portly gentleman,                                        75
   And, to say truth, Verona brags of him
   To be a virtuous and well-governed youth.

I would not for the wealth of all this town
Here in my house do him disparagement.
Therefore be patient. Take no note of him.                    80
It is my will, the which if thou respect,
Show a fair presence and put off these frowns,
An ill-beseeming semblance for a feast.

**(GROUP THREE—2 ROLES)**

TYBALT
    It fits when such a villain is a guest.
    I'll not endure him.                                      85

CAPULET  He shall be endured.
    What, goodman boy? I say he shall. Go to.
    Am I the master here or you? Go to.
    You'll not endure him! God shall mend my soul,
    You'll make a mutiny among my guests,                     90
    You will set cock-a-hoop, you'll be the man!

TYBALT
    Why, uncle, 'tis a shame.

CAPULET  Go to, go to.
    You are a saucy boy. Is 't so indeed?
    This trick may chance to scathe you. I know what.         95
    You must contrary me. Marry, 'tis time—
    Well said, my hearts.—You are a princox, go.
    Be quiet, or—More light, more light!—for shame,
    I'll make you quiet.—What, cheerly, my hearts!

TYBALT
    Patience perforce with willful choler meeting             100
    Makes my flesh tremble in their different greeting.
    I will withdraw, but this intrusion shall,
    Now seeming sweet, convert to bitt'rest gall.
                                        *He exits.*

**(GROUP FOUR—2 ROLES)**

ROMEO, *taking Juliet's hand*
    If I profane with my unworthiest hand
    This holy shrine, the gentle sin is this:                 105
    My lips, two blushing pilgrims, ready stand
    To smooth that rough touch with a tender kiss.

JULIET

Good pilgrim, you do wrong your hand too much,
Which mannerly devotion shows in this;
For saints have hands that pilgrims' hands do touch,      110
And palm to palm is holy palmers' kiss.

ROMEO

Have not saints lips, and holy palmers too?

JULIET

Ay, pilgrim, lips that they must use in prayer.

ROMEO

O then, dear saint, let lips do what hands do.
They pray: grant thou, lest faith turn to despair.      115

JULIET

Saints do not move, though grant for prayers' sake.

ROMEO

Then move not while my prayer's effect I take.
                              *He kisses her.*
Thus from my lips, by thine, my sin is purged.

JULIET

Then have my lips the sin that they have took.

ROMEO

Sin from my lips? O trespass sweetly urged!      120
Give me my sin again.            *He kisses her.*

JULIET  You kiss by th' book.


## (GROUP FIVE—4 ROLES)

NURSE

Madam, your mother craves a word with you.
                        *Juliet moves toward her mother.*

ROMEO

What is her mother?

NURSE  Marry, bachelor,      125
Her mother is the lady of the house,
And a good lady, and a wise and virtuous.
I nursed her daughter that you talked withal.

I tell you, he that can lay hold of her
Shall have the chinks.                    *Nurse moves away.*          130

ROMEO, *aside* Is she a Capulet?
O dear account! My life is my foe's debt.

BENVOLIO
Away, begone. The sport is at the best.

ROMEO
Ay, so I fear. The more is my unrest.

CAPULET
Nay, gentlemen, prepare not to be gone.                            135
We have a trifling foolish banquet towards.—
Is it e'en so? Why then, I thank you all.
I thank you, honest gentlemen. Good night.—
More torches here.—Come on then, let's to bed.—
Ah, sirrah, by my fay, it waxes late.                              140
I'll to my rest.
                    *All but Juliet and the Nurse begin to exit.*

## (GROUP SIX—3 ROLES)

JULIET
Come hither, nurse. What is yond gentleman?

NURSE
The son and heir of old Tiberio.

JULIET
What's he that now is going out of door?

NURSE
Marry, that, I think, be young Petruchio.                          145

JULIET
What's he that follows here, that would not dance?

NURSE  I know not.

JULIET
Go ask his name. *The Nurse goes.* If he be marrièd,
My grave is like to be my wedding bed.

NURSE, *returning*
His name is Romeo, and a Montague,                                 150
The only son of your great enemy.

JULIET

My only love sprung from my only hate!
Too early seen unknown, and known too late!
Prodigious birth of love it is to me
That I must love a loathèd enemy.                                    155

NURSE

What's this? What's this?

JULIET  A rhyme I learned even now
Of one I danced withal.

*One calls within "Juliet."*

NURSE  Anon, anon.
Come, let's away. The strangers all are gone.                        160
*They exit.*

# All of 1.5 in Motion, *and* Defining Beauty Across Time and Culture: "I'll make thee think thy swan a crow"

## Here's What We're Doing and Why

We're going to warm up today with a promptbook relay of 1.5, based on the decisions and promptbooks that students made yesterday. They'll produce all of 1.5 with their groups as relay teams. Then they will dive into one of Romeo's speeches in that scene along with another from Act 2, taking a close look at part of what we call at the Folger the "real thing." It's important to get Shakespeare off his pedestal and in conversation with contemporary writers because literature can often be a safe, generative space for taking note of differences—then and now, there and here.

The comparison that students will consider today points to something important to note in *Romeo and Juliet,* and in all of Shakespeare—language that assigns negative connotative value to words describing blackness or darkness, and that assigns positive value to words describing whiteness. For example, in Act 1, Benvolio coaches a heartsick Romeo to "examine other beauties." During this speech, Benvolio says that his advice will allow Romeo to think "thy swan (Rosaline) [is] a crow." Here, Benvolio uses the whiteness and fairness of a swan to represent beauty, and the blackness and harshness of a crow to represent ugliness. Similar imagery—beauty and virtue ascribed in words that focus on whiteness—*fair, swan,* and more—and ugliness and lack of virtue with words that describe blackness or darkness—is evident in all of Shakespeare's plays.

Today, students will create a conversation in which a brilliant and celebrated 21st-century author "talks back to Shakespeare" because she defines beauty very differently. We wildly encourage these conversations that cross centuries and cultures because they allow students to observe and question, and this encourages them to talk back to Shakespeare themselves.

## What Will I Need?

- Students will come to class armed with their promptbook notes from yesterday.

- Copies of Romeo's 1.5 monologue, edited, for each student – **RESOURCE #2.3A**

- Copies of Romeo's 2.2 monologue, edited, for each student – **RESOURCE #2.3B**

- Copies of Maya Angelou's "Ain't That Bad?" for each student – **RESOURCE #2.3C**

- If needed, copies of the Shakespeare-Angelou mashup – **OPTIONAL RESOURCE #2.3D**

## How Should I Prepare?

- List on the board the scene sections in order, so that each group knows their spot in the relay.

- Arrange your classroom so that there's a performance space.

- Make copies of 1.5 and 2.2 – **RESOURCE #2.3A** and **RESOURCE #2.3B**

- Make copies of Maya Angelou's "Aint That Bad?" – **RESOURCE #2.3C**

- Check out **OPTIONAL RESOURCE #2.3D** in case you might use it.

## Agenda (~ 45-minute period)

- ❏ 1.5 Relay Performance: 10 minutes
- ❏ Reading Romeo's two monologues: 10 minutes
- ❏ Reading "Ain't That Bad?": 10 minutes
- ❏ Creating mashup poems: 10 minutes
- ❏ Reflection: 5 minutes

## Here's What Students Hear (From You) and (Then What They'll) Do

### Part One: The Party Scene in Relay

1. Reconvene in your groups and take a few minutes to go over the decisions you made yesterday. Check the board to see where your piece comes within the whole scene so you'll know who you're following, and who will follow you. Be ready to head to the performance space when your group's turn comes up. We're eager to put on this scene with energy and spirit, so—as in any relay—let's keep this scene moving!

2. Let the relay begin! Much celebration on its completion!

### Part Two: A Look at Beauty, Shakespeare-style

1. Now that we're experts on Act 1, scene 5, we're going to look even more closely at two speeches of Romeo's. First let's look at Romeo in 1.5 – **RESOURCE #2.3A**. During this first read, we are going to circle up and read the passage all together. What did you notice after the first read?

[TEACHER NOTE: As always, leave the question open. Students might mention something about Shakespeare's usage of birds again to depict beauty. Probe them on the colors that he uses to create the image of the birds. This will lead to more insight about colors throughout the rest of the lesson.]

2. Let's all read again. This time we are going to shout instances of the word *light*, or a word that refers to light or white, and whisper when we see a word that refers to darkness. What do you notice here?

[**TEACHER NOTE:** They will likely ask you to define an *Ethiope*. If any students have knowledge or insight to share about the country of Ethiopia or the skin color of Ethiopians, this is great. If not, ask them to look the word up quickly and share. This may tie into all kinds of questions about Shakespeare choosing to focus on the jewel instead of the Ethiope and how this fits into how beauty was defined in the world in which he wrote.]

3. Now let's look at a passage from the upcoming balcony scene – **RESOURCE #2.3B**. Who will volunteer to read it? Or will a pair of you read it chorally?

    a. What did you notice when listening to this monologue?

       Does it bring forward any of the descriptions of beauty you noticed in the first speech?

    b. Does Romeo believe Juliet to be beautiful? How do we know?

    c. What patterns of words do you notice about Romeo's language in defining Juliet's beauty? What larger ideas do we see being explored about Romeo's idea of what is beautiful?

    d. What does this say about this society?

## Part Three: Listening to Maya Angelou

1. Now let's get involved with a poem by another excellent writer. I'm not going to tell you much about this writer.

2. Let's all read it together – **RESOURCE #2.3C**. We'll keep it moving, but we want to have multiple exposures to the poet's language while also exploring different sound techniques she uses.

3. Next, we are going to go around in the circle. Each student is going to read to the end of each poetic line, and the next student will pick up.

[**TEACHER NOTE:** The group now reads sequentially—singly, one speaker after another, switching readers when they get to the end of the poetic line—and these are short lines!]

4. Now we are going to read the whole poem chorally again, but this time **whispering** every instance of the word *black*.

5. Now we are going to read the whole poem chorally again, but this time **shouting** instances of the word *black*.

6. What have we learned about the perception of beauty in this poem?

[**TEACHER NOTE:** These questions may help, but only if students can't get there themselves]:

    a. What do you observe about the language of the poem?

    b. What are some juicy words that jump out at you?

    c. What do we know about how the author perceives beauty? How do you know? How is this different from Romeo's perception of beauty?

    **d.** What seems to be celebrated in this poem that is not celebrated in Romeo's monologue?

    **e.** Do we see beauty in different ways today? How do we know?

## Part Four: Dr. Angelou and Mr. Shakespeare in Conversation

  **1.** Find a partner and first discuss briefly how you define beauty. Then, select lines from 1.5, 2.2, and "Ain't That Bad?" and cut the texts together to create a 14-line mashup poem. In your mashup, use lines from both Romeo and "Ain't That Bad?" to create a monologue that celebrates how you both define beauty.

[**TEACHER NOTE:** If time is tight or student hesitation intervenes, consider using **OPTIONAL RESOURCE #2.3D** instead. Students can do their own—and better—mashup for homework.]

## Part Five: Reflection

Go around the room, with each student sharing a response to one of the following:

- I was surprised that . . .
- This class made me think about . . .

## Here's What Just Happened in Class

- Students collaborated to put Shakespeare's text on its feet by performing their promptbook scenes.

- Students discovered how repeated readings of a passage can reveal historical and social subtext.

- Students considered some ways in which beauty is described in the text of *Romeo and Juliet* and discussed the limitations of these definitions.

- Students spoke the words of another great poet, Maya Angelou.

- Students worked together to talk back to Shakespeare by putting him in conversation with another writer who defines beauty differently across space and time.

## RESOURCE #2.3A

## 1.5.51–60

ROMEO
    O, she doth teach the torches to burn bright!
    It seems she hangs upon the cheek of night
    As a rich jewel in an Ethiop's ear—
    Beauty too rich for use, for Earth too dear.
    So shows a snowy dove trooping with crows
    As yonder lady o'er her fellows shows.
    The measure done, I'll watch her place of stand
    And, touching hers, make blessèd my rude hand.
    Did my heart love till now? Forswear it, sight,
    For I ne'er saw true beauty till this night.

## RESOURCE #2.3B

## 2.2.1–26

*Enter Juliet above.*

ROMEO

But soft, what light through yonder window breaks?
It is the East, and Juliet is the sun.
Arise, fair sun, and kill the envious moon,
Who is already sick and pale with grief
That thou, her maid, art far more fair than she.
Be not her maid since she is envious.
Her vestal livery is but sick and green,
And none but fools do wear it. Cast it off.
It is my lady. O, it is my love!
O, that she knew she were!
She speaks, yet she says nothing. What of that?
Her eye discourses; I will answer it.
I am too bold. 'Tis not to me she speaks.
Two of the fairest stars in all the heaven,
Having some business, do entreat her eyes
To twinkle in their spheres till they return.
What if her eyes were there, they in her head?
The brightness of her cheek would shame those
    stars
As daylight doth a lamp; her eye in heaven
Would through the airy region stream so bright
That birds would sing and think it were not night.
See how she leans her cheek upon her hand.
O, that I were a glove upon that hand,
That I might touch that cheek!

## RESOURCE #2.3C

Dancin' the funky chicken
Eatin' ribs and tips
Diggin' all the latest sounds
And drinkin' gin in sips.

Puttin' down that do-rag
Tighten' up my 'fro
Wrappin' up in Blackness
Don't I shine and glow?

Hearin' Stevie Wonder
Cookin' beans and rice
Goin' to the opera
Checkin' out Leontyne Price.

Get down, Jesse Jackson
Dance on, Alvin Ailey
Talk, Miss Barbara Jordan
Groove, Miss Pearlie Bailey.

Now ain't they bad?
An' ain't they Black?
An' ain't they Black?
An' ain't they Bad?
An ain't they bad?
An' ain't they Black?
An' ain't they fine?

Black like the hour of the night
When your love turns and wriggles close to your side
Black as the earth which has given birth
To nations, and when all else is gone will abide.

Bad as the storm that leaps raging from the heavens
Bringing the welcome rain
Bad as the sun burning orange hot at midday
Lifting the waters again.

Arthur Ashe on the tennis court
Mohammed Ali in the ring
Andre Watts and Andrew Young
Black men doing their thing.

*Dressing in purples and pinks and greens*
*Exotic as rum and Cokes*
*Living our lives with flash and style*
*Ain't we colorful folks?*

*Now ain't we bad?*
*An' ain't we Black?*
*An' ain't we Black?*
*An' ain't we bad?*
*An' ain't we bad?*
*An' ain't we Black?*
*An' ain't we fine?*

# Mr. Shakespeare and Dr. Angelou Talk to Each Other

Divide your class in two, standing on opposite sides of the room. One group reads the text in bold, the other group reads the text in italics.

**O, she doth teach the torches to burn bright!**
*An' ain't they Black?*
*An' ain't they fine?*
*Wrappin' up in Blackness*
*Don't she shine and glow?*

**It seems she hangs upon the cheek of night**
*Black as the earth which has given birth*
**Beauty too rich for use, for Earth too dear.**
*Bad as the storm that leaps raging from the heavens*
**Make blessèd my rude hand**
*Black like the hour of the night*

**True beauty**
**This night**
*When your love turns and wriggles close to your side*
**Did my heart love till now?**
**I'll watch her place of stand**
*Dancin' the funky chicken*
**The measure done,**
*Tightenin' up my 'fro,*
**Touching hers,**
*Ain't we colorful folks?*
*An ain't we fine?*

Angelou, Maya. "Ain't That Bad?" In *And Still I Rise*, 1978
Shakespeare, William. *Romeo and Juliet*, c. 1595

# On the Balcony: *Romeo and Juliet*, 2.2

## Here's What We're Doing and Why

Today students will take on the balcony scene, one of the most famous scenes in all of Shakespeare. They will consider how Shakespeare characterizes Juliet and Romeo as they make plans to defy their families' hatred and speed ahead in their declarations of love—and every student will play an active part.

## What Will I Need?

- *Romeo and Juliet* 2.2.53–205, slightly edited – **RESOURCE #2.4A**

## How Should I Prepare?

- Set up your classroom to have space for students to move about.

- Make copies of *Romeo and Juliet* 2.2.53–205, slightly edited – **RESOURCE #2.4A.**

## Agenda (~ 45-minute class period)

- ❏ Read through 2.2.53–205, slightly edited: 20 minutes

- ❏ Revealing meaning by physicalizing the conflicting emotions of Romeo and Juliet: 15 minutes

- ❏ Discovery and Reflection: 10 minutes

## Here's What Students Hear (From You) and (Then What They'll) Do

### Part One: Performing and Processing the Balcony Scene

1. First Reading: We are going to do a first-draft reading of the famous balcony scene today—it's a long scene and one of the most famous scenes in all of Shakespeare. We'll do this first reading chorally—everyone together—just to get a sense of what's happening in the scene before we dig deeper. As usual, don't worry about pronunciation, stay together, and keep it moving!

   Great job in the first reading. Now let's get some thoughts and observations out in a whole-class reflection round. First round, each of you complete the first sentence; the second round, the second sentence:

   – I noticed . . .

   – I wondered . . .

   Any observations on our observations?

2. Second Reading: We're going to reread, and we need four pairs to volunteer. In each pair, one of you will read Romeo and the other Juliet. One pair will read Page 1, another Page 2, then Page 3 and Page 4. Anyone can be a great Romeo or Juliet!

Read a bit slowly, as the rest of the class will be processing your words in a new way. Listeners, feel free to mark up your texts as you notice more that's going on in this scene.

3. Third Reading: I'm going to ask our readers to read a second time, and I'll divide the rest of you into two groups. One group will stand toward one end of the room and focus on Juliet's lines; the other will stand toward the opposite wall and focus on Romeo's.

4. As our readers read the scene again, each of the listeners will do these things:

   Step forward when you hear a word or phrase that emphasizes your character's **hesitance** with their future love plans, and . . .

   Step back when you hear a word or phrase that emphasizes your character's **eagerness**.

[**TEACHER NOTE:** Modification—for students who have different mobility needs or in confined spaces, this can be achieved with Legos or chess pieces at a desk or around tables.]

5. As we've now gone through the scene in this way, let's take a minute to see where you are in the room and where your classmates are, and think about what this tells us about what's going on in this scene. Check in with a partner about what you saw in terms of hesitancy and eagerness, and then share with the class.

### Part Two: Reflection

With respect to all of the work on the balcony scene today:

- I observed . . .

- I realized that . . .

## Here's What Just Happened in Class

- Students carried forward the critical analysis skills developed in the previous lesson to an almost entirely new and extended piece of text.

- Students had a chance to continue to consider the cultural and societal subtext of language.

- Students closely read this scene, enhanced by using their bodies in a different way in order to aid their analysis. They used information gleaned from that movement to make meaning from Shakespeare's language.

- Students also used information gleaned from that analysis-in-motion movement to consider relationships and power dynamics of the characters.

## RESOURCE #2.4A

## 2.2.53–205, edited

## Page 1

ROMEO  I take thee at thy word.
    Call me but love, and I'll be new baptized.
    Henceforth I never will be Romeo.                       55

JULIET
    What man art thou that, thus bescreened in night,
    So stumblest on my counsel?

ROMEO  By a name
    I know not how to tell thee who I am.
    My name, dear saint, is hateful to myself               60
    Because it is an enemy to thee.
    Had I it written, I would tear the word.

JULIET
    My ears have yet not drunk a hundred words
    Of thy tongue's uttering, yet I know the sound.
    Art thou not Romeo, and a Montague?               65

ROMEO
    Neither, fair maid, if either thee dislike.

JULIET
    How camest thou hither, tell me, and wherefore?
    The orchard walls are high and hard to climb,
    And the place death, considering who thou art,
    If any of my kinsmen find thee here.               70

ROMEO
    With love's light wings did I o'erperch these walls,
    For stony limits cannot hold love out,
    And what love can do, that dares love attempt.
    Therefore thy kinsmen are no stop to me.

JULIET
    If they do see thee, they will murder thee.          75

ROMEO

    Alack, there lies more peril in thine eye
    Than twenty of their swords. Look thou but sweet,
    And I am proof against their enmity.

JULIET

    I would not for the world they saw thee here.

ROMEO

    I have night's cloak to hide me from their eyes,     80
    And, but thou love me, let them find me here.
    My life were better ended by their hate
    Than death prorLguèd, wanting of thy love.

JULIET

    By whose direction found'st thou out this place?

ROMEO

    By love, that first did prompt me to inquire.     85
    He lent me counsel, and I lent him eyes.
    I am no pilot; yet, wert thou as far
    As that vast shore washed with the farthest sea,
    I should adventure for such merchandise.

---

## Page 2

JULIET

    Thou knowest the mask of night is on my face,     90
    Else would a maiden blush bepaint my cheek
    For that which thou hast heard me speak tonight.
    Fain would I dwell on form; fain, fain deny
    What I have spoke. But farewell compliment.
    Dost thou love me? I know thou wilt say "Ay,"     95
    And I will take thy word. Yet, if thou swear'st,
    Thou mayst prove false. At lovers' perjuries,
    They say, Jove laughs. O gentle Romeo,
    If thou dost love, pronounce it faithfully.
    Or, if thou thinkest I am too quickly won,     100
    I'll frown and be perverse and say thee nay,
    So thou wilt woo, but else not for the world.
    In truth, fair Montague, I am too fond,
    And therefore thou mayst think my havior light.
    But trust me, gentleman, I'll prove more true     105
    Than those that have more coying to be strange.
    I should have been more strange, I must confess,
    But that thou overheard'st ere I was ware

My true-love passion. Therefore pardon me,
And not impute this yielding to light love, 110
Which the dark night hath so discoverèd.

ROMEO

Lady, by yonder blessèd moon I vow,
That tips with silver all these fruit-tree tops—

JULIET

O, swear not by the moon, th' inconstant moon,
That monthly changes in her circled orb, 115
Lest that thy love prove likewise variable.

ROMEO

What shall I swear by?

JULIET  Do not swear at all.

Or, if thou wilt, swear by thy gracious self,
Which is the god of my idolatry, 120
And I'll believe thee.

ROMEO  If my heart's dear love—

JULIET

Well, do not swear. Although I joy in thee,
I have no joy of this contract tonight.
It is too rash, too unadvised, too sudden, 125
Too like the lightning, which doth cease to be
Ere one can say "It lightens." Sweet, good night.
This bud of love, by summer's ripening breath,
May prove a beauteous flower when next we meet.
Good night, good night. As sweet repose and rest 130
Come to thy heart as that within my breast.

ROMEO

O, wilt thou leave me so unsatisfied?

JULIET

What satisfaction canst thou have tonight?

ROMEO

Th' exchange of thy love's faithful vow for mine.

JULIET

I gave thee mine before thou didst request it, 135

## Page 3

And yet I would it were to give again.

ROMEO

Wouldst thou withdraw it? For what purpose, love?

JULIET

But to be frank and give it thee again.
And yet I wish but for the thing I have.
My bounty is as boundless as the sea,                                       140
My love as deep. The more I give to thee,
The more I have, for both are infinite.
                              *Nurse calls from within.*
I hear some noise within. Dear love, adieu.—
Anon, good nurse.—Sweet Montague, be true.
Stay but a little; I will come again.          *She exits.*          145

ROMEO

O blessèd, blessèd night! I am afeard,
Being in night, all this is but a dream,
Too flattering sweet to be substantial.
                              *Reenter Juliet above.*

JULIET

Three words, dear Romeo, and good night indeed.
If that thy bent of love be honorable,                                       150
Thy purpose marriage, send me word tomorrow,
By one that I'll procure to come to thee,
Where and what time thou wilt perform the rite,
And all my fortunes at thy foot I'll lay
And follow thee my lord throughout the world.                          155

NURSE, *within* Madam.

JULIET

I come anon.—But if thou meanest not well,
I do beseech thee—

NURSE, *within* Madam.

JULIET  By and by, I come.—                                               160
To cease thy strife and leave me to my grief.
Tomorrow will I send.

ROMEO  So thrive my soul—

JULIET  A thousand times good night.     *She exits.*

# Page 4

ROMEO

    A thousand times the worse to want thy light.     165
    Love goes toward love as schoolboys from their
      books,
    But love from love, toward school with heavy looks.
                              *Going.*
                     *Enter Juliet above again.*

JULIET

    Romeo.

ROMEO  My dear.

JULIET  What o'clock tomorrow     180
    Shall I send to thee?

ROMEO  By the hour of nine.

JULIET

    I will not fail. 'Tis twenty year till then.
    I have forgot why I did call thee back.

ROMEO

    Let me stand here till thou remember it.     185

JULIET

    I shall forget, to have thee still stand there,
    Rememb'ring how I love thy company.

ROMEO

    And I'll still stay, to have thee still forget,
    Forgetting any other home but this.

JULIET

    Good night, good night. Parting is such sweet
      sorrow     200
    That I shall say "Good night" till it be morrow.
                       *She exits.*

ROMEO

    Sleep dwell upon thine eyes, peace in thy breast.
    Would I were sleep and peace so sweet to rest.
    Hence will I to my ghostly friar's close cell,
    His help to crave, and my dear hap to tell.     205
                       *He exits.*

# "I'll thy assistant be": Evaluating the Friar's Advice in 2.3 and 2.6

## Here's What We're Doing and Why

In our last few lessons, we have focused on Romeo and Juliet (because they've been focused on each other!), but what about their families and the other adults in their lives? What sort of support do Romeo and Juliet need in order to build a healthy relationship? What sort of support will they receive? In Act 1, we hear Juliet's mother make plans about Juliet's future. In today's scene, Romeo is meeting with the adult he trusts most, Friar Lawrence.

Today, students will cut a scene (with a twist!) to close read Friar Lawrence's conversation with a lovestruck Romeo. Then, they will compare the Friar's counsel to Lady Capulet's and Clint Smith's advice from last week's lesson and think about the advice a trusted adult might give to Romeo today.

This lesson involves three main components: cutting the scene with a "mission" (more on that later), discussing cuts, and chorally reading the Friar's 2.6 advice. If you have extra time for some performances, you can have students cut the scene and then perform the cut versions. These performances really deepen students' understanding of the text and the possibilities of interpretation.

In our game plan for these lessons, we mentioned how *Romeo and Juliet* is a play that asks big questions about the significance of community support, what parents owe to their teenagers, and what teenagers owe to their parents. This lesson is a chance to dig into that theme and help students make personal connections with the plot and characters.

## What Will I Need?

- Copies of *Romeo and Juliet* 2.3.1–58, slightly edited, for each student – **RESOURCE #2.5A**

- Copies of *Romeo and Juliet* 2.6.9–15 for each student – **RESOURCE #2.5B**

- Pens/pencils/markers

## How Should I Prepare?

- Put students in groups of 3–4

- Decide how many groups will be assigned to each of the three "missions"

- Make a copy of 2.3 and 2.6 (**RESOURCES #2.5A and #2.5B**) for each student.

[**TEACHER NOTE:** You could also do this lesson digitally with electronic versions of the scene to which every student has editing rights.]

## Agenda (~ 45-minute period)

❏ Scene cutting with a mission: 20 minutes

❏ Discussion of cuts and connections to other parental advice: 15 minutes

❏ Choral reading of the Friar's wedding-day advice: 5 minutes

❏ Fast, whole-class discussion: 5 minutes

## Here's What Students Hear (From You) and (Then What They'll) Do:

This should be the students' first encounter with this scene, at least in your class.

1. After Romeo "proposes" to Juliet in the Capulets' orchard, he visits his friend (and a clergyman who could perform the wedding ceremony) Friar Lawrence, just after the friar has gathered some herbs in his garden. We're going to cut Romeo's conversation with Friar Lawrence with a "mission," a particular goal, in mind.

2. As with anytime we cut a text:

   a. You must read the scene aloud before you begin cutting.

   b. You have to understand the gist of a line before you cut it.

   c. You should discuss and come to a consensus in each group about what to cut.

3. These groups will cut the scene to focus on Friar Lawrence SUPPORTING Romeo: [Name the groups]

4. These groups will cut the scene to focus on Friar Lawrence SCOLDING Romeo: [Name the groups]

5. These groups will cut the scene to focus on Friar Lawrence ADVISING Romeo: [Name the groups]

6. There are about 60 lines in this edited version of 2.3. As you cut, try to reduce the length of the scene by half—roughly 30 lines.

7. You have 15 minutes to cut the scene.

[**TEACHER NOTE:** Provide no further instructions, and get out of the way.]

8. Let's talk about what you cut and what you kept.

   a. Which lines show Friar Lawrence SUPPORTING Romeo? What led you to choose them?

   b. Which lines show Friar Lawrence SCOLDING Romeo? What led you to choose them?

   c. Which lines show Friar Lawrence ADVISING Romeo? What led you to choose them?

   d. Think back to the conversation Juliet and Lady Capulet had before the Capulets' party. How is Friar Lawrence's advice similar to or different from Lady Capulet's? How is his advice similar to or different from Clint Smith's advice in his letter to his son?

    **e.** We know that Romeo and Juliet are defying their parents' rules and expectations by falling in love and trying to marry each other. Do you agree with the Friar's decision to perform their marriage ceremony? Why or why not?

    **f.** If you had a friend in Romeo's or Juliet's situation, how would you want the adults in their life to support them? Do you think Friar Lawrence has offered the right support and advice here? Why or why not?

9. Let's look at **RESOURCE #2.5B**. At the end of this act, Romeo and Juliet meet in Friar Lawrence's cell for their wedding ceremony. As Romeo is waiting for Juliet to arrive, Friar Lawrence shares one more piece of advice. Let's read it together as we've done other choral readings. The first time, we'll read it loud and fast.

10. Great! Let's read it again, a little slower this time. Listen to your neighbors to keep pace with one another.

11. On a scale of 1 to 5, how well do you understand what the Friar is saying?

12. What advice is he giving the almost-newlyweds? How do you know?

13. Let's read it one more time. I'm going to divide the room into two sides. Side A, you'll begin and read until the first end-punctuation. Side B, you'll read to the next end-punctuation. And then we will keep alternating back and forth until the passage is finished.

14. What did you notice about hearing this passage read by two "sides" or two voices? What do you notice about the Friar's language in this passage? Do you see any connections to his conversation in 2.3 with Romeo?

[**TEACHER NOTE:** Students may point out vivid phrases or even the language of violence. Students might recognize some pairing of opposite concepts or extremes (violence and love, loathsomeness and sweetness/deliciousness).]

15. Do you think the Friar is advising, scolding, or supporting here? Which words or phrases are guiding your answer?

16. Great work! Let's close today with two quick rounds:

    **a.** I realized . . .

    **b.** Today's work made me wonder . . .

## Here's What Just Happened in Class

- Students collaborated with each other (and with Shakespeare!) to make decisions about the text.

- Students spoke Shakespeare's words together.

- Students used textual evidence to support their thinking.

- Students connected new learning to prior knowledge of the play.

- Students discussed their own and others' social/emotional needs through the lens of the plot and characters of *Romeo and Juliet*.

**RESOURCE #2.5A**

---

# 2.3.1–58, slightly edited

*Enter Friar Lawrence alone with a basket.*

ROMEO

Good morrow, father.

FRIAR LAWRENCE

Young son, it argues a distempered head
So soon to bid "Good morrow" to thy bed.
Care keeps his watch in every old man's eye,
And, where care lodges, sleep will never lie;                5
But where unbruisèd youth with unstuffed brain
Doth couch his limbs, there golden sleep doth
    reign.
Therefore thy earliness doth me assure
Thou art uproused with some distemp'rature,
Or, if not so, then here I hit it right:                    10
Our Romeo hath not been in bed tonight.

ROMEO

That last is true. The sweeter rest was mine.

FRIAR LAWRENCE

God pardon sin! Wast thou with Rosaline?

ROMEO

With Rosaline, my ghostly father? No.
I have forgot that name and that name's woe.               15

FRIAR LAWRENCE

That's my good son. But where hast thou been
    then?

ROMEO

I'll tell thee ere thou ask it me again.
I have been feasting with mine enemy.

FRIAR LAWRENCE

Be plain, good son, and homely in thy drift.
Riddling confession finds but riddling shrift.            20

ROMEO

    Then plainly know my heart's dear love is set
    On the fair daughter of rich Capulet.
    As mine on hers, so hers is set on mine,
    And all combined, save what thou must combine
    By holy marriage. When and where and how     25
    We met, we wooed, and made exchange of vow
    I'll tell thee as we pass, but this I pray,
    That thou consent to marry us today.

FRIAR LAWRENCE

    Holy Saint Francis, what a change is here!
    Is Rosaline, that thou didst love so dear,     30
    So soon forsaken? Young men's love then lies
    Not truly in their hearts, but in their eyes.
    Jesu Maria, what a deal of brine
    Hath washed thy sallow cheeks for Rosaline!
    How much salt water thrown away in waste     35
    To season love, that of it doth not taste!
    The sun not yet thy sighs from heaven clears,
    Thy old groans yet ringing in mine ancient ears.
    Lo, here upon thy cheek the stain doth sit
    Of an old tear that is not washed off yet.     40
    If e'er thou wast thyself, and these woes thine,
    Thou and these woes were all for Rosaline.
    And art thou changed? Pronounce this sentence
      then:
    Women may fall when there's no strength in men.

ROMEO

    Thou chid'st me oft for loving Rosaline.     45

FRIAR LAWRENCE

    For doting, not for loving, pupil mine.

ROMEO

    And bad'st me bury love.

FRIAR LAWRENCE  Not in a grave
    To lay one in, another out to have.

ROMEO

    I pray thee, chide me not. Her I love now     50
    Doth grace for grace and love for love allow.
    The other did not so.

FRIAR LAWRENCE

But come, young waverer, come, go with me.
In one respect I'll thy assistant be,
For this alliance may so happy prove                                55
To turn your households' rancor to pure love.

ROMEO

O, let us hence. I stand on sudden haste.

FRIAR LAWRENCE

Wisely and slow. They stumble that run fast.
                                        *They exit.*

**RESOURCE #2.5B**

## 2.6.9–15

FRIAR LAWRENCE
These violent delights have violent ends
And in their triumph die, like fire and powder,                    10
Which, as they kiss, consume. The sweetest honey
Is loathsome in his own deliciousness
And in the taste confounds the appetite.
Therefore love moderately. Long love doth so.
Too swift arrives as tardy as too slow.                            15

WEEK THREE: LESSON 1

# "We Shall Not 'Scape a Brawl": Creating and Analyzing Action in 3.1

## Here's What We're Doing and Why

Students will collaborate on approaching this passionate, complicated scene, digging into the language and the action—and there is plenty of both here! Today we'll start with choral reading, getting the whole scene in our heads, then move to working in depth in small groups through digestible sections of 3.1 as you promptbook them with a focus on meaning and action.

The action in this scene changes both the direction and the underpinnings of the play. This lesson will give students a chance to get into all of that as they discover the implied stage action that is heavily embedded in the language. Students take ownership of the scene (and Shakespeare) by locating the small, implied moments of action and deciding how they will bring them to life. We'll end with a second choral reading of the whole scene so that students can demonstrate to themselves a greater sense of meaning. Tomorrow's lesson will begin with a relay warm-up of 3.1 . . . and we'll invite a guest artist into this scene as well!

## What Will I Need?

- Copies of 3.1, divided into sections – **RESOURCE #3.1**

## How Should I Prepare?

- Print copies of 3.1 divided into sections – **RESOURCE #3.1**. Each student should have a copy of the complete scene.

- Be ready to assign students for group work.

## Agenda (~ 45-minute class period)

- ❏ Choral Reading of entire scene and quick initial discussion: 10 minutes

- ❏ Small-group work: reading and collaborating on their sections of 3.1: 15 minutes

- ❏ Second Choral Reading of entire scene and discussion of these two "bookend" readings: 10 minutes

- ❏ Reflection: 10 minutes

## Here's What Students Hear (From You) and (Then What They'll) Do

1. Today, we are going to be working with one of the most important scenes in *Romeo and Juliet*—a scene that changes everything! It's a complicated fight scene. You are going to work in six small groups; each group will have a small chunk

of the scene. There is a lot to dig into here: you'll be deciding on meaning and action, working collaboratively in your groups. Together you'll be performing the entire scene tomorrow.

2. First Choral Reading: We're going to start off, though, getting a sense of the whole scene. Let's circle up and read it all together as we usually do. Then let's read it sequentially, speech-to-speech.

3. Then, a quick all-class reflection to gather initial thoughts on what's happening here:

   a. I observed . . .

   b. I wonder about . . .

4. Gather in your groups and read aloud the part of the scene that you've been assigned.

[**TEACHER NOTE:** As students are reading, circulate around the room. By now, they are used to pushing through words without worry of pronunciation and are beginning to take ownership of Shakespeare's language and bring life to it.]

5. As we've done before, read through again and mark up your text with initial questions and thoughts about words, meaning, and action. Talk through these thoughts together.

6. Continue to figure out together how you will bring your scene to life. In preparing your part of 3.1 for performance, be aware that you must integrate at least these certain actions in your performances.

[**TEACHER NOTE:** It might be helpful to have these actions posted on a board or wall for students to reference throughout:]

   a. a whisper

   b. a yell

   c. a prop

   d. a pointing finger

   e. a kneel

   f. a chest thump

   g. a smile or a frown

7. Continue to discuss, experiment, and mark up your scripts in terms of where actions, shifts in tone of voice, etc., will take place. The list on the board might help with visualizing action.

8. Second, Wrap-Up Choral Reading: Let's all read the whole scene the way we started out.

9. Reflection:

   – I was surprised that . . .

   – This reading sounds different to me because . . .

   – I wonder if . . .

## Here's What Just Happened in Class

- Students collaborated to perform a turning-point scene with very little assistance from you.

- Students made discoveries about how stage directions are embedded in dialogue, and they made decisions about performance that were grounded in an understanding of the text.

- Students had a chance to compare their own learning pre- and post- their group promptbook work.

- Students had fun! (And we bet you did, too.)

## 3.1.1–143
## Group 1: 1–35

**Scene 1**

*Enter Mercutio, Benvolio, and their men.*

BENVOLIO
I pray thee, good Mercutio, let's retire.
The day is hot, the Capels are abroad,
And if we meet we shall not 'scape a brawl,
For now, these hot days, is the mad blood stirring.

MERCUTIO  Thou art like one of these fellows that, when        5
he enters the confines of a tavern, claps me his
sword upon the table and says "God send me no
need of thee" and, by the operation of the second
cup, draws him on the drawer when indeed there is
no need.                                                       10

BENVOLIO  Am I like such a fellow?

MERCUTIO  Come, come, thou art as hot a jack in thy
mood as any in Italy, and as soon moved to be
moody, and as soon moody to be moved.

BENVOLIO  And what to?                                         15

MERCUTIO  Nay, an there were two such, we should
have none shortly, for one would kill the other.
Thou—why, thou wilt quarrel with a man that
hath a hair more or a hair less in his beard than
thou hast. Thou wilt quarrel with a man for cracking        20
nuts, having no other reason but because thou
hast hazel eyes. What eye but such an eye would spy
out such a quarrel? Thy head is as full of quarrels as
an egg is full of meat, and yet thy head hath been
beaten as addle as an egg for quarreling. Thou hast        25
quarreled with a man for coughing in the street
because he hath wakened thy dog that hath lain
asleep in the sun. Didst thou not fall out with a tailor
for wearing his new doublet before Easter? With
another, for tying his new shoes with old ribbon?          30
And yet thou wilt tutor me from quarreling?

BENVOLIO  An I were so apt to quarrel as thou art, any
man should buy the fee simple of my life for an
hour and a quarter.

MERCUTIO  The fee simple? O simple!                    35

---

# 3.1.1–143
# Group 2: 36–56

*Enter Tybalt, Petruchio, and others.*

BENVOLIO  By my head, here comes the Capulets.

MERCUTIO  By my heel, I care not.

TYBALT, *to his companions*
Follow me close, for I will speak to them.—
Gentlemen, good e'en. A word with one of you.

MERCUTIO  And but one word with one of us? Couple it       40
with something. Make it a word and a blow.

TYBALT  You shall find me apt enough to that, sir, and
you will give me occasion.

MERCUTIO  Could you not take some occasion without
giving?                                                    45

TYBALT  Mercutio, thou consortest with Romeo.

MERCUTIO  Consort? What, dost thou make us minstrels?
An thou make minstrels of us, look to hear
nothing but discords. Here's my fiddlestick; here's
that shall make you dance. Zounds, consort!               50

BENVOLIO
We talk here in the public haunt of men.
Either withdraw unto some private place,
Or reason coldly of your grievances,
Or else depart. Here all eyes gaze on us.

MERCUTIO
Men's eyes were made to look, and let them gaze.         55
I will not budge for no man's pleasure, I.
*Enter Romeo.*

## 3.1.1–143
## Group 3: 57–77

TYBALT
Well, peace be with you, sir. Here comes my man.

MERCUTIO
But I'll be hanged, sir, if he wear your livery.
Marry, go before to field, he'll be your follower.
Your Worship in that sense may call him "man."                              60

TYBALT
Romeo, the love I bear thee can afford
No better term than this: thou art a villain.

ROMEO
Tybalt, the reason that I have to love thee
Doth much excuse the appertaining rage
To such a greeting. Villain am I none.                                      65
Therefore farewell. I see thou knowest me not.

TYBALT
Boy, this shall not excuse the injuries
That thou hast done me. Therefore turn and draw.

ROMEO
I do protest I never injured thee
But love thee better than thou canst devise                                 70
Till thou shalt know the reason of my love.
And so, good Capulet, which name I tender
As dearly as mine own, be satisfied.

MERCUTIO
O calm, dishonorable, vile submission!
*Alla stoccato* carries it away.              *He draws.*                    75
Tybalt, you ratcatcher, will you walk?

TYBALT  What wouldst thou have with me?

## 3.1.1–143
## Group 4: 78–98

MERCUTIO  Good king of cats, nothing but one of your
    nine lives, that I mean to make bold withal, and, as
    you shall use me hereafter, dry-beat the rest of the        80
    eight. Will you pluck your sword out of his pilcher
    by the ears? Make haste, lest mine be about your
    ears ere it be out.

TYBALT  I am for you.            *He draws.*

ROMEO
    Gentle Mercutio, put thy rapier up.          85

MERCUTIO  Come, sir, your *passado.*    *They fight.*

ROMEO
    Draw, Benvolio, beat down their weapons.
                    *Romeo draws.*
    Gentlemen, for shame forbear this outrage!
    Tybalt! Mercutio! The Prince expressly hath
    Forbid this bandying in Verona streets.        90
    Hold, Tybalt! Good Mercutio!
              *Romeo attempts to beat down their rapiers.*
              *Tybalt stabs Mercutio.*

PETRUCHIO  Away, Tybalt!

              *Tybalt, Petruchio, and their followers exit.*

MERCUTIO  I am hurt.
    A plague o' both houses! I am sped.
    Is he gone and hath nothing?         95

BENVOLIO  What, art thou hurt?

MERCUTIO
    Ay, ay, a scratch, a scratch. Marry, 'tis enough.
    Where is my page?—Go, villain, fetch a surgeon.
                    *Page exits.*

## 3.1.1–143
## Group 5: 99–120

ROMEO

    Courage, man, the hurt cannot be much.

MERCUTIO  No, 'tis not so deep as a well, nor so wide as      100
    a church door, but 'tis enough. 'Twill serve. Ask for
    me tomorrow, and you shall find me a grave man. I
    am peppered, I warrant, for this world. A plague o'
    both your houses! Zounds, a dog, a rat, a mouse, a
    cat, to scratch a man to death! A braggart, a rogue, a      105
    villain that fights by the book of arithmetic! Why the
    devil came you between us? I was hurt under your
    arm.

ROMEO  I thought all for the best.

MERCUTIO

    Help me into some house, Benvolio,      110
    Or I shall faint. A plague o' both your houses!
    They have made worms' meat of me.
    I have it, and soundly, too. Your houses!

                            *All but Romeo exit.*

ROMEO

    This gentleman, the Prince's near ally,
    My very friend, hath got this mortal hurt      115
    In my behalf. My reputation stained
    With Tybalt's slander—Tybalt, that an hour
    Hath been my cousin! O sweet Juliet,
    Thy beauty hath made me effeminate
    And in my temper softened valor's steel.      120

                            *Enter Benvolio.*

## 3.1.1–143
## Group 6: 121–143

BENVOLIO

    O Romeo, Romeo, brave Mercutio is dead.
    That gallant spirit hath aspired the clouds,
    Which too untimely here did scorn the earth.

ROMEO

This day's black fate on more days doth depend.
This but begins the woe others must end.                          125
*Enter Tybalt.*

BENVOLIO

Here comes the furious Tybalt back again.

ROMEO

Alive in triumph, and Mercutio slain!
Away to heaven, respective lenity,
And fire-eyed fury be my conduct now.—
Now, Tybalt, take the "villain" back again                        130
That late thou gavest me, for Mercutio's soul
Is but a little way above our heads,
Staying for thine to keep him company.
Either thou or I, or both, must go with him.

TYBALT

Thou wretched boy that didst consort him here                     135
Shalt with him hence.

ROMEO  This shall determine that.
*They fight. Tybalt falls.*

BENVOLIO

Romeo, away, begone!
The citizens are up, and Tybalt slain.
Stand not amazed. The Prince will doom thee death                 140
If thou art taken. Hence, be gone, away.

ROMEO

O, I am Fortune's fool!

BENVOLIO  Why dost thou stay?
*Romeo exits.*

# Performing 3.1 with a Mystery Guest from 3.2!

## Here's What We're Doing and Why

Students will carry forward yesterday's analysis of 3.1 in a couple of different ways. They'll start by warming up with their relay performance of 3.1, and then layer in a "voice-over" that connects the action of 3.1 with 3.2. This literally creates the collision of the worlds of Romeo and Juliet. Your students hold all the power here. Step back and let the magic happen!

## What Will I Need?

- Students need the promptbook scripts they created yesterday.

- Copies of 3.1.1–143 (whole scene, undivided) for each student – **RESOURCE #3.2A**

- Copies of the same text with Juliet's voice-over – **RESOURCE #3.2B**

## How Should I Prepare?

- List on the board the scene sections in order, so that each group knows their spot in the relay.

- Set up your classroom so that students can perform the relay and pull all of 3.1 together.

- Make copies of **RESOURCE #3.2A** and **RESOURCE #3.2B.**

## Agenda (~ 45-minute period)

- ❏ Relay of 3.1 and quick follow-on comments from all groups: 20 minutes
- ❏ "Voice-over" Choral Readings of the entire scene: 15 minutes
- ❏ Share with a partner and whole-class discussion: 10 minutes

## Here's What Students Hear (From You) and (Then What They'll) Do

### Part One: 3.1 in Relay

1. As we did last week, reconvene in your groups and take a few minutes to go over the promptbook decisions you made yesterday. Check the board to see where your piece comes within the whole scene so you'll know who you're following, and who will follow you. Be ready to head to the performance space when your group's turn comes up. Remember, this scene is loaded with energy and action!

2. Let the relay begin! Much celebration on its completion!

**Part Two: Juliet's Presence**

1. Now we're going to add a new voice into the mix. First, we've had this extraordinary performance, and coming off that energy, we're going to read the whole scene together as we did yesterday – **RESOURCE #3.2A**. Let's read it chorally—all together—a couple of times. Any further thoughts or discoveries about this scene?

2. Let's think for a minute about Juliet. If Juliet were out in the hall watching your performance of 3.1, what might she be thinking or saying as she took in the words and the action? We're going to borrow Juliet and some of her lines from the next scene—3.2—and move them right into this scene . . . and see what that tells us.

3. Could we have a volunteer or two to read Juliet's lines?

[**TEACHER NOTE:** They can alternate lines or read them together chorally.]

4. Let's have relay groups gather in different parts of the room. Juliets, you'll be at the head or in the center of the room. I'm going to distribute copies of 3.1 into which Juliet has found her way – **RESOURCE #3.2B**.

5. As we present the whole scene through: Groups, you perform your scenes. And Juliets, you read her lines when they appear in the text, a voice-over from the future.

6. Repeat this reading with the Juliets whispering her lines, then again with her shouting her lines.

7. Turn to a partner and discuss for a few minutes the effect of Juliet's voice in this scene, and how you arrived at this analysis. Let's wrap up with everyone sharing their observations with the class.

## Here's What Just Happened in Class

- Students demonstrated their in-depth knowledge of 3.1 by working together to decide on meaning, action, and tone in a complex scene, and then collaboratively performing it in its entirety.

- Students considered the effect of this scene on the thinking and on the life of Juliet by "borrowing" her from 3.2 and performing the scene with the addition of her voice.

- Students partnered up to consider their analyses of the effect on Juliet, and shared these analyses with the class.

## RESOURCE #3.2A

## 3.1.1–143

BENVOLIO
    I pray thee, good Mercutio, let's retire.
    The day is hot, the Capels are abroad,
    And if we meet we shall not 'scape a brawl,
    For now, these hot days, is the mad blood stirring.

MERCUTIO  Thou art like one of these fellows that, when          5
    he enters the confines of a tavern, claps me his
    sword upon the table and says "God send me no
    need of thee" and, by the operation of the second
    cup, draws him on the drawer when indeed there is
    no need.                                                      10

BENVOLIO  Am I like such a fellow?

MERCUTIO  Come, come, thou art as hot a jack in thy
    mood as any in Italy, and as soon moved to be
    moody, and as soon moody to be moved.

BENVOLIO  And what to?                                            15

MERCUTIO  Nay, an there were two such, we should
    have none shortly, for one would kill the other.
    Thou—why, thou wilt quarrel with a man that
    hath a hair more or a hair less in his beard than
    thou hast. Thou wilt quarrel with a man for cracking          20
    nuts, having no other reason but because thou
    hast hazel eyes. What eye but such an eye would spy
    out such a quarrel? Thy head is as full of quarrels as
    an egg is full of meat, and yet thy head hath been
    beaten as addle as an egg for quarreling. Thou hast           25
    quarreled with a man for coughing in the street
    because he hath wakened thy dog that hath lain
    asleep in the sun. Didst thou not fall out with a tailor
    for wearing his new doublet before Easter? With
    another, for tying his new shoes with old ribbon?             30
    And yet thou wilt tutor me from quarreling?

BENVOLIO  An I were so apt to quarrel as thou art, any
    man should buy the fee simple of my life for an
        hour and a quarter.

MERCUTIO  The fee simple? O simple!                                     35

*Enter Tybalt, Petruchio, and others.*

BENVOLIO  By my head, here comes the Capulets.

MERCUTIO  By my heel, I care not.

TYBALT, *to his companions*
    Follow me close, for I will speak to them.—
    Gentlemen, good e'en. A word with one of you.

MERCUTIO  And but one word with one of us? Couple it              40
    with something. Make it a word and a blow.

TYBALT  You shall find me apt enough to that, sir, an
    you will give me occasion.

MERCUTIO  Could you not take some occasion without
    giving?                                                                     45

TYBALT  Mercutio, thou consortest with Romeo.

MERCUTIO  Consort? What, dost thou make us minstrels?
    An thou make minstrels of us, look to hear
    nothing but discords. Here's my fiddlestick; here's
    that shall make you dance. Zounds, consort!              50

BENVOLIO
    We talk here in the public haunt of men.
    Either withdraw unto some private place,
    Or reason coldly of your grievances,
    Or else depart. Here all eyes gaze on us.

MERCUTIO
    Men's eyes were made to look, and let them gaze.         55
    I will not budge for no man's pleasure, I.

*Enter Romeo.*

TYBALT
    Well, peace be with you, sir. Here comes my man.

MERCUTIO
    But I'll be hanged, sir, if he wear your livery.
    Marry, go before to field, he'll be your follower.
    Your Worship in that sense may call him "man."             60

TYBALT

    Romeo, the love I bear thee can afford
    No better term than this: thou art a villain.

ROMEO

    Tybalt, the reason that I have to love thee
    Doth much excuse the appertaining rage
    To such a greeting. Villain am I none.             65
    Therefore farewell. I see thou knowest me not.

TYBALT

    Boy, this shall not excuse the injuries
    That thou hast done me. Therefore turn and draw.

ROMEO

    I do protest I never injured thee
    But love thee better than thou canst devise       70
    Till thou shalt know the reason of my love.
    And so, good Capulet, which name I tender
    As dearly as mine own, be satisfied.

MERCUTIO

    O calm, dishonorable, vile submission!
    *Alla stoccato* carries it away.        *He draws.*     75
    Tybalt, you ratcatcher, will you walk?

TYBALT  What wouldst thou have with me?

MERCUTIO  Good king of cats, nothing but one of your
    nine lives, that I mean to make bold withal, and, as
    you shall use me hereafter, dry-beat the rest of the     80
    eight. Will you pluck your sword out of his pilcher
    by the ears? Make haste, lest mine be about your
    ears ere it be out.

TYBALT  I am for you.               *He draws.*

ROMEO

    Gentle Mercutio, put thy rapier up.            85

MERCUTIO  Come, sir, your *passado*.    *They fight.*

ROMEO

    Draw, Benvolio, beat down their weapons.
                                *Romeo draws.*
    Gentlemen, for shame forbear this outrage!
    Tybalt! Mercutio! The Prince expressly hath

Forbid this bandying in Verona streets. 90
Hold, Tybalt! Good Mercutio!

*Romeo attempts to beat down their rapiers.*
*Tybalt stabs Mercutio.*

PETRUCHIO  Away, Tybalt!

*Tybalt, Petruchio, and their followers exit.*

MERCUTIO  I am hurt.
A plague o' both houses! I am sped.
Is he gone and hath nothing? 95

BENVOLIO  What, art thou hurt?

MERCUTIO
Ay, ay, a scratch, a scratch. Marry, 'tis enough.
Where is my page?—Go, villain, fetch a surgeon.
*Page exits.*

ROMEO
Courage, man, the hurt cannot be much.

MERCUTIO  No, 'tis not so deep as a well, nor so wide as 100
a church door, but 'tis enough. 'Twill serve. Ask for
me tomorrow, and you shall find me a grave man. I
am peppered, I warrant, for this world. A plague o'
both your houses! Zounds, a dog, a rat, a mouse, a
cat, to scratch a man to death! A braggart, a rogue, a 105
villain that fights by the book of arithmetic! Why the
devil came you between us? I was hurt under your
arm.

ROMEO  I thought all for the best.

MERCUTIO
Help me into some house, Benvolio, 110
Or I shall faint. A plague o' both your houses!
They have made worms' meat of me.
I have it, and soundly, too. Your houses!
*All but Romeo exit.*

ROMEO
This gentleman, the Prince's near ally,
My very friend, hath got this mortal hurt 115
In my behalf. My reputation stained
With Tybalt's slander—Tybalt, that an hour
Hath been my cousin! O sweet Juliet,

Thy beauty hath made me effeminate
And in my temper softened valor's steel.                              120

*Enter Benvolio.*

BENVOLIO

O Romeo, Romeo, brave Mercutio is dead.
That gallant spirit hath aspired the clouds,
Which too untimely here did scorn the earth.

ROMEO

This day's black fate on more days doth depend.
This but begins the woe others must end.                             125

*Enter Tybalt.*

BENVOLIO

Here comes the furious Tybalt back again.

ROMEO

Alive in triumph, and Mercutio slain!
Away to heaven, respective lenity,
And fire-eyed fury be my conduct now.—
Now, Tybalt, take the "villain" back again                           130
That late thou gavest me, for Mercutio's soul
Is but a little way above our heads,
Staying for thine to keep him company.
Either thou or I, or both, must go with him.

TYBALT

Thou wretched boy that didst consort him here                        135
Shalt with him hence.

ROMEO  This shall determine that.

*They fight. Tybalt falls.*

BENVOLIO

Romeo, away, begone!
The citizens are up, and Tybalt slain.
Stand not amazed. The Prince will doom thee death                    140
If thou art taken. Hence, be gone, away.

ROMEO

O, I am Fortune's fool!

BENVOLIO  Why dost thou stay?

*Romeo exits.*

**RESOURCE #3.2B**

# 3.1.1–143 with Juliet's "voice-over" from 3.2.1–155

*Enter Mercutio, Benvolio, and their men.*

BENVOLIO

I pray thee, good Mercutio, let's retire.
The day is hot, the Capels are abroad,
And if we meet we shall not 'scape a brawl,
For now, these hot days, is the mad blood stirring.

MERCUTIO  Thou art like one of these fellows that, when                     5
he enters the confines of a tavern, claps me his
sword upon the table and says "God send me no
need of thee" and, by the operation of the second
cup, draws him on the drawer when indeed there is
no need.                                                                    10

BENVOLIO  Am I like such a fellow?

MERCUTIO  Come, come, thou art as hot a jack in thy
mood as any in Italy, and as soon moved to be
moody, and as soon moody to be moved.

JULIET

**Gallop apace, you fiery-footed steeds,**
**Toward Phoebus' lodging. Such a wagoner**
**As Phaëton would whip you to the west**
**And bring in cloudy night immediately.**

BENVOLIO  And what to?                                                      15

MERCUTIO  Nay, an there were two such, we should
have none shortly, for one would kill the other.
Thou—why, thou wilt quarrel with a man that
hath a hair more or a hair less in his beard than
thou hast. Thou wilt quarrel with a man for cracking                        20
nuts, having no other reason but because thou
hast hazel eyes. What eye but such an eye would spy
out such a quarrel? Thy head is as full of quarrels as
an egg is full of meat, and yet thy head hath been
beaten as addle as an egg for quarreling. Thou hast                         25
quarreled with a man for coughing in the street
because he hath wakened thy dog that hath lain
asleep in the sun. Didst thou not fall out with a tailor

for wearing his new doublet before Easter? With
another, for tying his new shoes with old ribbon?                    30
And yet thou wilt tutor me from quarreling?

BENVOLIO  An I were so apt to quarrel as thou art, any
man should buy the fee simple of my life for an
hour and a quarter.

MERCUTIO  The fee simple? O simple!                                  35

*Enter Tybalt, Petruchio, and others.*

BENVOLIO  By my head, here comes the Capulets.

MERCUTIO  By my heel, I care not.

TYBALT, *to his companions*
Follow me close, for I will speak to them.—
Gentlemen, good e'en. A word with one of you.

MERCUTIO  And but one word with one of us? Couple it            40
with something. Make it a word and a blow.

TYBALT  You shall find me apt enough to that, sir, an
you will give me occasion.

MERCUTIO  Could you not take some occasion without
giving?                                                              45

TYBALT  Mercutio, thou consortest with Romeo.

JULIET
Spread thy close curtain, love-performing night,
That runaways' eyes may wink, and Romeo
Leap to these arms, untalked of and unseen.

MERCUTIO  Consort? What, dost thou make us minstrels?
An thou make minstrels of us, look to hear
nothing but discords. Here's my fiddlestick; here's
that shall make you dance. Zounds, consort!                          50

BENVOLIO
We talk here in the public haunt of men.
Either withdraw unto some private place,
Or reason coldly of your grievances,
Or else depart. Here all eyes gaze on us.

MERCUTIO

Men's eyes were made to look, and let them gaze.       55
I will not budge for no man's pleasure, I.
                        *Enter Romeo.*

TYBALT

Well, peace be with you, sir. Here comes my man.

JULIET

**Hood my unmanned blood, bating in my cheeks,**
**With thy black mantle till strange love grow bold,**
**Think true love acted simple modesty.**

MERCUTIO

But I'll be hanged, sir, if he wear your livery.
Marry, go before to field, he'll be your follower.
Your Worship in that sense may call him "man."       60

TYBALT

Romeo, the love I bear thee can afford
No better term than this: thou art a villain.

ROMEO

Tybalt, the reason that I have to love thee
Doth much excuse the appertaining rage
To such a greeting. Villain am I none.       65
Therefore farewell. I see thou knowest me not.

JULIET

**Come, night. Come, Romeo. Come, thou day in night.**

TYBALT

Boy, this shall not excuse the injuries
That thou hast done me. Therefore turn and draw.

JULIET

**If love be blind, it best agrees with night.**

ROMEO

I do protest I never injured thee
But love thee better than thou canst devise       70
Till thou shalt know the reason of my love.
And so, good Capulet, which name I tender
As dearly as mine own, be satisfied.

MERCUTIO

O calm, dishonorable, vile submission!

*Alla stoccato* carries it away.        *He draws.*        75
Tybalt, you ratcatcher, will you walk?

TYBALT  What wouldst thou have with me?

MERCUTIO  Good king of cats, nothing but one of your
nine lives, that I mean to make bold withal, and, as
you shall use me hereafter, dry-beat the rest of the        80
eight. Will you pluck your sword out of his pilcher
by the ears? Make haste, lest mine be about your
ears ere it be out.

TYBALT  I am for you.        *He draws.*

ROMEO
Gentle Mercutio, put thy rapier up.        85

JULIET
. . . **Learn me how to lose a winning match**
**Played for a pair of stainless maidenhoods.**

MERCUTIO  Come, sir, your *passado.*    *They fight.*

ROMEO
Draw, Benvolio, beat down their weapons.
                                        *Romeo draws.*
Gentlemen, for shame forbear this outrage!
Tybalt! Mercutio! The Prince expressly hath
Forbid this bandying in Verona streets.        90
Hold, Tybalt! Good Mercutio!

JULIET
**Come, night. Come, Romeo. Come, thou day in night.**
                *Romeo attempts to beat down their rapiers.*
                *Tybalt stabs Mercutio.*

PETRUCHIO  Away, Tybalt!

                *Tybalt, Petruchio, and their followers exit.*

MERCUTIO  I am hurt.
A plague o' both houses! I am sped.
Is he gone and hath nothing?        95

BENVOLIO  What, art thou hurt?

MERCUTIO
Ay, ay, a scratch, a scratch. Marry, 'tis enough.

Where is my page?—Go, villain, fetch a surgeon.

*Page exits.*

ROMEO

Courage, man, the hurt cannot be much.

MERCUTIO  No, 'tis not so deep as a well, nor so wide as                    100
a church door, but 'tis enough. 'Twill serve. Ask for
me tomorrow, and you shall find me a grave man. I
am peppered, I warrant, for this world. A plague o'
both your houses! Zounds, a dog, a rat, a mouse, a
cat, to scratch a man to death! A braggart, a rogue, a                     105
villain that fights by the book of arithmetic! Why the
devil came you between us? I was hurt under your
arm.

ROMEO  I thought all for the best.

JULIET

**So tedious is this day**
**As is the night before some festival**
**To an impatient child that hath new robes**
**And may not wear them.**

MERCUTIO

Help me into some house, Benvolio,                                         110
Or I shall faint. A plague o' both your houses!
They have made worms' meat of me.
I have it, and soundly, too. Your houses!

*All but Romeo exit.*

ROMEO

This gentleman, the Prince's near ally,
My very friend, hath got this mortal hurt                                  115
In my behalf. My reputation stained
With Tybalt's slander—Tybalt, that an hour
Hath been my cousin! O sweet Juliet,
Thy beauty hath made me effeminate
And in my temper softened valor's steel.                                   120

JULIET

**O, I have bought the mansion of a love**
**But not possessed it, and, though I am sold,**
**Not yet enjoyed. Come, night.**

*Enter Benvolio.*

BENVOLIO

O Romeo, Romeo, brave Mercutio is dead.
That gallant spirit hath aspired the clouds,
Which too untimely here did scorn the earth.

ROMEO

This day's black fate on more days doth depend.
This but begins the woe others must end.                                    125

*Enter Tybalt.*

BENVOLIO

Here comes the furious Tybalt back again.

ROMEO

Alive in triumph, and Mercutio slain!
Away to heaven, respective lenity,
And fire-eyed fury be my conduct now.—
Now, Tybalt, take the "villain" back again                                  130
That late thou gavest me, for Mercutio's soul
Is but a little way above our heads,
Staying for thine to keep him company.
Either thou or I, or both, must go with him.

TYBALT

Thou wretched boy that didst consort him here                               135
Shalt with him hence.

ROMEO  This shall determine that.

JULIET

**Ay me, what news?**

*They fight. Tybalt falls.*

BENVOLIO

Romeo, away, begone!
The citizens are up, and Tybalt slain.
Stand not amazed. The Prince will doom thee death                           140
If thou art taken. Hence, be gone, away.

JULIET

**O break, my heart, poor bankrout, break at once!**
**To prison, eyes; ne'er look on liberty.**
**My husband lives, that Tybalt would have slain,**
**And Tybalt's dead, that would have slain my husband.**
**All this is comfort. Wherefore weep I then?**

ROMEO

O, I am Fortune's fool!

BENVOLIO  Why dost thou stay?

*Romeo exits.*

JULIET

**Give me my Romeo, and when I shall die,**
**Take him and cut him out in little stars,**
**And he will make the face of heaven so fine**
**That all the world will be in love with night**
**And pay no worship to the garish sun.**

# Advice to Teenagers Through Time and Space

## Here's What We're Doing and Why

Students will closely examine the support systems—or lack of them—that are available to Juliet and Romeo. Though the play leaves us guessing about the paternal support within the Montague household itself, we see that Friar Lawrence has plenty of advice for Romeo. In cutting 3.3, students will look at the advice that the Friar offers Romeo after he has committed a fatal error, and they'll reflect on which bits are most valuable to Romeo.

By way of comparison, students will also read an excerpt from Toni Morrison's *Song of Solomon* in which another character is receiving advice while recovering from a "fatal love" quite like Romeo and Juliet. Drawing students closer to these ideas of "fatal love" and how it might look different across space, time, gender, or race will help draw them closer to the world of the text.

## What Will I Need?

- Copies of Act 3.3.1–80 – **RESOURCE #3.3A**

- Copies of excerpt from Toni Morrison's *Song of Solomon* – **RESOURCE #3.3B**

## How Should I Prepare?

- Print copies of **RESOURCE #3.3A** and **RESOURCE #3.3B**.

- Set up your classroom for group work

## Agenda (~ 45-minute class period)

- ❏ Cutting the Scene, 3.3: 15 minutes

- ❏ Read cut scenes aloud and discuss: 10 minutes

- ❏ Read excerpt from Toni Morrison's *Song of Solomon*: 10 minutes

- ❏ Comparing passages, discoveries discussion, and closing reflection: 10 minutes

## Here's What Students Hear (From You) and (Then What They'll) Do

### Part One: Getting with Friar Lawrence and Romeo

1. Take a look at this conversation between Romeo and the Friar in **RESOURCE #3.3A**. With a partner, cut this conversation down to ten lines.

2. Let's share the scenes you created!

[**TEACHER NOTE:** If you don't have many groups, everyone should read their scenes; if you have many pairs, invite a few volunteers to read and then ask which pairs have used different lines from those they have already heard performed.]

**3.** Let's discuss this scene:

  **a.** What were some of your reasons for keeping what you kept or cutting what you cut?

  **b.** What are you seeing or hearing in this scene?

  **c.** What are some juicy words that jump out at you? (Juicy words are words that feel good to say, have high connotative value.)

  **d.** How does Friar Lawrence feel in this moment? How do we know?

  **e.** What was some of the best advice that Friar Lawrence offered Romeo? Why do you think that was good advice?

  **f.** Does it seem like Friar Lawrence and Romeo have the same sort of relationship that they had in earlier acts? Why or why not?

**Part Two: Holding Shakespeare Up to Toni Morrison**

**1.** Now we're going to consider a short excerpt from a 20th-century novel called *Song of Solomon*. I'm distributing **RESOURCE #3.3B** without much context.

**2.** Read this excerpt silently at your desk and circle what you think are the "wisest" lines.

**3.** Read this excerpt again, marking any other "wise" lines that you notice.

**4.** Let's discuss:

  **a.** What do you observe about the language of the text?

  **b.** What have you learned about the conflict the two characters are experiencing?

  **c.** What is the impact of never getting to hear from the character who isn't speaking? What forces seem to be contributing to her conflict? What language tells us this?

  **d.** Which lines did you highlight as "wise" or offering good advice? Why?

**5.** Now, we'll discuss these two passages together:

  **a.** How are the supportive relationships portrayed differently? Similarly?

  **b.** What does the world of the *Song of Solomon* passage value? How do you know?

  **c.** How is that world different from the world of Romeo and Juliet? How do you know?

  **d.** What concerns from these passages are still very real and present for us today?

**6.** Let's close with some rounds:

  – I learned . . .

  – I was surprised that . . .

## Here's What Just Happened in Class

- Students collaborated to close read a scene by cutting 3.3.

- Students spoke Shakespeare's language aloud to demonstrate their understanding of the text.

- Students put Shakespeare in conversation with a 20th-century text by comparing 3.3 and an excerpt from *Song of Solomon* by Toni Morrison.

- Students thought critically about the relationships between young people and adults in *Romeo and Juliet*.

- Students made connections between their world and the worlds of Shakespeare and Morrison.

## RESOURCE #3.3A

# Act 3, Scene 3

*Enter Friar Lawrence.*

FRIAR LAWRENCE

    Romeo, come forth; come forth, thou fearful man.
    Affliction is enamored of thy parts,
    And thou art wedded to calamity.

                     *Enter Romeo.*

ROMEO

    Father, what news? What is the Prince's doom?
    What sorrow craves acquaintance at my hand          5
    That I yet know not?

FRIAR LAWRENCE  Too familiar

    Is my dear son with such sour company.
    I bring thee tidings of the Prince's doom.

ROMEO

    What less than doomsday is the Prince's doom?        10

FRIAR LAWRENCE

    A gentler judgment vanished from his lips:
    Not body's death, but body's banishment.

ROMEO

    Ha, banishment? Be merciful, say "death,"
    For exile hath more terror in his look,
    Much more than death. Do not say "banishment."    15

FRIAR LAWRENCE

    Here from Verona art thou banishèd.
    Be patient, for the world is broad and wide.

ROMEO

    There is no world without Verona walls
    But purgatory, torture, hell itself.
    Hence "banishèd" is "banished from the world,"    20
    And world's exile is death. Then "banishèd"
    Is death mistermed. Calling death "banishèd,"
    Thou cutt'st my head off with a golden ax
    And smilest upon the stroke that murders me.

FRIAR LAWRENCE

O deadly sin, O rude unthankfulness!                              25
Thy fault our law calls death, but the kind prince,
Taking thy part, hath rushed aside the law
And turned that black word "death" to
    "banishment."
This is dear mercy, and thou seest it not.                        30

ROMEO

'Tis torture and not mercy. Heaven is here
Where Juliet lives, and every cat and dog
And little mouse, every unworthy thing,
Live here in heaven and may look on her,
But Romeo may not. More validity,                                 35
More honorable state, more courtship lives
In carrion flies than Romeo. They may seize
On the white wonder of dear Juliet's hand
And steal immortal blessing from her lips,
Who even in pure and vestal modesty                               40
Still blush, as thinking their own kisses sin;
But Romeo may not; he is banishèd.
Flies may do this, but I from this must fly.
They are free men, but I am banishèd.
And sayest thou yet that exile is not death?                      45
Hadst thou no poison mixed, no sharp-ground
    knife,
No sudden mean of death, though ne'er so mean,
But "banishèd" to kill me? "Banishèd"?
O friar, the damnèd use that word in hell.                        50
Howling attends it. How hast thou the heart,
Being a divine, a ghostly confessor,
A sin absolver, and my friend professed,
To mangle me with that word "banishèd"?

FRIAR LAWRENCE

Thou fond mad man, hear me a little speak.                        55

ROMEO

O, thou wilt speak again of banishment.

FRIAR LAWRENCE

I'll give thee armor to keep off that word,
Adversity's sweet milk, philosophy,
To comfort thee, though thou art banishèd.

ROMEO

Yet "banishèd"? Hang up philosophy.                               60

Unless philosophy can make a Juliet,
Displant a town, reverse a prince's doom,
It helps not, it prevails not. Talk no more.

**FRIAR LAWRENCE**

O, then I see that madmen have no ears.

**ROMEO**

How should they when that wise men have no eyes?          65

**FRIAR LAWRENCE**

Let me dispute with thee of thy estate.

**ROMEO**

Thou canst not speak of that thou dost not feel.
Wert thou as young as I, Juliet thy love,
An hour but married, Tybalt murderèd,
Doting like me, and like me banishèd,          70
Then mightst thou speak, then mightst thou tear thy
    hair
And fall upon the ground as I do now,
                    *Romeo throws himself down.*
Taking the measure of an unmade grave.
                    *Knock within.*

**FRIAR LAWRENCE**

Arise. One knocks. Good Romeo, hide thyself.          75

**ROMEO**

Not I, unless the breath of heartsick groans,
Mistlike, enfold me from the search of eyes.
                    *Knock.*

**FRIAR LAWRENCE**

Hark, how they knock!—Who's there?—Romeo,
    arise.
Thou wilt be taken.—Stay awhile.—Stand up.          80
                    *Knock.*

RESOURCE #3.3B

# A Short Excerpt from Toni Morrison's *Song of Solomon*

The engine of the old car he'd borrowed roared, but spoke softly to her.

"You think because he doesn't love you that you are worthless. You think because he doesn't want you anymore that he is right—that his judgment and opinion of you are correct. If he throws you out, then you are garbage. You think he belongs to you because you want to belong to him. Hagar, don't. It's a bad word, 'belong.' Especially when you put it with somebody you love. Love shouldn't be like that. Did you ever see the way the clouds love a mountain? They circle all around it; sometimes you can't even see the mountain for the clouds. But you know what? You go up top and what do you see? His head. The clouds never cover the head. His head pokes through, because the clouds let him; they don't wrap him up. They let him keep his head up high, free, with nothing to hide him or bind him. Hear me, Hagar?"

He spoke to her as he would to a very young child.

"You can't own a human being. You can't lose what you don't own. Suppose you did own him. Could you really love somebody who was absolutely nobody without you? You really want somebody like that? Somebody who falls apart when you walk out the door? You don't, do you? And neither does he. You're turning over your whole life to him. Your whole life, girl. And if it means so little to you that you can just give it away, hand it to him, then why should it mean any more to him? He can't value you more than you value yourself."

He stopped. She did not move or give any sign that she had heard him. Pretty woman, he thought. They were always women who had been spoiled children. Whose whims had been taken seriously by adults and who grew up to be the stingiest, greediest people on earth and out of their stinginess grew their stingy little love that ate everything in sight. They could not believe or accept the fact that they were unloved; they believed that the world itself was off balance when it appeared as though they were not loved.

And they loved their love so much they would kill anybody who got in its way. He looked at her again. Pretty. Pretty little black girl. Pretty little black-skinned girl. What had Pilate done to her? Hadn't anybody told her the things she ought to know? She needed what most colored girls needed: a chorus of mamas, grandmamas, aunts, cousins, sisters, neighbors, Sunday school teachers, best girlfriends, and what all to give her the strength life demanded of her—and the humor with which to live it.

# "Hear me with patience": Revisiting Parenting in 3.5

## Here's What We're Doing and Why

During Week One, we examined the pre-party scene in which Juliet and Lady Capulet discuss Juliet's disinterest in a marriage with the County Paris. We compared Lady Capulet's parental advice for Juliet with Clint Smith's hopes, dreams, and fears for a future son. In another take at comparison mode, students will now look at Juliet's support system—Lord Capulet, Lady Capulet, and the Nurse—and compare their relationships with Juliet to Romeo's relationship with the Friar.

In 3.3, the Friar consoled Romeo about his banishment. Will Juliet's father and mother be as kind about her continued disinterest in marrying Paris? Students will discover the answer to that question as they read 3.5 and make promptbooks for Juliet's interaction with each parental figure.

A lot of action is embedded in the dialogue of this scene, so it lends itself well to making promptbooks. As students make decisions about how Lord Capulet, Lady Capulet, or the Nurse move and what tone of voice they use, they will also think about whether or not Juliet is receiving the support she needs from those in charge of caring for her. Exploring the answer to that question can help students understand the choices that Juliet makes in Act 4.

## What Will I Need?

- 3.5.109–255 of *Romeo and Juliet* – **RESOURCES #3.4A, #3.4B, and #3.4C**
  - Note: **#3.4A** focuses on Juliet and Lady Capulet, **#3.4B** focuses on Juliet and Lord Capulet, and **#3.4C** focuses on Juliet and the Nurse.
  - Organize your class into 3, 6, or 9 groups (depending on your class size—these groups will each make a promptbook for ONE of the three parts of this scene).

## How Should I Prepare?

- Set up your classroom for group work.

- Make copies of **RESOURCES #3.4A, #3.4B, and #3.4C** (enough for each group that will study the assigned excerpt)—OR share digital copies of these scripts with students so that they can edit electronically.

## Agenda (~ 45-minute class period)

❏ Introduction to the lesson: 5 minutes

❏ Read and make promptbooks: 20 minutes

❏ "Table read" scenes with stage directions: 10 minutes

❏ Discussion and reflection: 10 minutes

## Here's What Students Hear (From You) and (Then What They'll) Do

### Part One: Keeping On with Promptbooks

1. Today, we're going to continue with promptbooks, the scripts that directors and actors make to guide their performance of a scene. You will work in groups to make promptbooks for three different parts of Act 3, scene 5. I'll pass out scripts to assigned groups.

2. Each group should:
    - Read their part of the scene out loud at least once
    - Decide together what is happening in the scene
    - Cut the scene in half
    - Write in directions for how characters will move and speak in the scene (aim for at least five significant movements and two directions for tone of voice; think back to our work on 3.1 and consider adding changes in volume or particular props, too!)

3. Assemble in your groups and start working!

[**TEACHER NOTE:** As groups work together, listen in to hear negotiations about students' understanding of the scene. If needed, encourage students to use the text to support their suggestions for movement and tone.]

### Part Two: Promptbooks in a "Table Read" and Discussion!

1. Now that everyone has created their promptbooks, we will present at least one version of each part of the scene in a "table read" style. Group members will sit together and read the characters' dialogue while a director reads the stage directions aloud in the places where your group has added them. For example, the first line of the script might "sound" something like this:

DIRECTOR: *Lady Capulet enters Juliet's room and closes the door behind her.*

LADY CAPULET: But now I'll tell thee joyful tidings, girl.

DIRECTOR: *She places a kind but commanding hand on Juliet's shoulder.*

2. Let's talk about this scene and reflect on our work today:
    - What did you notice about the language of this scene? Were there any words or phrases that stood out? Why?
    - What did you notice about how Lady Capulet, Lord Capulet, and the Nurse reacted to Juliet's feelings and wishes in this scene?
    - What do each of these adults seem to value? How do you know? Do their values align with Juliet's needs? Why or why not?

- Think about the scene we read yesterday between Romeo and the Friar. How would you compare the Friar's words to Romeo with what Lady Capulet, Lord Capulet, or the Nurse says to Juliet?
- How do you think the Capulet adults should have reacted to Juliet's refusal to marry Paris?
- How do you think Juliet feels at the end of this scene? Which words or phrases support your thinking?

[TEACHER NOTE: You may want to make sure that students recognize how Juliet is hatching a plot with her plan to visit Friar Lawrence's cell.]

### Part Three: Reflection

Let's close today's work with rounds:

- I realized . . .
- I wonder . . .

## Here's What Just Happened in Class

- Students collaborated and negotiated to understand and interpret the language of a scene (with very little input from you!).
- Students recognized how action is often embedded in the dialogue of a Shakespeare play.
- Students taught each other about the scene by sharing their promptbooks in a table-read style.
- Students supported their thinking with textual evidence during class discussion.
- Students made connections to other scenes, texts, and time periods by comparing how parent-child relationships and societal values are portrayed in this scene and 3.3.
- Students practiced an important step of the final performance: making a promptbook.

## RESOURCE #3.4A

## 3.5.109–145

*Note: Lady Capulet has entered Juliet's chambers just after Romeo, who snuck into Juliet's room overnight, left to begin his banishment in Mantua.*

LADY CAPULET

But now I'll tell thee joyful tidings, girl.

JULIET

And joy comes well in such a needy time.                                110
What are they, beseech your Ladyship?

LADY CAPULET

Well, well, thou hast a careful father, child,
One who, to put thee from thy heaviness,
Hath sorted out a sudden day of joy
That thou expects not, nor I looked not for.                             115

JULIET

Madam, in happy time! What day is that?

LADY CAPULET

Marry, my child, early next Thursday morn
The gallant, young, and noble gentleman,
The County Paris, at Saint Peter's Church
Shall happily make thee there a joyful bride.                            120

JULIET

Now, by Saint Peter's Church, and Peter too,
He shall not make me there a joyful bride!
I wonder at this haste, that I must wed
Ere he that should be husband comes to woo.
I pray you, tell my lord and father, madam,                              125
I will not marry yet, and when I do I swear
It shall be Romeo, whom you know I hate,
Rather than Paris. These are news indeed!

LADY CAPULET

Here comes your father. Tell him so yourself,
And see how he will take it at your hands.                               130

*Enter Capulet and Nurse.*
*[Juliet and Lady Capulet are already present.]*

CAPULET

    When the sun sets, the earth doth drizzle dew,
    But for the sunset of my brother's son
    It rains downright.
    How now, a conduit, girl? What, still in tears?
    Evermore show'ring? In one little body                135
    Thou counterfeits a bark, a sea, a wind.
    For still thy eyes, which I may call the sea,
    Do ebb and flow with tears; the bark thy body is,
    Sailing in this salt flood; the winds thy sighs,
    Who, raging with thy tears and they with them,        140
    Without a sudden calm, will overset
    Thy tempest-tossèd body.—How now, wife?
    Have you delivered to her our decree?

LADY CAPULET

    Ay, sir, but she will none, she gives you thanks.
    I would the fool were married to her grave.             145

**RESOURCE #3.4B**

## 3.5.146–207

*Note: Lady Capulet has told Lord Capulet that Juliet isn't interested in marrying Paris.*

CAPULET

    Soft, take me with you, take me with you, wife.
    How, will she none? Doth she not give us thanks?
    Is she not proud? Doth she not count her blessed,
    Unworthy as she is, that we have wrought
    So worthy a gentleman to be her bride?          150

JULIET

    Not proud you have, but thankful that you have.
    Proud can I never be of what I hate,
    But thankful even for hate that is meant love.

CAPULET

    How, how, how, how? Chopped logic? What is this?
    "Proud," and "I thank you," and "I thank you not,"       155
    And yet "not proud"? Mistress minion you,
    Thank me no thankings, nor proud me no prouds,
    But fettle your fine joints 'gainst Thursday next
    To go with Paris to Saint Peter's Church,
    Or I will drag thee on a hurdle thither.          160
    Out, you green-sickness carrion! Out, you baggage!
    You tallow face!

LADY CAPULET  Fie, fie, what, are you mad?

JULIET, *kneeling*

    Good father, I beseech you on my knees,
    Hear me with patience but to speak a word.       165

CAPULET

    Hang thee, young baggage, disobedient wretch!
    I tell thee what: get thee to church o' Thursday,
    Or never after look me in the face.
    Speak not; reply not; do not answer me.
    My fingers itch.—Wife, we scarce thought us     170
      blessed
    That God had lent us but this only child,
    But now I see this one is one too much,
    And that we have a curse in having her.
    Out on her, hilding.             175

NURSE  God in heaven bless her!
  You are to blame, my lord, to rate her so.

CAPULET
  And why, my Lady Wisdom? Hold your tongue.
  Good Prudence, smatter with your gossips, go.

NURSE
  I speak no treason.                                            180

CAPULET  O, God 'i' g' eden!

NURSE
  May not one speak?

CAPULET  Peace, you mumbling fool!
  Utter your gravity o'er a gossip's bowl,
  For here we need it not.                                       185

LADY CAPULET  You are too hot.

CAPULET  God's bread, it makes me mad.
  Day, night, hour, tide, time, work, play,
  Alone, in company, still my care hath been
  To have her matched. And having now provided                  190
  A gentleman of noble parentage,
  Of fair demesnes, youthful, and nobly ligned,
  Stuffed, as they say, with honorable parts,
  Proportioned as one's thought would wish a man—
  And then to have a wretched puling fool,                       195
  A whining mammet, in her fortune's tender,
  To answer "I'll not wed. I cannot love.
  I am too young. I pray you, pardon me."
  But, an you will not wed, I'll pardon you!
  Graze where you will, you shall not house with me.             200
  Look to 't; think on 't. I do not use to jest.
  Thursday is near. Lay hand on heart; advise.
  An you be mine, I'll give you to my friend.
  An you be not, hang, beg, starve, die in the streets,
  For, by my soul, I'll ne'er acknowledge thee,                  205
  Nor what is mine shall never do thee good.
  Trust to 't; bethink you. I'll not be forsworn.
                                      *He exits.*

**RESOURCE #3.4C**

## 3.5.208–255

JULIET

    Is there no pity sitting in the clouds
    That sees into the bottom of my grief?—
    O sweet my mother, cast me not away.            210
    Delay this marriage for a month, a week,
    Or, if you do not, make the bridal bed
    In that dim monument where Tybalt lies.

LADY CAPULET

    Talk not to me, for I'll not speak a word.
    Do as thou wilt, for I have done with thee.       215

                                *She exits.*

JULIET, *rising*

    O God! O nurse, how shall this be prevented?
    My husband is on Earth, my faith in heaven.
    How shall that faith return again to Earth
    Unless that husband send it me from heaven
    By leaving Earth? Comfort me; counsel me.—     220
    Alack, alack, that heaven should practice stratagems
    Upon so soft a subject as myself.—
    What sayst thou? Hast thou not a word of joy?
    Some comfort, nurse.

NURSE  Faith, here it is.                          225

    Romeo is banished, and all the world to nothing
    That he dares ne'er come back to challenge you,
    Or, if he do, it needs must be by stealth.
    Then, since the case so stands as now it doth,
    I think it best you married with the County.     230
    O, he's a lovely gentleman!
    Romeo's a dishclout to him. An eagle, madam,
    Hath not so green, so quick, so fair an eye
    As Paris hath. Beshrew my very heart,
    I think you are happy in this second match,     235
    For it excels your first, or, if it did not,
    Your first is dead, or 'twere as good he were
    As living here and you no use of him.

JULIET

   Speak'st thou from thy heart?

NURSE

   And from my soul too, else beshrew them both.          240

JULIET  Amen.

NURSE  What?

JULIET

   Well, thou hast comforted me marvelous much.
   Go in and tell my lady I am gone,
   Having displeased my father, to Lawrence' cell       245
   To make confession and to be absolved.

NURSE

   Marry, I will; and this is wisely done.    *She exits.*

JULIET

   Ancient damnation, O most wicked fiend!
   Is it more sin to wish me thus forsworn
   Or to dispraise my lord with that same tongue     250
   Which she hath praised him with above compare
   So many thousand times? Go, counselor.
   Thou and my bosom henceforth shall be twain.
   I'll to the Friar to know his remedy.
   If all else fail, myself have power to die.       255
                        *She exits.*

**WEEK THREE: LESSON 5**

# "Let them gaze...": Visualizing Acts 1, 2, and 3

## Here's What We're Doing and Why

Using images from the Folger collection expands students' own visual libraries and can help them see the characters in the play, envision the scenes, and determine tone, mood, power, and emotion by making connections between the language, the images, and their imaginations. Most often, working with images engages them far more than video versions do; images seem to spur analysis of many possible interpretations of scenes instead of showing them just one. In addition, your students can dip into the world's largest Shakespeare collection and get a sense of how these scenes have been interpreted through time.

In this lesson, students will use images of various moments in *Romeo and Juliet* from the Folger collection to review the characters and events of Acts 1, 2, and 3. They will observe how artists (both visual and theatrical) use faces and bodies to communicate relationships, actions, conflict, and character. Once students have discussed what they observe in the images, they will pair lines from Acts 1, 2, and 3 with those images, once again making connections between language and action, and practicing the creative thinking and decision-making they will need when crafting their final scenes for performance.

## What Will I Need?

- *Romeo and Juliet* text, in Folger paperback or free Folger Shakespeare online folger.edu/shakespeares-works

- Nine Folger collection images of *Romeo and Juliet* – **RESOURCE #3.5A** through **RESOURCE #3.5I**

## How Should I Prepare?

- Set up your classroom to give space for students to walk around as if in an art gallery.

- Print the images and attach them to larger paper the students can write on. Post the images in different parts of the classroom. You may want to have sticky notes available in case spacing on the poster becomes limited.

## Agenda (~ 45-minute class period)

- ❏ Gallery walk as individuals: 5 minutes

- ❏ Gallery walk in groups (if each group receives 2 minutes at each image): 18 minutes

- ❏ Labeling images with lines: 15 minutes

- ❏ Reflection: 5 minutes

## Here's What Students Hear (From You) and (Then What They'll) Do

### Part One: Gallery Walk and Observation

1. Wander the room and examine the images. Get close, back up, look at small parts, look at the bigger picture. Jot on the paper some initial thoughts. What do you see? What do you notice? What jumps out at you? Wander and look at all of the images and jot down first impressions on the paper around them. I'll give you enough time to quickly examine each image.

2. Next, in groups of 3–4, gather around each image and compare the characters in that image. First look as an individual and then discuss with your group. Here are some suggestions of things to look for:
   - Look at where the characters are standing or sitting in the image, what their arms and legs are doing, where they are leaning, what they are wearing and what color that clothing is, and what their facial expressions imply.
   - Examine how love or hate or family (or whatever motif you want to discuss) is portrayed in the image. Is it through physical touch? Eye glances? Body language?
   - Really LOOK at the image and decide how the actors are "speaking" with no words on the page.

   After analyzing, have one person in the group write your thoughts and observations on the paper around the image. Visit each image and comment on the papers.

3. Now, look at these images for a third time and determine who in the image holds the power.
   - Who is the dominant figure? How can you tell? Write the name of the character on the paper.
   - Let's discuss your decisions and how they are supported by details from the image.

### Part Two: Pairing Lines with Images

1. Now find two lines in the text—from Act 1 through Act 3—that seem to go with each image and write those lines on the posters.

[**TEACHER NOTE:** You could divide this part into group assignments and allow each group to work on one image. Students can try to figure out the exact lines or they can find any lines that connect to the scene in the image. Students will start to discover the images can be universal to the play.]

### Part Three: Reflection

Debrief by asking everyone to finish the sentence:
- "I noticed . . ."

[**TEACHER NOTE:** Students will likely tie this to predictions for how they see some of the lines foreshadowing the tragic end and pick up on the violence that continues throughout the rest of the play.]

## Here's What Just Happened in Class

- Students owned the process of discovering the meaning behind the images.

- Students' comprehension of the images increased over time.

- Students realized that they could interpret images without teacher explanation.

- Language-forward lines from the rest of the play allowed students to express excitement and make predictions for the conclusion of the play.

## RESOURCE #3.5A

Watercolor and pencil drawing by John Massey Wright,
*Drawings for or after engravings designed by J.M. Wright*
(late 18th century or 19th century).
Used by permission of the Folger Shakespeare Library.

## RESOURCE #3.5B

Photograph of 2013 Folger Theatre production of *Romeo and Juliet*. Jeff Malet, photographer. Used by permission of the Folger Shakespeare Library.

## RESOURCE #3.5C

Pen-and-ink drawing by Louis Rhead, *Tybalt's duel* (before 1918).
Used by permission of the Folger Shakespeare Library.

## RESOURCE #3.5D

Photograph of 1997 Folger Theatre production of *Romeo and Juliet*. Ken Cobb, photographer. Used by permission of the Folger Shakespeare Library.

## RESOURCE #3.5E

Ink drawing by Alfred Edward Chalon, *Romeo and Juliet* (late 18th century or 19th century). Used by permission of the Folger Shakespeare Library.

**RESOURCE #3.5F**

Watercolor drawing by John Hayter, *Romeo and Juliet*, Juliet [Miss F. Kemble] & Friar
Laurence (19th century). Used by permission of the Folger Shakespeare Library.

**RESOURCE #3.5G**

Watercolor drawing by W.T. Dennis, *Romeo and Juliet*: Friar Lawrence's cell
(19th century). Used by permission of the Folger Shakespeare Library.

## RESOURCE #3.5H

Oil painting by James Northcote, *Romeo and Juliet, Monument belonging to the Capulets: Romeo and Paris dead, Juliet and Friar Laurence* (1790). This painting hangs in the Reading Room of the Folger Shakespeare Library and is the largest item in the Folger collection. Used by permission of the Folger Shakespeare Library.

## RESOURCE #3.51

Photograph of 2018 Oregon Shakespeare Festival production
of *Romeo and Juliet*. Jenny Graham, photographer.
Used by permission of the Oregon Shakespeare Festival.

# Intermission and Review:
# 10-Minute Plays from Single Points of View!

## Here's What We're Doing and Why

We know that a 20-minute play is an essential way of introducing the whole play to students. In this lesson, your students will create 10-minute plays that look at the action in Acts 1 through 3 through the lenses of individual characters. Students will end up owning juicy lines from *Romeo and Juliet*—and be an expert on their characters. They will also get a review of that character's journey and just enough of the plot, characters, and conflict to leave them wanting more, propelling them toward the end of the play.

## What Will I Need?

- A copy of *Romeo and Juliet*, Folger Edition, or free Folger Shakespeare online folger.edu/shakespeares-works

- Pencils, markers, paper, chart paper

- A list of the play's important characters, most likely:
    - Romeo
    - Juliet
    - Tybalt
    - Mercutio
    - Benvolio
    - Nurse
    - Friar Lawrence
    - Paris
    - Lord Capulet, Lady Capulet? (You'll be dividing your class up in groups of 3–4 or in pairs to work on 10-minute plays for each important character, so do a little math and figure out the number of characters you need in advance.)

## How Should I Prepare?

- Set up your classroom conducive to working in groups or pairs.

- Be ready to share your list of important characters.

- Be ready to organize students in groups of 3–4 or in pairs (see above), and to connect who will be working with which character.

## Agenda (~ 45-minute class period)

- ❏ Explain the assignment, and give them time to search for/find their 10 Shakespeare lines: 15 minutes

❑ Students add 10 lines of analysis and rehearse their plays: 15 minutes

❑ Students perform their character plays and informally discuss: 15 minutes

## Here's What Students Hear (From You) and (Then What They'll) Do

1. At this point, we're going to take a creative intermission in which we'll review important characters by creating a 10-minute version of *Romeo and Juliet* through the lens of each of those characters.

[**TEACHER NOTE:** Divide students into groups of 3–4 or in pairs. Assign each group a character or have them choose from the list. Each group should have a different character.]

2. You'll be considering the events of the play through the lens of your character. This is because each character experiences the play from a different perspective. With your partner(s), search through Acts 1, 2, and 3 for lines that encompass your character's journey thus far. Decide on the 10 most important lines that depict your character's journey in the play and write them on paper—large pieces of paper to post around the room, or small-scale in your group. Keep the lines in the order of the play so that we can follow the main plot points and character development that are true to the play as Shakespeare wrote it.

3. After you've decided on and noted your character's 10 lines, add your own original line of analysis or explanation after each line to augment your study of this character. When you finish this, you will have 20 lines total—10 lines that Shakespeare wrote and 10 original lines that you have written. You have created an original, very short play that presents *Romeo and Juliet* through the lens of a single key character.

4. Take 10 minutes to rehearse the play you have created. You can alternate reading the parts if you're a pair, or if you are in a larger group, you can split the lines evenly to be read. You'll figure it out! Be sure to add physical movements to go along with the lines!

5. Performance Festival: We'll perform all of your character plays and discuss as we go!

## Here's What Just Happened in Class

- Students combined their words with Shakespeare's to review the action of Acts 1 through 3 (with very little input from you!).

- Students collaborated to analyze characters and understand the feelings and motivations that might guide their choices in Act 4.

- Students practiced a valuable skill for their final performance: compression. Selecting 10 significant lines is another means of "cutting a scene," something everyone will need to do when preparing for their final performance.

- All students spoke Shakespeare's words.

- When physicalizing some of their 10 lines, students considered how language guides action.

WEEK FOUR: LESSON 2

# Juliet, Friar Lawrence, and Paris: Multiple Perspectives in 4.1

## Here's What We're Doing and Why

In this lesson, students will use the tools they have been practicing and perfecting throughout this unit to dig into the overlapping and kind of amazing conversations that take place between Juliet, Paris, and Friar Lawrence in 4.1.

At this point, students know the characters well, and in our previous lesson, they had a recent catch-up. Today, they will inhabit these characters—their roles will switch around during class. They'll discuss what each character wants, and how that may shift as the scene progresses.

Since this is the scene in which Juliet tells Friar Lawrence that she would consider dying by suicide, we feel that this can be the point to call out the suicide in the play . . . even though your students know how the play ends. Teen mental health experts recommend that we not gloss over this issue, but rather use it to spark a conversation among your students about what resources are available to them today.

## What Will I Need?

- Copies of 4.1 – **RESOURCE #4.2** – for each student

- Resources available to your students (or their friends) who are contemplating injuring themselves or suicide.

## How Should I Prepare?

- Set up your classroom so that there is room for three groups to gather in different parts of the room. Label group areas as Juliet, Paris, and Friar Lawrence.

- Ask students to have a pen, pencil, or highlighter ready to mark up their texts.

## Agenda (~ 45-minute class period)

- ❏ Collaborative reading and analysis of Section One (4.1.1–44): 10 minutes

- ❏ Collaborative reading and analysis of Section Two (4.1.45–128): 25 minutes

- ❏ Reflection: 10 minutes

## Here's What Students Hear (From You) and (Then What They'll) Do

### Part One:

1. Let's really dig into these two overlapping conversations so that we can get clear on everything that is happening within and between the Friar, Paris, and Juliet.

Let's get into three groups in three different parts of the room. One group will be Paris, one will be Juliet, and one Friar Lawrence.

2. Huddle up with your group and focus on Section One— the conversation between Juliet, Paris, and Friar Lawrence, 4.1.1–44, **RESOURCE #4.2**. Read only your character's lines—chorally, as we've been doing for weeks—and then do some thinking and talking in your group about what's going on just in this conversation. Read your character's lines again and add tone, gesture, all that seems right. Discuss in your groups:

   – what the language tells you about what your character wants

   – what the language tells you about what your character is feeling

   Note that wants and feelings are complicated, right? No easy answers to these questions. It's all about your character at this point.

3. Then all groups will read the whole conversation chorally, across the room. Afterward, share your thoughts about wants and feelings across all the characters.

**Part Two:**

1. Let's move to a similar kind of analysis in lines 45–128 (labeled Section Two). As we do, I'll mention that, in this scene, Juliet tells Friar Lawrence that she is thinking about suicide. You know how the play ends, but it's important to note these difficult parts of the play. This is a sensitive topic because these feelings and actions are difficult and painful parts of Juliet's life—and later Romeo's—but they also can be difficult and painful parts of our lives today.

   As you'll read, Juliet asked for help from Friar Lawrence. We all need help when we feel desperate. What do you do, or what would you recommend, when a friend feels desperate? What help could you arrange for them to receive? Advice for them? (Text 988 to reach 988 Suicide and Crisis Lifeline.)

**[TEACHER NOTE:** Give time for this conversation, and distribute a resource sheet if you have one.]

2. Let's investigate what the scene tells us, as we did with Section One. If you read Paris in the last section, rotate to Juliet, Juliet to Friar Lawrence, and Friar Lawrence to Paris for this section. Character groups, read just your character's lines aloud, and ask each other questions:

   – What does the language tell you about what **your character wants**?

   – What does the language tell you about what **your character is feeling**?

   – What are three words that **your group would use to describe your character?**

3. Let's read/perform this whole scene chorally now. We're going to listen for those wants and feelings and descriptors in the choral reading.

**Part Three: Reflection**

Around the room, pick one statement and complete it quickly:

- At this point, Friar Lawrence's advice to Juliet SEEMS HELPFUL to her because . . .

    OR

- At this point, Friar Lawrence's advice to Juliet SEEMS NOT HELPFUL to her because . . .

## Here's What Just Happened in Class

- Students interrogated deeply two small and pivotal scenes in *Romeo and Juliet*.

- Students considered both language and character, and brought forward their previous knowledge of Juliet, Paris, and the Friar to their analyses.

- Their careful analyses will provide them with a solid foundation as they go forward to the end of the play.

- Their analyses enabled them to make connections among Juliet's seemingly hopeless and desperate situation, circumstances in our own lives that can cause us to feel that way today, and sources of help and support.

## RESOURCE #4.2

## Section One. 4.1.1–44, edited

FRIAR LAWRENCE
> On Thursday, sir? The time is very short.

PARIS
> My father Capulet will have it so,
> And I am nothing slow to slack his haste.

FRIAR LAWRENCE
> You say you do not know the lady's mind?
> Uneven is the course. I like it not.

PARIS
> Immoderately she weeps for Tybalt's death,
> And therefore have I little talk of love.
> Now, sir, her father . . .
> . . . in his wisdom hastes our marriage
> To stop the inundation of her tears.
> Now do you know the reason of this haste.

FRIAR LAWRENCE, *aside*
> I would I knew not why it should be slowed.—
> Look, sir, here comes the lady toward my cell.
> > *Enter Juliet.*

PARIS
> Happily met, my lady and my wife.

JULIET
> That may be, sir, when I may be a wife.

PARIS
> That "may be" must be, love, on Thursday next.

JULIET
> What must be shall be.

FRIAR LAWRENCE  That's a certain text.

PARIS
> Come you to make confession to this father?

JULIET

To answer that, I should confess to you.

PARIS

Do not deny to him that you love me.

JULIET

I will confess to you that I love him.

PARIS

So will you, I am sure, that you love me.

JULIET

If I do so, it will be of more price
Being spoke behind your back than to your face.

PARIS

Poor soul, thy face is much abused with tears.

JULIET

The tears have got small victory by that,
For it was bad enough before their spite.

PARIS

Thou wrong'st it more than tears with that report.

JULIET

That is no slander, sir, which is a truth,
And what I spake, I spake it to my face.

PARIS

Thy face is mine, and thou hast slandered it.

JULIET

It may be so, for it is not mine own.—
Are you at leisure, holy father, now,
Or shall I come to you at evening Mass?

FRIAR LAWRENCE

My leisure serves me, pensive daughter, now.—
My lord, we must entreat the time alone.

PARIS

God shield I should disturb devotion!—
Juliet, on Thursday early will I rouse you.
Till then, adieu, and keep this holy kiss.          *He exits.*

## Section Two. 4.1.45–128, edited

JULIET

    O, shut the door, and when thou hast done so,
    Come weep with me, past hope, past care, past help.

FRIAR LAWRENCE

    O Juliet, I already know thy grief.
    It strains me past the compass of my wits.
    I hear thou must . . .
    On Thursday next be married to this County.

JULIET

    Tell me not, friar, that thou hearest of this,
    Unless thou tell me how I may prevent it.
    God joined my heart and Romeo's, thou our hands;
    Therefore out of thy long-experienced time
    Give me some present counsel, or, behold,
    'Twixt my extremes and me this bloody knife
    Shall play the umpire. I long to die
    If what thou speak'st speak not of remedy.

FRIAR LAWRENCE

    Hold, daughter, I do spy a kind of hope,
    If, rather than to marry County Paris,
    Thou hast the strength of will to slay thyself,
    Then is it likely thou wilt undertake
    A thing like death to chide away this shame.
    And if thou darest, I'll give thee remedy.

JULIET

    O, bid me leap, rather than marry Paris,
    From off the battlements of any tower,
    Or walk in thievish ways, or bid me lurk
    Where serpents are.
    And I will do it without fear or doubt,
    To live an unstained wife to my sweet love.

FRIAR LAWRENCE

    Hold, then. Go home; be merry; give consent
    To marry Paris. Wednesday is tomorrow.
    Tomorrow night look that thou lie alone;
    Let not the Nurse lie with thee in thy chamber.
                                    *Holding out a vial.*
    Take thou this vial, being then in bed,
    And this distilling liquor drink thou off;
    When presently through all thy veins shall run

A cold and drowsy humor; for no pulse
Shall keep his native progress, but surcease.
No warmth, no breath shall testify thou livest.
And in this borrowed likeness of shrunk death
Thou shalt continue two and forty hours
And then awake as from a pleasant sleep.
Now, when the bridegroom in the morning comes
To rouse thee from thy bed, there art thou dead.
Thou shalt be borne to that same ancient vault
Where all the kindred of the Capulets lie.
In the meantime,
Shall Romeo by my letters know our drift,
And hither shall he come, and he and I
Will watch thy waking, and that very night
Shall Romeo bear thee hence to Mantua.
If no womanish fear
Abate thy valor in the acting it.

JULIET
Give me, give me! O, tell not me of fear!

FRIAR LAWRENCE, *giving Juliet the vial*
Be strong and prosperous
In this resolve. I'll send a friar with speed
To Mantua with my letters to thy lord.

JULIET
Love give me strength, and strength shall help
afford.
Farewell, dear father.

*They exit in different directions.*

# "I Drink to Thee": Breaking Up Juliet's Soliloquy in 4.3

## Here's What We're Doing and Why

Soliloquies are conversations that characters have with themselves. They present the characters' innermost thoughts and provide an opportunity for audiences and readers to see inside them. Most often, soliloquies show us characters' thinking as they are trying to work something out for themselves. Getting students inside a soliloquy can lead to all kinds of deep reading and surprising discoveries about the words, the characters, and the big questions that plays ask. *Romeo and Juliet* is somewhat short on soliloquies, but Juliet's in 4.3 is an excellent one to dive into.

Breaking the soliloquy into parts helps "break" apart the confusion and complexity of the text, providing students with another chance to read Shakespeare with little teacher intervention and to understand the message the character is delivering all on their own.

This lesson combines several of the essential practices of the Folger Method. It includes Two-Line Scenes, Cutting a Scene, and Choral Reading. At this point in the unit, these exercises will be familiar to students, and the students will be ready to layer them and build their skills.

By the end of this exercise, ALL students will have spoken and read Shakespeare's original language multiple times, discovered that soliloquies are internal arguments, discussed various interpretations of this soliloquy, and, in a lively and authentic way, explored all those cool things going on with this complex text: tone, structure, characterization, and big ideas.

## What Will I Need?

- One copy for each student of *Romeo and Juliet*, 4.3.15–60 – **RESOURCE #4.3**

- Pen, pencil, highlighter

- Blank note cards or half-sheets of paper

## How Should I Prepare?

- Set up your classroom so that students can stand in two lines, facing each other, then rearrange the room for partner work.

- On the board or on chart paper, write a list to reveal as Part Two begins:
    - a line of fear
    - a line of doubt
    - a line of acquiescence
    - a line of independence
    - a line of concern

      – a line of confidence

      – a line of confusion

      – a line of power

      – a line when Juliet expresses her own identity

      – a line of _____ (your own observation of a different emotion)

- Give each student a copy of Juliet's soliloquy, 4.3.15–60 – **RESOURCE #4.3**

- Give each student a blank note card.

## Agenda (~ 45-minute class period)

❑ Directions: 5 minutes

❑ Choral Reading (3 times): 10 minutes

❑ Analysis with a partner: 20 minutes

❑ Performances: 10 minutes

## Here's What Students Hear (From You) and (Then What They'll) Do

### Part One: Reading and Rereading

1. This scene—4.3.15–60—is Juliet before she drinks the potion, part of Friar Lawrence's plan. While this scene is all of Juliet's thoughts, you're going to read it in a way that might make you think about it a little differently. As always, let the language work, and see what you can glean from the process of reading and rereading in the way we'll do it today.

2. Stand in two straight lines facing each other. One line is Juliet #1 and the other, Juliet #2. I'll distribute **RESOURCE #4.3**, and you will see that the speech is separated into parts. Juliet #1 or Juliet #2, you will read your lines chorally.

3. We will read it twice. Let's start with just our basic warm-up round, reading it loudly at a moderate pace.

After choral reading: What is going on in this speech? What do you notice? Look at the punctuation—what do you notice about that?

4. Let's read again, this time paying close attention to accentuating the questions and pausing at dashes.

Post–second reading: Do you have any new observations? What did you notice as we read the scene a second time? What do the question marks imply? What are Juliet's questions specifically about? What is she thinking when she asks these questions? What are ways you read a question so that the audience knows it's a question? What do the dashes imply? Where do you notice they are placed? What do you think is happening in Juliet's mind when there is a dash in the text?

**Part Two: Analysis with a Partner**

1. Find a partner and sit together with your script, note card, pen/pencil, and highlighter. We are going to highlight and label some parts of the scene.

2. Juliet is having a lot of big feelings in the soliloquy. With your partner, read through the scene again, being mindful of her emotions and her worries. Highlight and label any or all of these feelings you can find. This list might help you:
   - a line of fear
   - a line of doubt
   - a line of acquiescence
   - a line of independence
   - a line of concern
   - a line of confidence
   - a line of confusion
   - a line of power
   - a line when Juliet expresses her own identity
   - a line of _____ (your own observation of an emotion)

   When you finish highlighting, discuss with your partner what these big, mixed feelings imply.

3. With your partner, choose two different, possibly conflicting, emotions you observed in the soliloquy. Read through the soliloquy and highlight six words that display one of the emotions and six words that display the other emotion. The words you pull from the soliloquy can be six individual words, a mix of phrases that totals six words, or a line that you cut to six words. Just make sure the six words convey that emotion. Put the words in an order that makes sense to you—they could be chronological in Juliet's soliloquy, in order of intensity, or simply in the order you think they sound best. Then add either a dash, a question mark, or another punctuation mark that adds meaning to your scene. Try to create a rhythm with your words.

4. Write the six words of one emotion on one note card and the other emotion's six words on the other note card. On the backs of the note cards, write the emotion you're conveying. Practice speaking the six words to each other. Create a scene demonstrating the contrast between the two emotions. Use intonation and movement to help convey your tone. Make sure you stress the punctuation you included.

5. We are now going to perform these six-word lines you cut from the soliloquy as two-line scenes. We'll move around the room and when we get to you and your partner, each of you stand up and perform your six words. After your performance we will try to guess what the intended emotion was, and you can turn over the note card and show us if we're right.

**6.** OK, let's talk about what we learned:

  – Did you notice any patterns or trends in the words that your classmates used? What were they?

  – If you had to give Juliet #1 and Juliet #2 a name (or assign one emotion to each Juliet), what would you label them? Why?

  – What seems to be Juliet's predominant emotion in this soliloquy? How do you know?

  – How do you think Juliet's interactions with the adults in her life—the Nurse, Lord Capulet, Lady Capulet, and Friar Lawrence—have influenced her feelings in this scene?

## Here's What Just Happened in Class

- Students owned the process of uncovering Juliet's language.

- Students' comprehension of Juliet's speech increased with repeated readings.

- Every student made decisions about meaning through the manipulation of Shakespeare's words.

- Students broke apart a soliloquy with little to no teacher explanation and created new meaning from cutting and rearranging the words.

- Students reflected on the effect of words and punctuation on tone.

- Students made connections between conflict and action when reflecting on how Juliet's relationships with adults in the play may have influenced her feelings in the soliloquy.

## RESOURCE #4.3

## 4.3.15–60

JULIET #1: Farewell.

JULIET #2: God knows when we shall meet again.                    15

JULIET #1: I have a faint cold fear thrills through my veins
    That almost freezes up the heat of life.

JULIET #2: I'll call them back again to comfort me.—

JULIET #1: Nurse!

JULIET #2: —What should she do here?

JULIET #1: My dismal scene I needs must act alone.              20

JULIET #2: Come, vial.                    *She takes out the vial.*

JULIET #1: What if this mixture do not work at all?

JULIET #2: Shall I be married then tomorrow morning?
                    *She takes out her knife*
                    *and puts it down beside her.*

JULIET #1: No, no, this shall forbid it.

JULIET #2: Lie thou there.

JULIET #1: What if it be a poison which the Friar              25
    Subtly hath ministered to have me dead,
    Lest in this marriage he should be dishonored
    Because he married me before to Romeo?

JULIET #2: I fear it is.

JULIET #1: And yet methinks it should not,
    For he hath still been tried a holy man.              30

JULIET #2: How if, when I am laid into the tomb,
    I wake before the time that Romeo
    Come to redeem me?

JULIET #1: There's a fearful point.
  Shall I not then be stifled in the vault,
  To whose foul mouth no healthsome air breathes in,                    35
  And there die strangled ere my Romeo comes?

JULIET #2: Or, if I live, is it not very like
  The horrible conceit of death and night,
  Together with the terror of the place—
  As in a vault, an ancient receptacle                                   40
  Where for this many hundred years the bones
  Of all my buried ancestors are packed;

JULIET #1: Where bloody Tybalt, yet but green in earth,
  Lies fest'ring in his shroud; where, as they say,
  At some hours in the night spirits resort—                             45

JULIET #2: Alack, alack, is it not like that I,
  So early waking, what with loathsome smells,
  And shrieks like mandrakes torn out of the earth,
  That living mortals, hearing them, run mad—

JULIET #1: O, if I wake, shall I not be distraught,                      50
  Environèd with all these hideous fears,
  And madly play with my forefathers' joints,
  And pluck the mangled Tybalt from his shroud,
  And, in this rage, with some great kinsman's bone,
  As with a club, dash out my desp'rate brains?                          55

JULIET #2: O look, methinks I see my cousin's ghost
  Seeking out Romeo that did spit his body
  Upon a rapier's point!

JULIET #1: Stay, Tybalt, stay!

JULIET #2: Romeo, Romeo, Romeo!

JULIET #1: Here's drink.

JULIET #2: I drink to thee.                                              60

  *She drinks and falls upon her bed within the curtains.*

# "Then I'll be brief": Creating a 5-Minute Act 5 in *Romeo and Juliet*

## Here's What We're Doing and Why

Act 5 moves quickly—a lot happens in a very short time. And this lesson will go at a similar pace! Students work with Act 5 chunked into 15 short sections as they head toward the resolution of the play. Close reading in many forms will be evident as they satisfy their desire to see how it all plays out when we get to that last line!

The lesson encourages high energy and movement, collaborative close reading, and ownership. It provides another opportunity for students to interpret the language and make meaning of it by themselves. This lesson is full of opportunities to practice the skills students will need for their final assessment: cutting the scene, using language to guide action, and making a promptbook. In tomorrow's lesson, we will connect what we've learned about Act 5 in today's lesson to life in the 20th and 21st centuries.

## What Will I Need?

- A copy of a section of Act 5 of *Romeo and Juliet* for each student—15 sections in all **RESOURCE #4.4A–#4.4O**

- Pen/pencil, markers

## How Should I Prepare?

- Determine how many students will work on each chunk of text. Pairs? Groups of three? Depending on how many students you have, some groups may work with more than one chunk.
    - 5.1.1–30 (2 roles; Romeo and Balthasar)
    - 5.1.31–60 (2 roles; Romeo and Balthasar)
    - 5.1.61–91 (2 roles; Apothecary and Romeo)
    - 5.2.1–30 (2 roles; Friar Lawrence and Friar John)
    - 5.3.1–21 (2 roles; Paris and Page)
    - 5.3.22–48 (2 roles; Romeo and Balthasar)
    - 5.3.49–73 (3 roles; Romeo, Paris, Page)
    - 5.3.74–120 (1 role; Romeo)
    - 5.3.121–152 (2 roles; Friar Lawrence and Balthasar)
    - 5.3.153–172 (2 roles; Friar Lawrence and Juliet)
    - 5.3.173–194 (5 roles; First Watch, Juliet, Page, Second Watch, Third Watch)
    - 5.3.195–215 (4 roles; Prince, Capulet, Lady Capulet; First Watch)
    - 5.3.216–237 (3 roles; Prince, Montague, Friar Lawrence)

- 5.3.238–280 (2 roles; Friar Lawrence, Prince)
- 5.3.281–321 (5 roles; Balthasar, Prince, Page, Capulet, Montague)

- Make the right amount of copies of **RESOURCE #4.4A** through **RESOURCE #4.4O** so that each student has a copy of the scene/chunk they will be working on.

- Set up your classroom conducive to students working in groups, then move the desks so students have space to perform in a large circle.

## Agenda (~ 45-minute class period)

❏ Group work/cutting/rehearsing: 30 minutes

❏ Performance (twice): 10 minutes

❏ One-word round: 5 minutes

## Here's What Students Hear (From You) and (Then What They'll) Do

1. Exciting day today—we're going to act out all of Act 5, and see how Shakespeare closes out this play! We have it divided into short scenes or chunks. You'll cut it, create quick scenes, and run a performance relay.

2. Here are the groups you'll work in.

[**TEACHER NOTE:** Each group will be assigned a chunk or two, depending upon number of students.]

3. In your groups:

   - Read your chunk with your partner(s), and discuss what is happening in the scene.

   - Cut your scene or scenes to ten lines, keeping the main idea intact. You may want to first use a pencil to cross out lines; then, once you are confident you want to cut the line, use a pen or marker to cross it out. As you cut, consider the process or reasoning you're using to eliminate or include a line. Jot down your elimination (or inclusion) strategy as you cut.

   - Assign reading parts. Read through your ten lines and time yourselves.

   - Practice reading the scene several times, and while still speaking clearly, determine how quickly you can perform your section of the act.

   - Be sure to include gestures and movement—help us understand the scene with your movement choices.

   - Add tone and/or volume shifts to the words that are most important.

4. Once every group has finished cutting and rehearsing (in about 30 minutes), you will perform Act 5!

   Move into a circle so that you are in the order of your scenes (5.1.1–30 starts, then moving clockwise, line up in order of scenes). The first group will perform; then, as soon as they finish, start your performance and keep moving! We want high energy and enthusiasm!

[**TEACHER NOTE:** The first run may be messy! Take the time for a second run if you can.]

5. After your performances, huddle with your group and collaboratively choose the ONE word that most stands out in your chunk of text, or that you all believe is the most important word in your chunk. You can only choose one word. Practice saying that one word in a tone that reflects what it means in context.

6. Let's go around the circle and say the one word—say it chorally with your group/partner.

7. Let's review! What happened in Act 5? What's the outcome of the play? What do your one-word choices tell you about the act or the resolution of the play? What do you think about the end of the play?

## Here's What Just Happened in Class

- Students put a full act of Shakespeare on its feet in less than 30 minutes with very little direction from you—whew!

- Students collaborated to understand and interpret Shakespeare's language.

- Students close read a complex text while negotiating which lines to keep and cut.

- Students made decisions about movement based on the language of the text.

- Students analyzed language, plot, theme, and character development when deciding which single word from their scene to emphasize.

- Students "rehearsed" the work of their final assessment—a scene performance—by assembling this lightning-fast Act 5 relay of mini-scenes.

**RESOURCE #4.4A**

## ACT 5, Scene 1

*Enter Romeo.*

ROMEO

If I may trust the flattering truth of sleep,
My dreams presage some joyful news at hand.
My bosom's lord sits lightly in his throne,
And all this day an unaccustomed spirit
Lifts me above the ground with cheerful thoughts.        5
I dreamt my lady came and found me dead
(Strange dream that gives a dead man leave to
    think!)
And breathed such life with kisses in my lips
That I revived and was an emperor.                       10
Ah me, how sweet is love itself possessed
When but love's shadows are so rich in joy!

                    *Enter Romeo's man Balthasar, in riding boots.*

News from Verona!—How now, Balthasar?
Dost thou not bring me letters from the Friar?
How doth my lady? Is my father well?                     15
How doth my Juliet? That I ask again,
For nothing can be ill if she be well.

BALTHASAR

Then she is well and nothing can be ill.
Her body sleeps in Capels' monument,
And her immortal part with angels lives.                 20
I saw her laid low in her kindred's vault
And presently took post to tell it you.
O, pardon me for bringing these ill news,
Since you did leave it for my office, sir.

ROMEO

Is it e'en so?—Then I deny you, stars!—                  25
Thou knowest my lodging. Get me ink and paper,
And hire post-horses. I will hence tonight.

BALTHASAR

I do beseech you, sir, have patience.
Your looks are pale and wild and do import
Some misadventure.                                       30

## RESOURCE #4.4B

ROMEO  Tush, thou art deceived.
    Leave me, and do the thing I bid thee do.
    Hast thou no letters to me from the Friar?

BALTHASAR
    No, my good lord.

ROMEO  No matter. Get thee gone,                    35
    And hire those horses. I'll be with thee straight.
                       *Balthasar exits.*
    Well, Juliet, I will lie with thee tonight.
    Let's see for means. O mischief, thou art swift
    To enter in the thoughts of desperate men.
    I do remember an apothecary                     40
    (And hereabouts he dwells) which late I noted
    In tattered weeds, with overwhelming brows,
    Culling of simples. Meager were his looks.
    Sharp misery had worn him to the bones.
    And in his needy shop a tortoise hung,             45
    An alligator stuffed, and other skins
    Of ill-shaped fishes; and about his shelves,
    A beggarly account of empty boxes,
    Green earthen pots, bladders, and musty seeds,
    Remnants of packthread, and old cakes of roses      50
    Were thinly scattered to make up a show.
    Noting this penury, to myself I said
    "An if a man did need a poison now,
    Whose sale is present death in Mantua,
    Here lives a caitiff wretch would sell it him."       55
    O, this same thought did but forerun my need,
    And this same needy man must sell it me.
    As I remember, this should be the house.
    Being holiday, the beggar's shop is shut.—
    What ho, Apothecary!                     60

## RESOURCE #4.4C

*Enter Apothecary.*

APOTHECARY  Who calls so loud?

ROMEO
 Come hither, man. I see that thou art poor.
                          *He offers money.*
 Hold, there is forty ducats. Let me have
 A dram of poison, such soon-speeding gear
 As will disperse itself through all the veins,                    65
 That the life-weary taker may fall dead,
 And that the trunk may be discharged of breath
 As violently as hasty powder fired
 Doth hurry from the fatal cannon's womb.

APOTHECARY
 Such mortal drugs I have, but Mantua's law                        70
 Is death to any he that utters them.

ROMEO
 Art thou so bare and full of wretchedness,
 And fearest to die? Famine is in thy cheeks,
 Need and oppression starveth in thy eyes,
 Contempt and beggary hangs upon thy back.                         75
 The world is not thy friend, nor the world's law.
 The world affords no law to make thee rich.
 Then be not poor, but break it, and take this.

APOTHECARY
 My poverty, but not my will, consents.

ROMEO
 I pay thy poverty and not thy will.                               80

APOTHECARY, *giving him the poison*
 Put this in any liquid thing you will
 And drink it off, and if you had the strength
 Of twenty men, it would dispatch you straight.

ROMEO, *handing him the money*

There is thy gold, worse poison to men's souls,
Doing more murder in this loathsome world                    85
Than these poor compounds that thou mayst not
   sell.
I sell thee poison; thou hast sold me none.
Farewell, buy food, and get thyself in flesh.

*Apothecary exits.*

Come, cordial and not poison, go with me                     90
To Juliet's grave, for there must I use thee.

*He exits.*

**RESOURCE #4.4D**

# Scene 2

*Enter Friar John.*

FRIAR JOHN
Holy Franciscan friar, brother, ho!
*Enter Friar Lawrence.*

FRIAR LAWRENCE
This same should be the voice of Friar John.—
Welcome from Mantua. What says Romeo?
Or, if his mind be writ, give me his letter.

FRIAR JOHN
  Going to find a barefoot brother out,                       5
  One of our order, to associate me,
  Here in this city visiting the sick,
  And finding him, the searchers of the town,
  Suspecting that we both were in a house
  Where the infectious pestilence did reign,             10
  Sealed up the doors and would not let us forth,
  So that my speed to Mantua there was stayed.

FRIAR LAWRENCE
  Who bare my letter, then, to Romeo?

FRIAR JOHN
  I could not send it—here it is again—
*Returning the letter.*
  Nor get a messenger to bring it thee,               15
  So fearful were they of infection.

FRIAR LAWRENCE
  Unhappy fortune! By my brotherhood,
  The letter was not nice but full of charge,
  Of dear import, and the neglecting it
  May do much danger. Friar John, go hence.        20
  Get me an iron crow and bring it straight
  Unto my cell.

FRIAR JOHN
  Brother, I'll go and bring it thee.       *He exits.*

FRIAR LAWRENCE

    Now must I to the monument alone.

    Within this three hours will fair Juliet wake.           25

    She will beshrew me much that Romeo

    Hath had no notice of these accidents.

    But I will write again to Mantua,

    And keep her at my cell till Romeo come.

    Poor living corse, closed in a dead man's tomb!       30

                          *He exits.*

RESOURCE #4.4E

# Scene 3

*Enter Paris and his Page.*

PARIS

    Give me thy torch, boy. Hence and stand aloof.
    Yet put it out, for I would not be seen.
    Under yond yew trees lay thee all along,
    Holding thy ear close to the hollow ground.
    So shall no foot upon the churchyard tread           5
    (Being loose, unfirm, with digging up of graves)
    But thou shalt hear it. Whistle then to me
    As signal that thou hearest something approach.
    Give me those flowers. Do as I bid thee. Go.

PAGE, *aside*

    I am almost afraid to stand alone           10
    Here in the churchyard. Yet I will adventure.
                        *He moves away from Paris.*

PARIS, *scattering flowers*

    Sweet flower, with flowers thy bridal bed I strew
    (O woe, thy canopy is dust and stones!)
    Which with sweet water nightly I will dew,
    Or, wanting that, with tears distilled by moans.           15
    The obsequies that I for thee will keep
    Nightly shall be to strew thy grave and weep.
                        *Page whistles.*
    The boy gives warning something doth approach.
    What cursèd foot wanders this way tonight,
    To cross my obsequies and true love's rite?           20
    What, with a torch? Muffle me, night, awhile.
                        *He steps aside.*

## RESOURCE #4.4F

*Enter Romeo and Balthasar.*

ROMEO

    Give me that mattock and the wrenching iron.
    Hold, take this letter. Early in the morning
    See thou deliver it to my lord and father.
    Give me the light. Upon thy life I charge thee,           25
    Whate'er thou hearest or seest, stand all aloof
    And do not interrupt me in my course.
    Why I descend into this bed of death
    Is partly to behold my lady's face,
    But chiefly to take thence from her dead finger       30
    A precious ring, a ring that I must use
    In dear employment. Therefore hence, begone.
    But, if thou, jealous, dost return to pry
    In what I farther shall intend to do,
    By heaven, I will tear thee joint by joint           35
    And strew this hungry churchyard with thy limbs.
    The time and my intents are savage-wild,
    More fierce and more inexorable far
    Than empty tigers or the roaring sea.

BALTHASAR

    I will be gone, sir, and not trouble you.           40

ROMEO

    So shalt thou show me friendship. Take thou that.
                           *Giving money.*
    Live and be prosperous, and farewell, good fellow.

BALTHASAR, *aside*

    For all this same, I'll hide me hereabout.
    His looks I fear, and his intents I doubt.
                            *He steps aside.*

ROMEO, *beginning to force open the tomb*

    Thou detestable maw, thou womb of death,        45
    Gorged with the dearest morsel of the earth,
    Thus I enforce thy rotten jaws to open,
    And in despite I'll cram thee with more food.

## RESOURCE #4.4G

PARIS

    This is that banished haughty Montague
    That murdered my love's cousin, with which grief          50
    It is supposèd the fair creature died,
    And here is come to do some villainous shame
    To the dead bodies. I will apprehend him.
                                  *Stepping forward.*
    Stop thy unhallowed toil, vile Montague.
    Can vengeance be pursued further than death?          55
    Condemnèd villain, I do apprehend thee.
    Obey and go with me, for thou must die.

ROMEO

    I must indeed, and therefore came I hither.
    Good gentle youth, tempt not a desp'rate man.
    Fly hence and leave me. Think upon these gone.      60
    Let them affright thee. I beseech thee, youth,
    Put not another sin upon my head
    By urging me to fury. O, begone!
    By heaven, I love thee better than myself,
    For I come hither armed against myself.             65
    Stay not, begone, live, and hereafter say
    A madman's mercy bid thee run away.

PARIS

    I do defy thy commination
    And apprehend thee for a felon here.

ROMEO

    Wilt thou provoke me? Then have at thee, boy!       70
                             *They draw and fight.*

PAGE

    O Lord, they fight! I will go call the watch.
                             *He exits.*

PARIS

    O, I am slain! If thou be merciful,
    Open the tomb; lay me with Juliet.    *He dies.*

**RESOURCE #4.4H**

ROMEO

In faith, I will.—Let me peruse this face.
Mercutio's kinsman, noble County Paris!                              75
What said my man when my betossèd soul
Did not attend him as we rode? I think
He told me Paris should have married Juliet.
Said he not so? Or did I dream it so?
Or am I mad, hearing him talk of Juliet,                            80
To think it was so?—O, give me thy hand,
One writ with me in sour misfortune's book!
I'll bury thee in a triumphant grave.—
                                    *He opens the tomb.*
A grave? O, no. A lantern, slaughtered youth,
For here lies Juliet, and her beauty makes                          85
This vault a feasting presence full of light.—
Death, lie thou there, by a dead man interred.
                                    *Laying Paris in the tomb.*
How oft when men are at the point of death
Have they been merry, which their keepers call
A light'ning before death! O, how may I                             90
Call this a light'ning?—O my love, my wife,
Death, that hath sucked the honey of thy breath,
Hath had no power yet upon thy beauty.
Thou art not conquered. Beauty's ensign yet
Is crimson in thy lips and in thy cheeks,                           95
And death's pale flag is not advancèd there.—
Tybalt, liest thou there in thy bloody sheet?
O, what more favor can I do to thee
Than with that hand that cut thy youth in twain
To sunder his that was thine enemy?                                100
Forgive me, cousin.—Ah, dear Juliet,
Why art thou yet so fair? Shall I believe
That unsubstantial death is amorous,
And that the lean abhorrèd monster keeps
Thee here in dark to be his paramour?                              105
For fear of that I still will stay with thee
And never from this palace of dim night
Depart again. Here, here will I remain
With worms that are thy chambermaids. O, here
Will I set up my everlasting rest                                  110
And shake the yoke of inauspicious stars
From this world-wearied flesh! Eyes, look your last.

Arms, take your last embrace. And, lips, O, you
The doors of breath, seal with a righteous kiss
A dateless bargain to engrossing death.                                    115
                              *Kissing Juliet.*
Come, bitter conduct, come, unsavory guide!
Thou desperate pilot, now at once run on
The dashing rocks thy seasick weary bark!
Here's to my love. *Drinking.* O true apothecary,
Thy drugs are quick. Thus with a kiss I die.                              120
                              *He dies.*

## RESOURCE #4.4I

*Enter Friar Lawrence with lantern, crow, and spade.*

FRIAR LAWRENCE
    Saint Francis be my speed! How oft tonight
    Have my old feet stumbled at graves!—Who's there?

BALTHASAR
    Here's one, a friend, and one that knows you well.

FRIAR LAWRENCE
    Bliss be upon you. Tell me, good my friend,
    What torch is yond that vainly lends his light          125
    To grubs and eyeless skulls? As I discern,
    It burneth in the Capels' monument.

BALTHASAR
    It doth so, holy sir, and there's my master,
    One that you love.

FRIAR LAWRENCE  Who is it?                   130

BALTHASAR  Romeo.

FRIAR LAWRENCE
    How long hath he been there?

BALTHASAR  Full half an hour.

FRIAR LAWRENCE
    Go with me to the vault.

BALTHASAR  I dare not, sir.               135
    My master knows not but I am gone hence,
    And fearfully did menace me with death
    If I did stay to look on his intents.

FRIAR LAWRENCE
    Stay, then. I'll go alone. Fear comes upon me.
    O, much I fear some ill unthrifty thing.         140

BALTHASAR
    As I did sleep under this yew tree here,
    I dreamt my master and another fought,
    And that my master slew him.

FRIAR LAWRENCE, *moving toward the tomb*
Romeo!—
Alack, alack, what blood is this which stains                    145
The stony entrance of this sepulcher?
What mean these masterless and gory swords
To lie discolored by this place of peace?
Romeo! O, pale! Who else? What, Paris too?
And steeped in blood? Ah, what an unkind hour              150
Is guilty of this lamentable chance!
The lady stirs.

## RESOURCE #4.4J

JULIET

    O comfortable friar, where is my lord?
    I do remember well where I should be,
    And there I am. Where is my Romeo?                    155

FRIAR LAWRENCE

    I hear some noise.—Lady, come from that nest
    Of death, contagion, and unnatural sleep.
    A greater power than we can contradict
    Hath thwarted our intents. Come, come away.
    Thy husband in thy bosom there lies dead,            160
    And Paris, too. Come, I'll dispose of thee
    Among a sisterhood of holy nuns.
    Stay not to question, for the watch is coming.
    Come, go, good Juliet. I dare no longer stay.

JULIET

    Go, get thee hence, for I will not away.               165
                              *He exits.*
    What's here? A cup closed in my true love's hand?
    Poison, I see, hath been his timeless end.—
    O churl, drunk all, and left no friendly drop
    To help me after! I will kiss thy lips.
    Haply some poison yet doth hang on them,           170
    To make me die with a restorative.     *She kisses him.*
    Thy lips are warm!

**RESOURCE #4.4K**

*Enter Paris's Page and Watch.*

FIRST WATCH  Lead, boy. Which way?

JULIET
  Yea, noise? Then I'll be brief. O, happy dagger,
  This is thy sheath. There rust, and let me die.                    175
                    *She takes Romeo's dagger, stabs herself, and dies.*

PAGE
  This is the place, there where the torch doth burn.

FIRST WATCH
  The ground is bloody.—Search about the
    churchyard.
  Go, some of you; whoe'er you find, attach.
                    *Some watchmen exit.*
  Pitiful sight! Here lies the County slain,                         180
  And Juliet bleeding, warm, and newly dead,
  Who here hath lain this two days burièd.—
  Go, tell the Prince. Run to the Capulets.
  Raise up the Montagues. Some others search.
                    *Others exit.*
  We see the ground whereon these woes do lie,                       185
  But the true ground of all these piteous woes
  We cannot without circumstance descry.
                    *Enter Watchmen with Romeo's man Balthasar.*

SECOND WATCH
  Here's Romeo's man. We found him in the
  churchyard.

FIRST WATCH
  Hold him in safety till the Prince come hither.                    190
                    *Enter Friar Lawrence and another Watchman.*

THIRD WATCH
  Here is a friar that trembles, sighs, and weeps.
  We took this mattock and this spade from him
  As he was coming from this churchyard's side.

FIRST WATCH
  A great suspicion. Stay the Friar too.

## RESOURCE #4.4L

*Enter the Prince with Attendants.*

PRINCE

What misadventure is so early up                                    195
That calls our person from our morning rest?
                                   *Enter Capulet and Lady Capulet.*

CAPULET

What should it be that is so shrieked abroad?

LADY CAPULET

O, the people in the street cry "Romeo,"
Some "Juliet," and some "Paris," and all run
With open outcry toward our monument.                               200

PRINCE

What fear is this which startles in our ears?

FIRST WATCH

Sovereign, here lies the County Paris slain,
And Romeo dead, and Juliet, dead before,
Warm and new killed.

PRINCE

Search, seek, and know how this foul murder               205
    comes.

FIRST WATCH

Here is a friar, and slaughtered Romeo's man,
With instruments upon them fit to open
These dead men's tombs.

CAPULET

O heavens! O wife, look how our daughter bleeds!          210
This dagger hath mista'en, for, lo, his house
Is empty on the back of Montague,
And it mis-sheathèd in my daughter's bosom.

LADY CAPULET

O me, this sight of death is as a bell
That warns my old age to a sepulcher.                              215

## RESOURCE #4.4M

*Enter Montague.*

PRINCE

> Come, Montague, for thou art early up
> To see thy son and heir now early down.

MONTAGUE

> Alas, my liege, my wife is dead tonight.
> Grief of my son's exile hath stopped her breath.
> What further woe conspires against mine age?                    220

PRINCE  Look, and thou shalt see.

MONTAGUE, *seeing Romeo dead*

> O thou untaught! What manners is in this,
> To press before thy father to a grave?

PRINCE

> Seal up the mouth of outrage for awhile,
> Till we can clear these ambiguities                             225
> And know their spring, their head, their true
>     descent,
> And then will I be general of your woes
> And lead you even to death. Meantime forbear,
> And let mischance be slave to patience.—                        230
> Bring forth the parties of suspicion.

FRIAR LAWRENCE

> I am the greatest, able to do least,
> Yet most suspected, as the time and place
> Doth make against me, of this direful murder.
> And here I stand, both to impeach and purge                     235
> Myself condemnèd and myself excused.

PRINCE

> Then say at once what thou dost know in this.

## RESOURCE #4.4N

FRIAR LAWRENCE

    I will be brief, for my short date of breath
    Is not so long as is a tedious tale.
    Romeo, there dead, was husband to that Juliet,          240
    And she, there dead, that Romeo's faithful wife.
    I married them, and their stol'n marriage day
    Was Tybalt's doomsday, whose untimely death
    Banished the new-made bridegroom from this city,
    For whom, and not for Tybalt, Juliet pined.          245
    You, to remove that siege of grief from her,
    Betrothed and would have married her perforce
    To County Paris. Then comes she to me,
    And with wild looks bid me devise some mean
    To rid her from this second marriage,          250
    Or in my cell there would she kill herself.
    Then gave I her (so tutored by my art)
    A sleeping potion, which so took effect
    As I intended, for it wrought on her
    The form of death. Meantime I writ to Romeo          255
    That he should hither come as this dire night
    To help to take her from her borrowed grave,
    Being the time the potion's force should cease.
    But he which bore my letter, Friar John,
    Was stayed by accident, and yesternight          260
    Returned my letter back. Then all alone
    At the prefixèd hour of her waking
    Came I to take her from her kindred's vault,
    Meaning to keep her closely at my cell
    Till I conveniently could send to Romeo.          265
    But when I came, some minute ere the time
    Of her awakening, here untimely lay
    The noble Paris and true Romeo dead.
    She wakes, and I entreated her come forth
    And bear this work of heaven with patience.          270
    But then a noise did scare me from the tomb,
    And she, too desperate, would not go with me
    But, as it seems, did violence on herself.
    All this I know, and to the marriage
    Her nurse is privy. And if aught in this          275

Miscarried by my fault, let my old life
Be sacrificed some hour before his time
Unto the rigor of severest law.

PRINCE
We still have known thee for a holy man.—
Where's Romeo's man? What can he say to this?                    280

## RESOURCE #4.40

BALTHASAR

I brought my master news of Juliet's death,
And then in post he came from Mantua
To this same place, to this same monument.
This letter he early bid me give his father
And threatened me with death, going in the vault,        285
If I departed not and left him there.

PRINCE

Give me the letter. I will look on it.—
                    *He takes Romeo's letter.*
Where is the County's page, that raised the
        watch?—
Sirrah, what made your master in this place?        290

PAGE

He came with flowers to strew his lady's grave
And bid me stand aloof, and so I did.
Anon comes one with light to ope the tomb,
And by and by my master drew on him,
And then I ran away to call the watch.        295

PRINCE

This letter doth make good the Friar's words,
Their course of love, the tidings of her death;
And here he writes that he did buy a poison
Of a poor 'pothecary, and therewithal
Came to this vault to die and lie with Juliet.        300
Where be these enemies?—Capulet, Montague,
See what a scourge is laid upon your hate,
That heaven finds means to kill your joys with love,
And I, for winking at your discords too,
Have lost a brace of kinsmen. All are punished.        305

CAPULET

O brother Montague, give me thy hand.
This is my daughter's jointure, for no more
Can I demand.

MONTAGUE        But I can give thee more,
For I will ray her statue in pure gold,        310
That whiles Verona by that name is known,

There shall no figure at such rate be set
As that of true and faithful Juliet.

CAPULET
As rich shall Romeo's by his lady's lie,
Poor sacrifices of our enmity.                                              315

PRINCE
A glooming peace this morning with it brings.
The sun for sorrow will not show his head.
Go hence to have more talk of these sad things.
Some shall be pardoned, and some punishèd.
For never was a story of more woe                                           320
Than this of Juliet and her Romeo.
                                                *All exit.*

# "See what a scourge is laid upon your hate": Resounding Words in *Romeo and Juliet* and Contemporary Poetry

## Here's What We're Doing and Why

We'll start this lesson with a quick performance of the Act 5 students created yesterday. Fabulous! Then we'll focus on the whole play and on the work that students have done to discover the relationships between the characters and their relationships with their community. By returning to the poems of unrest that lent lines to one of our first activities—Tossing Lines and Two-Line Scenes in Week One, Lesson 2—students will connect the events and questions posed by the play to their own histories and communities.

As you look at the set of poetry excerpts included in today's lesson, you may develop your own connections between the poems' language, allusions, or imagery and the events of *Romeo and Juliet*, but today's work is about the magic that happens when we simply place two seemingly disparate texts in front of students and they make powerful, authentic connections between the two. Throughout this unit, you've been the architect of rich and engaging paired text work, sometimes facilitating discussion through guided questions or very intentional groupings of passages. Now, students are in the driver's seat and pairing texts themselves in order to communicate their understanding of *Romeo and Juliet*. They will continue to grow their confidence with reading and interpreting Shakespeare while encountering other great writers who belong in conversation with him: Hughes, Brooks, Rodriguez, and Sanchez.

Just for you: take a look at **RESOURCE #5.1A**, the Teacher's Overview of Week 5. It's tucked in at the end of this lesson so you can get a heads-up on next week. You'll see it again—along with the Student Overview—at the top of the Week 5 lessons. Week 5: final projects when it all comes together!

## What Will I Need?

- A copy of *Romeo and Juliet*, Folger Edition, or free Folger Shakespeare online folger.edu/shakespeares-works

- Paper, pen/pencil

- Copies of Contemporary Poems About Unrest excerpts for each student – **RESOURCE #4.5A**. Make sure that every student has copies of all the excerpts. Check resources from the Academy of American Poets or the Poetry Foundation for complete copies of the poems if you'd like to use them.

- A few copies of Words of Advice and Warning, cut into strips and placed in a can or bowl (one strip for every student; maybe some students will have more than one line) – **RESOURCE #4.5B**

## How Should I Prepare?

- Set up your classroom conducive to students working in pairs.

## Agenda (~ 45-minute class period)

- ❏ Repeat performance of Act 5 Relay: 15 minutes
- ❏ Words of Advice pair study: 5 minutes
- ❏ Pair Words of Advice with contemporary poetry: 10 minutes
- ❏ Perform "mashup" choral readings: 10 minutes
- ❏ Wrap-up reflection: 5 minutes

## Here's What Students Hear (From You) and (Then When They'll) Do

Let's start today with a repeat performance of your great Act 5 from yesterday! Brought back by popular demand!

### Part One

1. Now that you've brought us to the end of the play, we're going to think about the play's connections to our contemporary lives and communities by pairing parts of *Romeo and Juliet* with some of the lines from poetry that we encountered at the very beginning of our study. Remember line tossing and two-line scenes?

2. First, let's look intentionally at some advice lines from the play. Each of you pick a strip of paper from the can, get a partner, and think together. Read the line of advice to yourself and think about that sentence or scene for a minute. With your partner, talk through your lines together. You can use your copy of *Romeo and Juliet* or check **folger.edu/shakespeares-works** for the play online.

   These questions might help: Where did it occur in the action? Who said this line to whom? What is the context? What was the advice? What was its purpose? Did the character listening to the advice follow it? What about the character giving the advice?

### Part Two

1. Now let's revisit some lines that we heard at the very beginning of our study. There were some lines from poetry mixed in with your *Romeo and Juliet* lines during our very first round of line tossing. Here is a set of those lines – **RESOURCE 4.5A** – plus a few extra from the poems they belong to.

2. Work with your partner to select two lines from these poem excerpts to group with the two lines that you pulled from the can. Arrange the four quotes in any order you'd like to create a new "Prologue" for *Romeo and Juliet*, something that you think speaks to the big ideas of the play and the connections it makes to the lives of a 21st-century audience.

3. Practice performing a choral reading of your new prologue. You can read all four lines in unison or take a back-and-forth approach as we sometimes have with two sides of the room. Read one line together, read one line apart—it's all up to you.

4. Now let's perform your new prologues! Bravo! Very quickly, let's share what we noticed about each other's performances.

   a. What did you notice about the combinations of Shakespeare and more modern poetry lines?

   b. What surprised you about these prologues?

   c. The Prologue to *Romeo and Juliet* tells the audience exactly what to expect in the plot and conclusion of the play. Do you think the poetry lines hinted at the action of the play or the end of the play? How?

   d. To make our new prologues, we brought together voices that were nearly 400 years apart. What can our communities still learn from *Romeo and Juliet* today? What might our communities teach the families of Verona?

**EXTENSION:** Need to include some writing practice or literary analysis? Ask students to defend their text pairing in a paragraph or short essay. A LOT of complex thinking goes into selecting paired texts; why not give students the opportunity to explain what's going on in their brilliant brains?

## Part Three

Finally, let's close with some rounds:

- Today, I heard . . .

- I realized . . .

## Here's What Just Happened in Class

- Students reviewed the entire text (plot and relationships between characters) through a student-directed "5-Minute Act 5" performance and close reading of lines of advice from the play.

- Students practiced close reading and critical thinking to decide which contemporary poetry to pair with their advice lines from Shakespeare.

- Students collaborated and negotiated to make choices about how to perform excerpts from several texts.

- Students synthesized poetry from Shakespeare and other great writers to draw conclusions about themes and the values and/or conflicts within their own communities.

# Contemporary Poems About Unrest

### "I Look at the World" by Langston Hughes

*I look then at the silly walls*
*Through dark eyes in a dark face—*
*And this is what I know:*
*That all these walls oppression builds*
*Will have to go!*

## Excerpts from "Boy Breaking Glass" by Gwendolyn Brooks

*"I shall create! If not a note, a hole.*
*If not an overture, a desecration."*

*"It was you, it was you who threw away my name!*
*And this is everything I have for me."*

### Excerpts from "Watts Bleeds" by Luis J. Rodriguez

*Watts bleeds*
*leaving stained reminders*
*on dusty sidewalks.*

*Watts bleeds*
*dripping from carcasses of dreams:*
*Where despair*
*is old people*
*sitting on torn patio sofas*
*with empty eyes*
*and children running down alleys*
*with big sticks.*

*Watts bleeds*
*on vacant lots*
*and burned-out buildings—*
*temples desolated by a people's rage.*

*Where fear is a deep river.*
*Where hate is an overgrown weed.*

*Oh bloom, you trampled flower!*
*Come alive as once*
*you tried to do from the ashes.*

## Excerpts from "Haiku and Tanka for Harriet Tubman" by Sonia Sanchez

*2*
*Picture her kissing*
*our spines saying no to*
*the eyes of slavery . . .*

*5*
*Picture this woman*
*saying no*

*6*
*Picture a woman*
*jumping rivers her*
*legs inhaling moons . . .*

*22*
*Picture this woman*
*of royalty . . . wearing a crown*
*of morning air . . .*

*23*
*Picture her walking,*
*running, reviving*
*a country's breath . . .*

*24*
*Picture black voices*
*leaving behind*
*lost tongues . . .*

RESOURCE #4.5B

# Words of Advice and Warning from *Romeo and Juliet*

Put up your swords, you know not what you do. 1.1
Thou shalt not stir one foot to seek a foe. 1.1
Throw your mistempered weapons to the ground. 1.1
Put up thy sword, or manage it to part these men with me. 1.1
Be ruled by me. Forget to think of her. 1.1
By giving liberty unto thine eyes. Examine other beauties. 1.1
'Tis not hard, I think, for men so old as we to keep the peace. 1.2
My child is yet a stranger in the world. 1.2
And too soon marred are those so early made. 1.2


But woo her, gentle Paris, get her heart;
My will to her consent is but a part. 1.2


Examine every married lineament
And see how one another lends content,
And what obscured in this fair volume lies
Find written in the margent of his eyes. 1.3


This precious book of love, this unbound lover,
To beautify him only lacks a cover.
That book in many's eyes doth share the glory
That in gold clasps locks in the golden story.
So shall you share all that he doth possess
By having him, making yourself no less. 1.3


Love is a smoke made with the fume of sighs;
Being purged, a fire sparkling in lovers' eyes;
Being vexed, a sea nourished with loving tears. 1.1


O, swear not by the moon, th' inconstant moon,
That monthly changes in her circled orb,
Lest that thy love prove likewise variable. 2.2


See what a scourge is laid upon your hate,
That heaven finds means to kill your joys with love,
And I, for winking at your discords too,
Have lost a brace of kinsmen. All are punished. 5.3

RESOURCE #5.1A

# Teacher's Overview

### Introducing the Final Week and the Final Project:
### Make *Romeo and Juliet* Your Own

## The Final Project's Learning Goals

This project is the culmination of everything your students have been doing all unit long. Students will work in groups to make a scene from *Romeo and Juliet* entirely their own.

By the end of this project, every student will have:

- Pulled together all the pieces of this unit, particularly essential practices like Cutting a Scene and Creating a Promptbook, Choral Reading, and 3D Lit, in order to get inside of and create a scene from *Romeo and Juliet*.

- Moved collaboratively through a complex process of reading, rereading, editing, adapting, embodying, imagining, re-editing, rehearsing, performing, deciding, and defending.

- Used the text to make choices about how to edit, adapt, and stage the scene.

- Performed their original interpretation of a *Romeo and Juliet* scene for an audience.

- Written and presented a group rationale for the text-based decisions that led to this performance (edits, additions, staging, etc.).

- Written a brief personal reflection on the experience of completing this project.

- Grappled with the whole play through work in class up to now and more collaborative work across the whole play this week.

Both the students and you, the teacher, should walk away with resounding evidence that everyone in your class can make meaning from Shakespeare's language—from complex texts—on their own.

## Advice and Reminders

**Time.** This learning experience is designed to take roughly 5 class periods of 45 minutes each. However, depending on your teaching context, it might take a longer or shorter time. For example, this plan is written with one day for final performances, but if you need more time and have the time, take it!

**Chaos.** Since it's all about turning the language and the learning over to the students, you can expect the process to get somewhat messy and noisy. As long as students are making *their own* way through their scenes, it's all good. **As you have been doing right along, resist the urge to explain the text to your students**. Trust the process—and trust your students to ask questions, find answers, create interpretations, and make meaning on their own, as they have been doing. (If they don't do this, then they're missing the deep learning and purpose of the project.) Throughout this process and this week, students are tracking their cutting, adding, and promptbooking decisions and preparing to present (along with their scene performance) an oral defense of their key decisions.

**Time and Less Chaos.** It works out best if you can decide how much time your schedule allows you for the final performances and scene rationales on the final day of the project. Then work backwards to schedule your groups within that time.

   An example: If you have 45 minutes of class time and 20 students, you might have 5 performing groups with 4 students each. That could mean that each group would have 7 to 8 minutes to share their work (their performance + then defense of their decisions). 8 minutes x 5 groups = 40 minutes, leaving 5 minutes for a whole-class reflection round. If this feels tight to you, give each group 7 minutes.

**Flexibility and Creativity.** You'll see that on the menu of scenes for this project, some scenes involve more than 4 actors, and some fewer than 4 actors. Students will add their own creativity to the mix by double-casting parts or using other means to make sure they have full participation.

## Suggested Guidance For You on Assessing Final Projects: A Seven-Point Checklist

1. Does the performance demonstrate a grasp of what the characters are saying and wanting?

2. Does the performance make strategic use of voice and body to convey effective tone and feeling?

3. Does the defense summarize the scene clearly, concisely, and accurately?

4. Does the defense comment on the scene's importance in the overall play and our world today?

5. Does the defense justify key decisions to cut, add, and perform language in this particular way? Is there strong and relevant textual evidence for this performance overall?

6. Does the defense describe how this process shaped new or different understandings of this play?

7. Does the personal reflection consider specific things that the student has learned, contributed, and discovered?

## WEEK FIVE: LESSON 1

# Your Final Projects!

### Here's What We're Doing This Week and Why

Today kicks off the culminating project, the student-driven process of making Shakespeare thoroughly their own by collaborating on creating for each other great scenes from *Romeo and Juliet*. By the end of this lesson, students will understand what's expected of them and why—both as individuals and as project groups. They will also have gathered with their groupmates and have their assigned scene for this project. Although we've divided the final project into 5 days, it's really one unified, cumulative process, so please **make whatever pacing adjustments your students need.** Different groups might be at different steps of the process on different days, and that's OK.

### What Will I Need?

- Final Project: The Teacher's Overview – **RESOURCE #5.1A** (Perhaps you got an early start and have read this already!)

- Final Project: The Student's Overview and Assignment – **RESOURCE #5.1B**

- The menu of *Romeo and Juliet* scenes for you to assign from, or for groups to choose from – **RESOURCE #5.1C**

[**TEACHER NOTE:** First on the menu are the two prologues—only 28 lines in total, so save this menu item for a special purpose. Someone who joined the class late? A new EL student, if that would work in a supportive way? Does your principal need an assignment?]

### How Should I Prepare?

- Make copies of the student's overview and assignment – **RESOURCE #5.1B** – for for everyone in class.

- Make a plan for grouping students.

- Make a plan for matching groups to scenes. (It's up to you whether you want to assign them the scenes we've provided, or scenes that you feel are key to the play, or allow them to make their own choices.)

- Figure out how much time students will have for their scenes and their defense so you can let them know today. (See Teacher's Overview, **RESOURCE #5.1A**.)

- Prepare yourself to get out of the way and let students figure things out on their own. You're assessing their ability to do exactly that.

### Agenda (~ 45-minute class period)

- ❏ Part 1: Intro to the assignment and scene menu: 20 minutes
- ❏ Part 2: Groups meet for the first time: 25 minutes

## Here's What Students Hear (From You) and (Then What They'll) Do

### Part One: Project Introduction

1. Give students the project assignment.

2. Check for understanding with reflection rounds:
   - I notice . . .
   - I wonder . . .

3. Assign scenes, answer any wonderings, and fill in any details that students missed.

### Part Two: Group Work

Students work in their groups and get started!

## Here's What Just Happened in Class

- Students met their final project and started working in groups to tackle the assignment!

- Every student read out loud some *Romeo and Juliet* new to them as groups and started to befriend their scenes.

RESOURCE #5.1A

# Teacher's Overview

## Introducing the Final Week and the Final Project:
## Make *Romeo and Juliet* Your Own

### The Final Project's Learning Goals

This project is the culmination of everything your students have been doing all unit long. Students will work in groups to make a scene from *Romeo and Juliet* entirely their own.

By the end of this project, every student will have:

- Pulled together all the pieces of this unit, particularly essential practices like Cutting a Scene and Creating a Promptbook, Choral Reading, and 3D Lit, in order to get inside of and create a scene from *Romeo and Juliet*.

- Moved collaboratively through a complex process of reading, rereading, editing, adapting, embodying, imagining, re-editing, rehearsing, performing, deciding, and defending.

- Used the text to make choices about how to edit, adapt, and stage the scene.

- Performed their original interpretation of a *Romeo and Juliet* scene for an audience.

- Written and presented a group rationale for the text-based decisions that led to this performance (edits, additions, staging, etc.).

- Written a brief personal reflection on the experience of completing this project.

- Grappled with the whole play through work in class up to now and more collaborative work across the whole play this week.

Both the students and you, the teacher, should walk away with resounding evidence that everyone in your class can make meaning from Shakespeare's language—from complex texts—on their own.

### Advice and Reminders

**Time.** This learning experience is designed to take roughly 5 class periods of 45 minutes each. However, depending on your teaching context, it might take a longer or shorter time. For example, this plan is written with one day for final performances, but if you need more time and have the time, take it!

**Chaos.** Since it's all about turning the language and the learning over to the students, you can expect the process to get somewhat messy and noisy. As long as students are making *their own* way through their scenes, it's all good. **As you have been doing right along, resist the urge to explain the text to your students**. Trust the process—and trust your students to ask questions, find answers, create interpretations, and make meaning on their own, as they have been doing. (If they don't do this, then they're missing the deep learning and purpose of the project.) Throughout this process and this week, students are tracking their cutting, adding, and promptbooking decisions and preparing to present (along with their scene performance) an oral defense of their key decisions.

**Time and Less Chaos.** It works out best if you can decide how much time your schedule allows you for the final performances and scene rationales on the final day of the project. Then work backwards to schedule your groups within that time.

An example: If you have 45 minutes of class time and 20 students, you might have 5 performing groups with 4 students each. That could mean that each group would have 7 to 8 minutes to share their work (their performance + then defense of their decisions). 8 minutes x 5 groups = 40 minutes, leaving 5 minutes for a whole-class reflection round. If this feels tight to you, give each group 7 minutes.

**Flexibility and Creativity.** You'll see that on the menu of scenes for this project, some scenes involve more than 4 actors, and some fewer than 4 actors. Students will add their own creativity to the mix by double-casting parts or using other means to make sure they have full participation.

## Suggested Guidance on Assessing Projects: A Seven-Point Checklist

1. Does the performance demonstrate a grasp of what the characters are saying and wanting?

2. Does the performance make strategic use of voice and body to convey effective tone and feeling?

3. Does the defense summarize the scene clearly, concisely, and accurately?

4. Does the defense comment on the scene's importance in the overall play and our world today?

5. Does the defense justify key decisions to cut, add, and perform language in this particular way? Is there strong and relevant textual evidence for this performance overall?

6. Does the defense describe how this process shaped new or different understandings of this play?

7. Does the personal reflection consider specific things that the student has learned, contributed, and discovered?

# Student's Overview and Assignment

### Introducing the Final Week and the Final Project:
### Make *Romeo and Juliet* Your Own

You will work in groups to make a scene from *Romeo and Juliet* entirely your own. This project is the culmination of everything you have been doing all unit long, and this week you will be demonstrating all that you have learned!

By the end of this project, you will have:

- Put together all the pieces of this unit, particularly essential practices like choral reading, cutting a scene, creating promptbooks, and 3D Lit, in order to get inside of and create a scene from *Romeo and Juliet*.

- Moved collaboratively through a complex process of reading, rereading, editing, adapting, embodying, imagining, re-editing, rehearsing, performing, deciding, and defending.

- Used the text to make choices about how to edit, adapt, and stage the scene.

- Performed your original interpretation of the scene for an audience.

- Written and presented a group rationale for the text-based decisions that led to this performance (edits, additions, staging, etc.).

- Written a brief personal reflection on the experience of completing this project.

- Grappled with the whole play (Acts 1 through 5) through work in class up to now and collaborative work on scenes throughout the play this week.

You, your classmates, and your teacher will walk away with resounding evidence that YOU can make meaning from Shakespeare's language—from complex texts—on your own.

## What You Will Produce

1. A performed scene from *Romeo and Juliet* (in a group)

2. A defense of your scene, delivered orally and in writing (in a group)

3. A personal reflection on this project (from you, as an individual)

## Your Action Steps

1. **Get your group and scene assignment** from your teacher.

2. Next, before anything else: with your group, **dive deeply into your scene.** Read it out loud as a group, just as we have done in class. Take notes on all of this—these will come in handy later. Collaboratively as a group, figure out:

    - What's happening in the scene
    - What the characters are saying

- What each of the characters wants
- Why the scene is important in the play
- Why someone should care about this scene today

3. Next, **consider the end goal:** your group is making a scene of **X** minutes and an oral defense of the scene that is no longer than **X** minutes. Your teacher will tell you the timing that you—like any group of actors—must work with. Keep this in mind as you work through the scene.

4. Next, work to **be directors and put the scene on its feet.** Each member of the group should be **creating a promptbook** for the scene along the way so that you're all working from the same script with the same notes. Together, make—and note—decisions about the following and be prepared to explain to your audience what in the text (and in your personal experience of reading it) motivated you to cut, add, and perform as you did:

    - **Cutting the scene.** Perhaps you must cut it so that it fits your time limit and still makes sense. What must stay? What can go?

    - **Locating the scene.** Where is it happening? What does this place look like? Feel like? Smell like? Sound like? How do you know this?

    - **Adding to the scene.** You may want to choose one or two outside texts to mash up with your scene. If you do, what is gained by putting these texts into your Shakespeare scene? What made you choose this/these text/texts? Why and where do they work best? If you choose to add outside texts, be sure that at least 80 percent of your scene is *Romeo and Juliet*.

    - **Getting ready to perform the scene.** Cast the parts. Which of you plays whom? Every group member must speak. What does each character want and think and feel? How can the audience tell? Who is moving where on what line, and why? Get on your feet and start moving, because some of these questions are answered when you get a scene on its feet. As you know, this is not about acting talent; it is about knowing what you are saying and doing as you bring life to this scene.

    - As you go, you're documenting your decisions and preparing your oral defense of the scene. What are the most significant or original decisions your group made? What drove those decisions? Let the audience into your interpretive process, your minds, ever so concisely. Your defense should involve every group member and do the following:

        - Summarize your scene.

        - Comment on the scene's importance in the overall play.

        - Justify your cutting, adding, and performing choices with textual evidence.

        - Conclude by describing how the process of preparing this performance shaped new or different understandings of *Romeo and Juliet*.

5. **Rehearse.** Yes, you should memorize your lines, though you can ask someone to serve as your prompter, as we think Shakespeare's company might have. Repeat: This is not about acting talent.

6. **Perform your scene and present your scene rationale** during your scheduled class period. After your performance, present your rationale for your scene. As with your performance, every group member must speak. Focus on just the most significant decisions and stick to your time limit. We will all watch all the final project scenes together so that we can celebrate wrapping up *Romeo and Juliet* with YOUR voices.

7. At that time, you will **submit the two written documents**:
   - The written version of your group's defense of your scene.
   - An individual reflection paper (400 to 500 words) reflecting on the experience—both the process and what you feel were your own contributions to the project.

# Menu: Juicy Scenes from *Romeo and Juliet*

| ACT & SCENES | LINES | # OF CHARACTERS |
|---|---|---|
| 1.1 and 2.1 | 1–14, 1–14 | 2–3 |
| 1.1 | 163–247 | 2 |
| 1.3 | 1–113 | 3 |
| 1.4 | 1–121 | 3 |
| 2.2 | 1–205 | 2 |
| 3.1 | 1–207 | roughly 6 |
| 3.2 | 34–157 | 2 |
| 3.5 | 69–207 | 4 |
| 4.1 | 45–129 | 2 |
| 5.3 | 74–120 | 3 |

# Your Final Project: Making *Romeo and Juliet* Your Own

## Here's What We're Doing and Why

We're here! Groups are making their way through the final project this week. They are working on scenes from *Romeo and Juliet*, demonstrating as they go what they have learned in terms of making the language, characters, and action their own—all infused with their own energy and creativity. They are also presenting scenes to each other as we wrap up *Romeo and Juliet*.

## Agenda for Lessons 2, 3, and 4 (~ THREE 45-minute periods)

### Lesson 2:

❑ Introduction/Warm-up: 10 minutes

❑ Cutting the scene/Group Work: 35 minutes

### Lesson 3:

❑ Introduction: 10 minutes

❑ Promptbook the newly edited scene and add outside texts if you choose to/ Group Work: 35 minutes

### Lesson 4:

❑ Frozen Scenes/Warm-up – **RESOURCE #5.4:** 10 minutes

❑ Rehearsing the scene and writing the scene rationale/Group Work: 35 minutes

## What Will I Need for These Three Lessons?

- Some print copies of the Folger Shakespeare edition of the play for student reference

- A few dictionaries or Shakespeare glossaries for student reference

- Space and time for students to make their way through this project

- Strength to resist the urge to explain or interpret the text for students (you're a pro by now)

- Access to outside books, songs, poems, films, etc. if they choose to add outside material to their scene

- A discreet eye to observe students as they work

## How Should I Prepare for These Three Lessons?

- As long as every student understands the task at hand, you're good. Students are doing the hard work now!

## Lesson 2: Here's What Students Hear (From You) and (Then What They'll) Do

### Part One: Introduction/Warm-up

1. Choose your favorite line from your scene.

2. Count off by 4. Meet with the other students with the same number.

3. Toss your lines in a circle; everyone should say their line three times (say it differently each time!).

4. Discuss as a class: Given the lines you heard in your circle, what do you think is happening in the scenes we are performing? Which delivery of your line felt like the best fit for your character or scene? Why?

### Part Two: Group Work

Groups are reading, rereading, and cutting their final scenes. You are also cooperating to compose a rationale for your unique performance of the scene. For a closer look at the steps in this process, please refer to the Student's Overview and Assignment – **RESOURCE #5.1B.**

[**TEACHER NOTE:** Students typically need to take this work home with them, especially the two writing tasks: the group rationale and the personal reflection. Check in with your students during each class to see where they are in the process, and help them set realistic goals for homework and classwork.]

## Lesson 3: Here's What Students Hear (From You) and (Then What They'll) Do

### Part One: Introduction/Warm Up

1. In your groups, agree on a song that best represents your scene.

2. Discuss with your small group. Share with the class.

### Part Two: Group Work

Groups are cutting, adapting, promptbooking, and rehearsing their final scenes. If they are including an outside text(s), they should decide what and how today. For a closer look at the steps in this process, please refer to the Student's Overview and Assignment – **RESOURCE #5.1B.**

[**TEACHER NOTE:** Once again, check in with your students during each class to see where they are in the process. Help them set realistic goals for homework and classwork, and see that they have a plan to complete the two writing tasks.]

## Lesson 4: Here's What Students Hear (From You) and (Then What They'll) Do

### Part One: Warm-up

1. In your group, decide on a great warm-up.

2. Either use it yourselves or pass it on to another group to do!

### Part Two: Group Work

Groups are rehearsing their final scenes. They are also cooperating to compose a rationale for their unique performance of their scene. For a closer look at the steps in this process, please refer to the Student's Overview and Assignment – **RESOURCE #5.1B.**

[**TEACHER NOTE:** Students typically need to work at home on these, especially the two writing tasks: the group rationale and the personal reflection. Check in with your students during each class to see where they are in the process, and help them set realistic goals for homework and classwork.]

## Here's What Just Happened in Class During These Three Classes

- You observed a class full of students in a state of flow, deeply engaged in the process of making a scene from *Romeo and Juliet* their own!

- You watched peers help one another by asking good questions, building comprehension, citing textual evidence, and encouraging creativity.

# The Final Project: Your Own *Romeo and Juliet*, Performed!

## Here's What We're Doing and Why

| CONSIDERATIONS | METRIC | CELEBRATIONS |
|---|---|---|
| | 1. Does the performance demonstrate a grasp of what the characters are saying and wanting? | |
| | 2. Does the performance make strategic use of voice and body to convey effective tone and feeling? | |
| | 3. Does the defense summarize the scene clearly, concisely, and accurately? | |
| | 4. Does the defense comment on the scene's importance in the overall play and our world today? | |
| | 5. Does the defense justify key decisions to cut, add, and perform language in this particular way? Is there strong and relevant textual evidence for this performance overall? | |
| | 6. Does the defense describe how this process shaped new or different understandings of this play? | |
| | 7. Does the personal reflection consider specific things that the student has learned, contributed, and discovered? | |

It's showtime! Watch and listen as your students demonstrate their ability to grapple with, respond to, and perform Shakespeare's language. Hear why they staged things as they did. Celebrate how far your students have come, not just as Shakespeareans but as thinkers and readers and makers. Don't forget to save time for a whole-class reflection round after all the performances. This is often just as enlightening as the scenes themselves, if not more so.

## Agenda (~ 45-minute period)

❏ Groups get organized: 5 minutes

❏ Scenes performed and defenses presented: 40 minutes

❏ Whole-class reflection: 10 minutes

## What Will I Need?

- Space and time for all groups to present their performances and rationales.

- Space and time for everyone to gather in a circle for a final reflection round.

- A notepad or digital doc to take notes on all the great learning you're witnessing. These notes will come in handy when you provide student feedback. (Revisit the seven-point checklist in your Teacher's Overview and the learning goals of the final project when it's time for feedback. You can also consider the chart included here.)

## How Should I Prepare?

- Create and share the "run of show" for today. Who's on and in what order? At the beginning of class, groups should know when they're on.

- Arrange your space so everyone can see each scene. A giant circle is our favorite.

- It's always nice to have a lighthearted but clear way to call "time" on a scene, too. Some teachers rely on a phone timer. Your call.

## Here's What Students Will Do

### Part One: Groups get organized.

- Students meet in their groups to organize props or make quick, last-minute changes for their scene.

### Part Two: Performances

- Each group presents their work to thunderous applause.

- Collect whatever project documentation you need to assess student learning.

### Part Three: Reflection Rounds

To conclude the performances, respond to the following prompts, thinking just about your work this week including this performance experience.

- I noticed . . .

- I learned . . .

- I wondered . . .

- *If responses stay focused on the language and activities, teachers should add:* What did you learn about **yourself** this week?

## Here's What Just Happened in Class

- Massive learning demonstrated and in action, all set up by you. WOW!

# Teaching Shakespeare—and *Romeo and Juliet*—with English Learners

## Christina Porter

I am Christina Porter and for the past 20 years I have worked in an urban school community right outside of Boston, Massachusetts. I began as an English teacher, then a literacy coach, and currently I am the district curriculum director for the humanities. I first started working with English Learners in 2006 when I became the literacy coach. Prior to that, I had little experience with these phenomenal students.

Also prior to working with them, I knew the general assumptions about ELs. For as long as they have sat in U.S. classrooms, ELs most often have been considered "other," having many "deficits" that need to be overcome. The "deficits" tend to be their native language and culture—seen as roadblocks that should be surmounted so that EL students can more closely match prevailing assumptions of "American" culture—white, middle-class, and English-speaking. In my work with EL students, I soon learned that this mindset can manifest itself in many ugly ways in schools, and it is both culturally and academically destructive.

Something I observed early on was that while our white, middle-class, English-speaking students were reading Shakespeare—the real thing, not that watered-down summarized stuff—our English Learners were not. Not even a watered-down version of Shakespeare! By "real Shakespeare" I mean his words in all their glorious Early Modern English (both with the full text of a play as well as in edited scenes from a play). Initially, I had the incorrect assumption myself: I assumed, like so many others, that because students were developing English, Shakespeare was probably too difficult for them to handle. I learned that this is incorrect. What I learned instead was that once we adults dismissed our own deficit-based thinking—and allowed our EL students to read, create, design, and imagine—the results were tremendous, with Shakespeare as well as with many other complex texts.

Coinciding with my start as a literacy coach, I spent a summer at the Folger Library's Teaching Shakespeare Institute. I learned about so many of the student-centered, get-them-on-their-feet methods that are one of the backbones of this book. As the new literacy coach at the high school, I was so excited to get into a classroom and use these, especially because I had the unique opportunity to work with many teachers in the building. One of the first colleagues to reach out was an English as a Second Language (ESL) teacher. We met to brainstorm, and I described how I had spent my summer at the Folger Library learning all of these innovative methods of engaging students. She was immediately onboard. Specifically, she wanted to tackle Shakespeare (again, REAL Shakespeare). Over the course of several years, we taught many plays together, and I did the same with other colleagues in the ESL department. Our ELs consistently destroyed any concern I or others could have had about their ability to read and perform something as intricate and complex as Shakespeare. Just one example: one of the first things I learned was that these students are uniquely attuned to the intricacy of language; it's how they exist on a daily basis! Sometimes when teaching a play with my native speakers, I found that they would want to rush. In this rushing, they would miss the depth and beauty of the words. ELs, on the other hand, take time with language—with the word, the line, the speech, and the scene. This is only one of the many strengths these students bring to working with Shakespeare, and other authors too.

Because the Folger understands the importance of ELs, I have been asked to share some of the knowledge I've gained working with these unique, intelligent, and resilient EL students and Shakespeare. My suggestions are based on years of scholarly research regarding second language acquisition coupled with my knowledge and experience working with ELs, Shakespeare, and the Folger Method. I am excited to share both what I've taught and what I've learned from EL students!

One important and perhaps obvious note here is that English Learners are not a monolith. You may have students in your class who have had exposure to English in their native country, you may also have students who have experienced gaps in schooling, and more. Though most of this chapter is focused on ELs generally, when I have found an approach that is particularly helpful for a specific subgroup of ELs, I point that out.

I build here on principles and classroom practices that you will find throughout this book and this series. Since teachers are the busiest people on the planet, this material is organized so that you can find what you need quickly:

❏ **Part One: ELs at Home in the Folger Method**

❏ **Part Two: Shakespeare with English Learners**

❏ **Part Three: *Romeo and Juliet* with English Learners**

## Part One: ELs at Home in the Folger Method

Many of the Folger Essentials are *already* excellent supports for ELs. Folger Essentials like choral reading, rereading, focusing on single words and lines, and then building to speeches and scenes—all of these support fluency and comprehension. In addition, these Teaching Guides include plot summaries and play maps, and the lesson plans include lots of other active instructional approaches.

When reading Shakespeare with ELs, I always give the option to read the scene summary in advance. I do this because it balances accessibility with giving them a chance to grapple with a complex text. Remember, Shakespeare borrowed most of his plots, so the plot is the least of our concerns. We never want the story to become the roadblock to working with the words. The Folger Shakespeare, both in print and online, includes brief play and scene synopses for all of the plays. The play maps may be helpful to ELs who may have had interruptions in their prior schooling or ELs who have not previously read a drama. It can be another structural support to "unveil" the characters and plot. You may choose to spend some time deconstructing the structure of a piece of drama—discussing, for example, scenes, acts, and character lists. For some students, drama may be completely new; for others, this quick activity can serve as an activator of prior knowledge.

Understanding text features is a solid support for comprehension. It is easy to assume that by high school when most students are reading this play, they have been exposed to drama, but this is not always the case, depending on the backgrounds of individual students.

# Part Two: Shakespeare with English Learners

With the Folger Method as my base, I build in additional resources to support English Learners in my urban school. This is because working with ELs is different from working with native English speakers. Equity is removing barriers. Equity is giving students what they need to be successful. Thus, I have come to four Truths that prevail when diving into Shakespeare—and other complex texts too—with EL students:

- TRUTH #1: **ELs need support with classroom practices.** We cannot assume that our ELs have had the same experience in classrooms as our other students. We need to offer specific guidance and support for common classroom practices such as having a small group discussion, acting out a piece of drama, or other Folger Essentials. Being clear in our expectations and directions, and offering scaffolds (for example, sentence starters for small group discussions) is good for all students and essential for ELs.

- TRUTH #2: **ELs need additional support in order to grapple with complex texts.** ELs are capable of reading Shakespeare. They also need supports for language comprehension. Important supports include chunking a scene/speech into smaller parts and using edited scenes or plays. To be clear, we always use Shakespeare's text (rather than the "simplified" versions), and we want to offer accessibility to those words through appropriate support for students who are in the process of acquiring English.

- TRUTH #3: **ELs need to have space for their unique language and culture to live in our classrooms.** Students' funds of knowledge are an asset, not a deficit. They need to bring their selves and their whole native culture to Shakespeare. This truth echoes the Folger principle about the importance of student voice.

- TRUTH #4: **ELs need support with the specific aspects of the English language and how words function** (individually, in a sentence, and more). This helps them to build academic vocabulary, in written as well as oral language.

Continuing from Truth #4 and parts of the Folger Method, I introduce my students to what I call the "actor's arsenal"—a toolbox of 5 elements of communication that actors (and all of us) have at their disposal in English: stress, inflection, pause, nonverbal communication, and tone.

At its simplest, it looks like this, and my students appreciate this visual:

**STRESS:** Emphasis placed on a **WORD** (or word, or <sub>word</sub>)

**INFLECTION:** The way the voice goes <sup>up</sup> or <sub>down</sub> when a word is pronounced

**PAUSE:** A break . . . . . in reading for emphasis

**NONVERBAL COMMUNICATION:** Without words, the gestures, posture, presence or absence of eye contact

**TONE:** The *emotional* sound in your voice

These five tools deserve attention because *they are not the same in all languages.* In some languages, some of these tools are nonexistent or used in different ways than they are in English. I have a distinct memory of teaching a lesson on tone for the first time to a class of ELs. Generally, students really enjoy practicing a word/line with varying tones of voice. In this class, I couldn't help but notice one student who had a puzzled look on his face. I didn't want to embarrass him in his small group, so I sought guidance from the ESL teacher I was working with. She explained to me that tone did not work the same way in his native language as it did in English. In some languages—Hmong, for example—tone alone literally changes the meaning of a word, while in other languages—English, for one—tone accompanied by nonverbal communication alters the subtext of a word/phrase.

When working with students who have varying language backgrounds, additional attention to tone and nonverbal communication is very helpful. I typically introduce this "arsenal" as a part of our pre-reading. Tone and Stress, the first Folger Essential, includes visuals and practice rounds, and is recommended for all students beginning their journey with Shakespeare's language. Learn more about it in the Folger Method chapter. What I describe here can be an additional and introductory support for EL students.

I often begin this communication work by asking students to consider a universal teenage dilemma—having a disagreement with your parents or caregivers. (I have found, after working with students from all over the world, that this is one of the few situations that transcend language and culture for most adolescents.) I then ask them to brainstorm all the different ways they can "show" their displeasure with words or actions. The list they generate generally includes items like volume, eye rolling, silence, additional gestures, and tone of voice. I then introduce the concept of tone vocabulary and include visuals with each element to further support comprehension. We pay particular attention to tone, as the English language offers infinite options for impacting the meaning of a word or phrase with tone alone. We define tone as the emotional sound in your voice, and I offer a specific list of tones for students' reference: love, hate, anger, joy, fear, and sorrow. While certainly not comprehensive of all the tones available in English, these six seem to capture the fundamentals. Students always enjoy taking a phrase like "That's great!" and applying these tones in small groups. For students coming from language backgrounds where tone is not utilized in the same way as it is in English, this activity offers additional practice in and added awareness of how tone functions in English. Using the Folger Essential, students practice with the word "Oh!," saying it in a variety of tones (happy, sad, angry, surprised, and more). Students on their own will automatically add accompanying nonverbal communication, crossing their arms if the tone is angry, for example.

In addition, you can use a film clip of a scene from a Shakespeare play to further explore tone. (There is a wide variety of clips on sites like YouTube, or check out folger .edu.) Initially, I hand out to the students a copy of the scene, and I play the audio only. Students can work individually or in small groups. They listen to the audio, following along with the lines. As they listen, I instruct them to focus on one character and note any tone of voice they hear (anger, love, joy, and more). Next, we watch the scene video only, with no audio at all. They continue to track the same character and note any non-verbal communication. Finally, we watch the scene with audio and video, and add any additional notes on tone, stress, nonverbal communication, inflection, or pause. After this, students share their notes and findings either in a pair (if they have been working individually) or with another small group. Later, when we get up on our feet as a class, we are able to draw upon this kind of analysis to support our version of the play!

## Part Three: *Romeo and Juliet* with English Learners

*Romeo and Juliet, Romeo y Julieta, Romeu e Julieta,* روميو وجوليت . . . . Perhaps more than any of Shakespeare's plays, *Romeo and Juliet* has a transcendence that bridges many cultures. Even though the plot of the play is familiar to many students, we still need to support our ELs in accessing this text. You will find that these strategies are useful for all students but essential for ELs!

Considering Truth #4 (ELs need support with aspects of English) and connecting to the Folger Arc (word, line, speech, scene, play), I begin *Romeo and Juliet* at the word level. Specifically, I use a word cloud generator (there are several of these available online; just search the term to find a few options) to let students "see" the play at the level of the words. A word cloud generator takes a text that you cut and paste and creates a visual of the most frequent words (by making the words that are used the most appear larger in the cloud). There are two sample word clouds for the play included below.

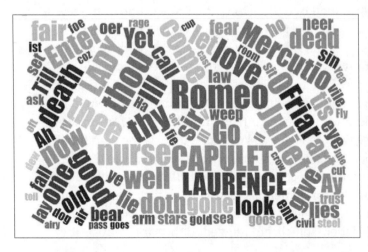

I arrange students in small groups and ask them to categorize the words from these clouds into the following groups: Characters, Nouns, Archaic Words (I explain that these are words we no longer use in modern English), Stage Directions/Locations, and Other. Below is a sample of the words from the clouds above placed into these categories.

| Characters | Nouns | Archaic (OLD) words | Stage directions/ Locations | Other |
|---|---|---|---|---|
| • Romeo | • Stars | • Doth | • Enter | • True love |
| • Mercutio | • Sea | • O'er | • Mantua | • II |
| • Juliet | • Death | • Coz | • Exeunt | • III |
| • Friar Lawrence | • Fear | • E'er | • Exit | • V |
| • Capulet | • Heaven | • Ye | | • IV |
| • Nurse | • Night | • Thy | | • Civil |
| • Benvolio | • Tears | • Oft | | • Woeful day |
| • Paris | • Kinsman | • Fie | | • Dead man |
| • Tybalt | • Peace | • Thee | | |
| • Servant | • Letter | • Thou wilt | | |
| • Prince | • Heart | • Morrow | | |
| | • Tomb | • Hath | | |
| | • Love | | | |
| | • Torch | | | |

Once the words are grouped, students can make predictions about the play. I have used starter sentences like, "Based on these words, this is a play about _____." Or "Something I predict will happen in this play is . . ." Students utilize the words to generate statements. I also use this as a formative assessment to see if there are students who have not read a play and need some support with text features of drama, such as stage directions, or acts and scenes. From the single word, we then move to the level of a line or lines of text to work with the element of tone.

Exploring the various tones of voice available in English connects to my Truth #4 (ELs need support with the intricacies of English). As I mentioned in Part One, tone— the emotional sound in your voice—is one of the tools in the actor's arsenal. Tone is not the same in all languages. To practice, I use the tone wheel (pictured on the next page) to give students the opportunity to try out different tones of voice using lines from the play. Since the Prologue gives students the plot in advance, I pull some famous lines from the play to experiment with. I begin by putting a line on the Smart Board. As a whole class, we then try that line out chorally using various tones. It's pretty entertaining to listen to a room full of teenagers read, "Do you bite your thumb at me, sir?" in tones of fear, and then love, and then apathy!

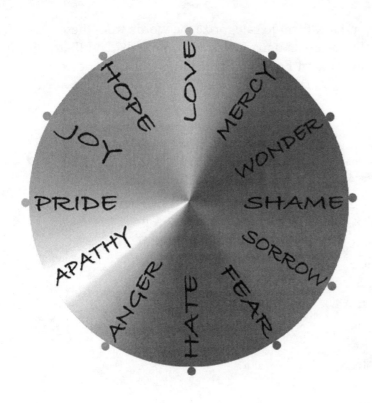

"My only love sprung from my only hate!
Too early seen unknown, and known too late!"
Juliet, 1.5.152–153

"Do you bite your thumb at us, sir?"
Abram, 1.1.45

"O, she doth teach the torches to burn bright!"
Romeo, 1.5.51

"O Romeo, Romeo, wherefore art thou Romeo?
Deny thy father and refuse thy name,
Or if thou wilt not, be but sworn my love,
And I'll no longer be a Capulet."
Juliet, 2.2.36–39

"A plague o' both your houses!"
Mercutio, 3.1.94

"O true apothecary,
Thy drugs are quick. Thus with a kiss I die."
Romeo, 5.3.119–120

Spending time working with tone on the individual line level is a good first step as students move toward taking on a scene as actors. Students feel more confident when they have had the opportunity to practice on the micro level before performing an entire scene!

Finally, Truth #3 (ELs need to have space for their unique language and culture to live in our classrooms) aligns perfectly with a play about forbidden teenage love. Regardless of their native language, culture, or country of origin, ALL adolescents have some level of experience with these intense feelings. Teaching a play on this topic when you are working with multicultural students offers them so many opportunities to share their beliefs on love and relationships.

I often open this play with a "four corners" activity, where I place four statements on topics connected to the play in the four corners of the classroom. Students move to the corner that best represents how they feel (see the next page for a few examples). Once they are in their corners, they have a conversation with their group about the statement. Next, we open the topic up to the whole class to discuss. This is a great way to use conversation skills in a small group and to hear the variety of beliefs around love, marriage, familial duty, rebellion, and more.

| |
|---|
| **TOPIC: Dating** |
| Corner 1: I make my own decisions about who I date. |
| Corner 2: I make my own decision about who I date, but I check in with my caregivers. |
| Corner 3: I don't share information about who I date with anyone. |
| Corner 4: I am not interested in dating right now. |
| **TOPIC: What My Friends Think** |
| Corner 1: I care what my friends think about the people I date. |
| Corner 2: I sort of care what my friends think about the people I date. |
| Corner 3: I don't really care what my friends think about the people I date. |
| Corner 4: If my friends did not approve of someone I was dating, I would stop talking to the person I was dating. |
| **TOPIC: Rules** |
| Corner 1: I break my caregivers' rules. |
| Corner 2: I break my caregivers' rules sometimes. |
| Corner 3: I don't break my caregivers' rules. |
| Corner 4: My caregivers do not really give me rules. |

I ask students to share with the class movies, stories, or folktales from their own culture that touch on the issues in the play; I also ask them to share their knowledge of any adaptations of the play in their language or culture. In our community, we have a large Brazilian population. One year, a student told me that we had to see parts of the 2005 Brazilian film *O Casamento de Romeu e Julieta* (*Romeo and Juliet Get Married*). In the movie, Romeu's and Julieta's families are fans of rival soccer clubs, and this is a source of the torture surrounding their love. Romeu must pretend to be a fan of her family's favorite team, a task that becomes more and more challenging. The film is hilarious, and we all had a wonderful time watching parts of it in class! Since many of our students are die-hard soccer fans, they could certainly understand the torture that could be caused by love of rival clubs!

I suggest these specific classroom ideas here because they have proven effective in supporting ELs in reading and performing *Romeo and Juliet*!

# Teaching Shakespeare—including *Romeo and Juliet*—to Students with Learning Differences

## Roni DiGenno

I am Roni DiGenno, a special education teacher with 10 years' experience teaching ninth- through twelfth-grade English in a District of Columbia public high school. My students' reading levels range from pre-primer to college level and their special education classifications include specific learning disabilities, ADHD, auditory disabilities, autism, as well as intellectual and emotional disabilities. I teach self-contained pull-out classes, each of about fifteen students, all with IEPs (Individualized Education Programs). Sometimes I have a teaching assistant, but most often I do not.

I love teaching. I love my students. And I love teaching Shakespeare to my students. I put to use what I have learned at the Folger; I use Shakespeare to inspire my students to believe in themselves. Most importantly, my students begin to see themselves as learners because I trust them with the hard stuff, the challenging content. I believe we can do it together, and my students know this. My passion for teaching these kids, who at times seem unreachable, comes from my own experience growing up with a reading difficulty. I could not sound out words, but this had nothing to do with my value or my intellect. My students, and all students, deserve the best, most engaging, intellectually stimulating lessons possible.

## Shakespeare Rewrites How Students See Themselves Learning

For the past several years, I have taught exclusively some of the most difficult students in my school—those with very large learning gaps, usually reading 5–8 years below grade level, and with emotional disturbances that make it difficult to build positive peer and adult relationships. They arrive in my classroom plagued with low expectations of themselves and of school, because for years other people have had low expectations of them. They are used to passing just by showing up and doing minimal work. Some have been through the criminal justice system, which adds another layer of low expectations. My first priority is to help my students see themselves as capable and val-

248

ued members of our classroom community. I do this by teaching lessons that empower them—lessons based on the Folger's philosophy. As a result, my students grow in exciting and surprising ways that no one could have anticipated.

I teach students like Armando, who had serious trust issues. He cut class frequently and was involved in groups that negatively influenced him in school. He repeated grades because he refused to do the work and he cursed teachers out regularly. In addition to being in and out of the criminal justice system, he was also a target of violent crime, which left him hospitalized for weeks and suffering from post-traumatic stress disorder. Through our class's collaborative work using Folger methods, Armando slowly began to discover and enjoy his strengths. He felt welcomed into the learning process and started to trust himself and others. He eventually became a peer leader who helped facilitate lessons.

I also taught Martin, a student who had such severe dyslexia that early on in my class he was reading at kindergarten level. He was withdrawn and shied away from participating for fear of judgment. Here again, by incorporating Folger principles and practices, I was able to give Martin the safe learning environment he needed and the confidence to try reading aloud. He learned to trust his peers and began to take risks—reading parts, participating, and giving amazing insight into discussion topics.

The Folger Method supports students like Armando and Martin, who have vastly different learning needs but who may also be in the same class. The teaching strategies offer students multiple entry points—tactical, visual, and aural—through which to engage and enjoy complex texts. Differentiation and scaffolding are built into the Folger's interactive lessons so students build a positive association with challenging texts. This is hugely important for students with learning differences and emotional difficulties. If content or concepts are overwhelming, or not taught in a way that they can grasp them, students will build a negative association. No one wants to struggle or feel like they can't learn something, which is often the root cause of behavior issues within classrooms. The Folger Method meets students' social and emotional learning needs through building a supportive and collaborative classroom community. Through the process, students begin to work through conflict, solve problems, and accept and support one another's learning differences.

## How the Folger Method Works for Students with IEPs

In the Folger Method chapter and in the *Romeo and Juliet* lessons in this book, you'll find the Folger Essentials that will throw your students right into the text through powerful practices like tossing words and phrases, two-line scenes, choral reading, and 3D Lit. Each Essential gives students exposure to the language and removes a barrier to learning and comprehension. Each builds on the others, increasing cognitive demand. Students master each step before moving to the next—words before lines, lines before scenes, choral reading before acting and reading parts solo. They don't feel left behind, because they learn the content and the skills simultaneously so that they understand more comprehensively.

Every year, my students look forward to our unit on Shakespeare. Typically about 10 weeks long, the unit allows us to slow down and dig into the text. Instead of skipping over difficult parts, we want to conquer them! It is important for us to embrace the struggle because it is an inevitable part of the learning process. In the Folger work, struggle is about joyful investigation and thinking hard together rather than a feeling of inadequacy. Students question, try out, and connect with the words and each other, and so they learn that there is no one right answer but rather a whole new way to discover a text. The Essentials get the language in the students' mouths, encourage collaboration, and shift focus away from the teacher so that students can practice navigating themselves through their learning. It's a different way of teaching and a different way of learning. At first, they are hesitant: They resist, they laugh, they feel weird, they are unsure, they can't believe they are talking this much in class—and I am encouraging all of it. Within a week or two, students are more willing to experiment and take risks with the language by reading really strange words they have never seen or heard before. And soon, students are reading Shakespeare and enjoying it.

Reading Shakespeare can be a great equalizer. While scholars and directors and actors never tire of decoding, interpreting, and defining Shakespeare, the truth is that no one knows exactly what Shakespeare really meant. He left no diary or notes. Everyone is entitled to their own interpretation. We also have no idea how the words were pronounced because we have no audio recordings of the performances in the Globe Theatre. The "funny" English (my students' term) in Shakespeare's works puts us all on the same playing field. Be vulnerable, mess up some words, and have fun! The students will ask, "How do you say this word?" and my only response is, "Not sure, let's figure it out." It's okay to do your best and sound "funny." We are all in this together and repeating that idea to students builds bridges.

The Folger Method gives students the scaffolding and tools needed to launch them from struggling readers to invested readers. Martin, my student with severe dyslexia and on a Beginning Reader level, struggled with sight words. As the rest of his class became more comfortable reading Shakespeare's words, he remained unsure. Could he read and understand Shakespeare? But he can't read! But he has a learning disability! But . . . nothing! Martin found his voice and his courage to try to read, and read he did. One day we were using the Folger Essential 3D Lit to explore a scene, and when his turn came to read, he chose not to pass. Previously, he'd always politely declined to read aloud, and the class and I obliged. On this day, though, he did not pass. Slowly, he began to read the words. Fumbling often, he kept reading, with the encouragement and support of his peers. They helped him sound out words when he didn't know how to start. He finished reading, and the room applauded him. Martin entered center stage that day because he had developed both belief in himself and trust in his peers. He wanted to join them and believed he could do it. Shakespeare is truly for everyone, and everyone is capable of "getting it." Martin "got it," not because he read the text flawlessly and was able to analyze the motifs in an essay. He got it because he was able to understand the text through a series of activities that led to his comprehension.

Shakespeare and other excellent complex texts are so important, especially for students who have IEPs, because they deserve an enriching learning experience with real, challenging content. Giving students access to appropriate, grade-level material is essential to meeting their IEP goals, regardless of the educational setting (resource, pullout, or inclusion). More than teaching Shakespeare, the Folger Method is also about instilling confidence in the students about the reality that they can do much of this work themselves. Even if it takes a while, even if they need a little help here and there— *they can do it.*

# My Students and *Romeo and Juliet*

## Connecting the Play to Their Own Lives

In general, multiple connections to any text build interest and improve comprehension. I have found that when my students connect elements of Shakespeare's plays to their own lives, they become more engaged in what they read and build stronger bonds to the text. In my classes, through the Folger approach, we have been building a safe, trusting community all along that makes it possible to explore these big ideas in the text.

*Romeo and Juliet* offers students any number of connections to their own lives. Here are a few, and ways in which you might use these in class:

**Fate/Personal Responsibility.** Romeo and Juliet, while considered "star-crossed lovers," are ultimately responsible for their own decisions in the play and toward their ultimate ending. Did Romeo have a choice in his actions, and could he have made other decisions along the way? Did Juliet have to follow through with the Friar's plan? These characters, and also Tybalt and Mercutio, continued to make decisions that led to their deaths. You can examine these decisions with students to analyze the cause and effect of each one made.

**Idea for class:** Create a flowchart or a thought tree for several characters to determine the different decisions each character could have made. For example, you can start with Romeo. 1. He made the decision to go to the ball—what other choices did he have? 2. He made the decision to jump over Juliet's wall to spy on her even after he learned who she was—what other choices did he have? 3. He made the decision to marry her knowing who she was and the consequences—again, what other choices did he have? By going through this process with Romeo, Juliet, Tybalt, and Friar Lawrence, students can see that each character had more choices and options for their lives and how their decisions impacted the story.

**Impulsivity and Immaturity.** Romeo and Juliet are teenaged characters, and that makes some wonder whether at their ages they would have had the ability to make responsible decisions for themselves. Some see Romeo as an impulsive character who acts out with immaturity and emotions that lead to poor decision-making and death. Some see Juliet's stubbornness and refusal to listen to others impacting her life choices as well. Were Romeo and Juliet equipped to make the consequential decisions they made? Even though these are characters and not real people, your students can look into the brain development of teenagers and consider how this knowledge might explain the behavior of these characters.

**Idea for class:** Introduce students to brain scans of children to young adults. Together, consider the differences in the brain scans. Then, together you can read an informational text about how the brain develops from childhood to young adulthood, especially the development of the prefrontal cortex (which operates executive functioning and judgment). Using this information, student groups can consider the decisions of Romeo or Juliet and if they were real people making real decisions, whether brain development might have had some influence on their falling quickly in love, jumping over walls, spying, lying to parents, keeping secrets, lashing out, or listening to others. Students should identify evidence from the text, explain what is happening, and then explain the relationship of this action to brain development.

## Focus on Key Scenes

The lessons in this book focus on key scenes and use the Folger Essentials to actively and immediately involve students. The choice of key scenes is up to you. Focus on whatever key scenes you'd like to, but I advise you to surely keep these juicy ones: the opening brawl (1.1); the party scene where Romeo and Juliet meet (1.5), the balcony scene (2.2), the pre-wedding scene (2.5), Tybalt's and Mercutio's deaths (3.1), the Friar's poisonous plan (4.1), and the tragic ending (5.3).

In working with key scenes, I pay attention to these important guidelines:

**Prioritize depth over breadth.** It is more important that students learn the skills to dig deep into a text, especially independently, than it is to read every line in the play. It may take your class of students with IEPs the same amount of time to analyze 4 key scenes as it takes your general education class to analyze 7. That's okay. Give your students the time they need to do this important work rather than rush through the text. The scripts we create and use in class are without footnotes or explanatory glosses. This allows students to decipher meaning on their own or collaboratively and removes distractions that impede their understanding.

**Keep the original language.** Always use Shakespeare's original language and not the modernized, made-easy versions. Do not substitute simplified language to make it easier. For one thing, it doesn't make it easier. More importantly, students with IEPs need to be given access to the original language and be able to make sense of it. And they can.

**Shorten the scenes if you need to.** You can cut key scenes to include just the most important information. Don't worry about cutting Shakespeare. For as long as Shakespeare has been performed, his plays have been cut by directors and editors. To guide you, ask yourself these questions: What do I want students to understand from this scene? In what part of the scene does that idea happen?

The cut version of *Romeo and Juliet* 2.2 below is about 40 lines; the original scene is 205 lines. You can find the full text here and folger.edu/romeo-and-juliet/read. Because the scene is brief, students can focus on meaning, setting, and characters on their own without getting lost. The cutting keeps the most important parts of the plot and character. Using Folger Shakespeare online makes finding and cutting scenes easy.

## ROMEO AND JULIET 2.2
### "Balcony Scene"

ROMEO

But soft, what light through yonder window breaks? It is the East, and Juliet is the sun.

JULIET

Ay me.

ROMEO

She speaks. O, speak again, bright angel!

JULIET

O Romeo, Romeo, wherefore art thou Romeo? Deny thy father and refuse thy name.

ROMEO

Shall I hear more, or shall I speak at this?

JULIET

What's in a name? That which we call a rose By any other word would smell as sweet.

ROMEO

I take thee at thy word. Call me but love, and I never will be Romeo.

JULIET

How camest thou hither, tell me, and wherefore?

ROMEO

With love's light wings did I o'erperch these walls, Therefore thy kinsmen are no stop to me.

JULIET

If they do see thee, they will murder thee.

ROMEO

I have night's cloak to hide me from their eyes, And, but thou love me, let them find me here.

JULIET

Dost thou love me?

ROMEO

Lady, by yonder blessèd moon I vow, That tips with silver all these fruit-tree tops—

JULIET

O, swear not by the moon.

ROMEO

What shall I swear by?

JULIET

Do not swear at all. Or, if thou wilt, swear by thy gracious self.

ROMEO

If my heart's dear love—

JULIET

Well, do not swear. Although I joy in thee,
I have no joy of this contract tonight. It is too rash, too unadvised, too sudden, Too like the lightning. Good night, good night.

ROMEO

O, wilt thou leave me so unsatisfied?

JULIET

What satisfaction canst thou have tonight?

ROMEO

Th' exchange of thy love's faithful vow for mine. Wouldst thou withdraw it? For what purpose, love?

JULIET

My bounty is as boundless as the sea, My love as deep. The more I give to thee, The more I have, for both are infinite.

ROMEO

O blessèd, blessèd night! I am afeard, Being in night, all this is but a dream, Too flattering sweet to be substantial.

JULIET

Three words, dear Romeo, and good night indeed. If that thy bent of love be honorable, Thy purpose marriage, send me word tomorrow,
Where and what time thou wilt perform the rite.

ROMEO

So thrive my soul—

JULIET

A thousand times good night.

ROMEO

A thousand times the worse to want thy light.

JULIET

Hist, Romeo, hist!
What o'clock tomorrow shall I send to thee?

ROMEO

By the hour of nine.

JULIET

I will not fail. 'Tis twenty year till then. I have forgot why I did call thee back.

ROMEO

Let me stand here till thou remember it.

JULIET

'Tis almost morning.
Good night, good night. Parting is such sweet sorrow.

## Annotate the Text

When I say "annotate," I mean make any notes about what is happening in the text; this practice helps students remember what is happening. Some may call this "marking the text"; it's all the same. Encourage students to take notes directly on the text during discussions because it leads them to analysis. **Make it purposeful.** Ensure that each time students annotate, they relate the underlined parts of the text to what is happening in the discussion. The annotations can be used for writing assignments.

**Show them what an annotated scene or speech looks like and how it's useful.** Model for students by annotating and thinking aloud with them. You can do this by using a projector or Smart Board, or by distributing copies of your own annotations. The example on the next page is a student's annotation of a cut version of Act 1, Scene 1 that we used in class.

*Romeo and Juliet*, 1.1

*A public place*

*Capulet*

*sword*

**GREGORY**

Draw thy tool! here comes two of the house of the Montagues.

**SAMPSON**

My naked weapon is out: quarrel, I will back thee.

**GREGORY**

How! turn thy back and run?

**SAMPSON**

*Montague*

I will bite my thumb at them;

which is a disgrace to them, if they bear it. — *an insult*

*Sampson bit his thumb @ abraham.*

**ABRAHAM**

Do you bite your thumb at us, sir?

**SAMPSON**

I do bite my thumb, sir.

**ABRAHAM**

Do you bite your thumb at us, sir?

**GREGORY**

Do you quarrel, sir?

**ABRAHAM**

Quarrel sir! no, sir.

**SAMPSON**

If you do, sir, I am for you: I serve as good a man as you. ← *insult again.*

**ABRAHAM**

No better.

**SAMPSON**

Well, sir.

**GREGORY**

Say 'better:' here comes one of my master's kinsmen. *(to Sampson)*

**SAMPSON**

Yes, better, sir.

**ABRAHAM**

You lie.

**SAMPSON**

*← to Abraham*

Draw, if you be men. Gregory, remember thy swashing blow. ← *to Gregory*

*Montague*

**BENVOLIO**

Part, fools! ——————— *STOP!*

Put up your swords; you know not what you do.

*Capulet*

**TYBALT**

What, art thou drawn among these heartless hinds?

Turn thee, Benvolio, look upon thy death.

*Why does he want to kill Benvolio? He's angry!*

**BENVOLIO**

I do but keep the peace: put up thy sword,

Or manage it to part these men with me.

**TYBALT**

What, drawn, and talk of peace! I hate the word,

As I hate hell, all Montagues, and thee:

Have at thee, coward!

*[handwritten: wants to keep peace]*

*[handwritten: fighting happens!]*

**FIRST CITIZEN**

Clubs, bills, and partisans! strike! beat them down!

Down with the Capulets! down with the Montagues!

**CAPULET**

What noise is this? Give me my long sword, ho!

**LADY CAPULET**

A crutch, a crutch! why call you for a sword?

*[handwritten: On one side]*

*[handwritten: He's too old to fight]*

**CAPULET**

My sword, I say! Old Montague is come,

And flourishes his blade in spite of me.

**MONTAGUE**

Thou villain Capulet,—Hold me not, let me go.

**LADY MONTAGUE**

Thou shalt not stir a foot to seek a foe.

*[handwritten: On other side]*

**PRINCE**

Rebellious subjects, enemies to peace,

What, ho! you men, you beasts,

That quench the fire of your pernicious rage

With purple fountains issuing from your veins,

On pain of torture, from those bloody hands

Throw your mistemper'd weapons to the ground,

Once more, on pain of death, all men depart.

*[handwritten: → The Prince is angry the families are fighting and destroying the city.]*

## Spread the Shakespeare Love

You and your students are on a Shakespeare journey together. As with everything you teach, the energy you give is the energy you get back. The more you LOVE teaching Shakespeare, the more your students will love it too. Keep in mind that it may take time, so fake it until you make it. When I started using the Folger Method, my students thought I was way too excited about Shakespeare. Over time, the energy is contagious, and they are just as excited to learn as I am to teach. Shakespeare has always been my favorite unit because it demonstrates that powerful literature belongs to them, and my students look forward to it because it is fun. From calling each other "greasy onion-eyed nut-hook" and "rank rump-fed giglet" to fake swordplay with foam weapons, and adding "thee" and "thou" to those words, I can see through their actions that they have fallen for Shakespeare as well.

Starting this journey with your students isn't always easy, but it is worth it. You are expecting more from them and teaching them more. Believe they can do the work and they will start to believe in themselves. Forgive yourself if a day does not work out. We are all works in progress, and it may take some tweaking to find out what extra things your students may need. Teaching Shakespeare or any other complex text using the Folger Method may be an adjustment to the way you teach now, so the more you do it, the better you will get at it. Students will become the drivers of the classroom, so get yourself ready for the show.

So, to my students who pop in to ask, "Hey Ms. DiGenno, you still doing that Shakespeare thing?" "Yes, I am, and so are you," I always say back as they rush out of the class again. Usually their last word: "Cool!"

# Pairing Texts: *Romeo and Juliet* Off the Pedestal and in Conversation with Other Voices

Donna Denizé

Something wildly important happens when we teach two very different works or authors together—like *Macbeth* and writings of Frederick Douglass; *Hamlet* and something by Claudia Rankine; *Othello* and the poetry of George Moses Horton, or *The Taming of the Shrew* and the poems of Audre Lorde.

*Paired texts* are two texts that you and your students dive into at the same time. Both texts have equal weight; each is strong and can stand fully on its own. You can pair whole works or segments of works, selected narratives, scenes, or stanzas. But there is no "primary" and "secondary" or "supplemental" hierarchy—ever. Two voices, two points of view, two writing styles, two characters, and each will illuminate the other.

It's important to note here, since we are in the world of Shakespeare, that a Shakespeare play and an adaptation of a Shakespeare play or plot are *not* paired texts. That's a primary text and most often some kind of supplemental one. Together, they don't have the power or the payoff of a set of paired texts.

Why pair texts? Because, taken together, they illuminate each other in powerful and surprising ways. Looking closely at paired works gives kids a sense of the sweep of literature and allows them to consider together two authors who wrote in vastly different times, places, cultures, genders, races, religions—you name it. These juxtapositions allow them to notice that in many cases, writers have been asking the same big questions for some time: about human identity—how we define ourselves through culture, our moral choices, how we navigate power or powerlessness, and more. In other instances, they are on very different wavelengths and . . . what might be the reasons for that?

I developed my love for paired texts in my thirty-eight years teaching in a variety of secondary school settings—public, private, urban, and rural—and in serving a term on the advisory board for all vocational schools in the state of Virginia. I currently teach at St. Albans School for Boys in Washington, DC, where I chair the English department. I love working with paired texts because two strong texts working together produce something marvelous in class: They create a space for meaningful conversations that come from students' experiences and questions, and this creates not just good analysis but empathy. Since students today must navigate an incredibly complex global society, they can only benefit by considering a sweep of literature that helps them deepen their empathy for others.

I've found that the more specific or particular the pairing, the better, since this inspires students' creativity and establishes new ways of thinking about both texts. It also strengthens students' analytical skills and increases their capacity for understanding complexity—qualities that are essential for navigating current human challenges and the promise of an ever-evolving world—and the worlds students inhabit.

The following section is designed in two parts: the first gives you two examples so that you can get a fuller sense of how paired texts work in general, and the second includes recommendations of pairings that in my experience work well with *Romeo and Juliet*.

# Part One: Two Examples of Paired Texts and How They Have Worked in Class

**1.** Pairing **Macbeth's "If it were done" soliloquy** (1.7.1–28; Macbeth weighs plans to murder King Duncan) with a passage from **Frederick Douglass's *Narrative of the Life of Frederick Douglass: An American Slave*** in which Douglass sits on a hillside watching freely moving passing ships while his movement is confined by slavery, its laws, and its customs.

| *Macbeth 1.7.1–28*<br>**by William Shakespeare** | *Narrative of the Life of Frederick Douglass*<br>**by Frederick Douglass** |
|---|---|
| MACBETH<br><br>If it were done when 'tis done, then 'twere well<br>It were done quickly. If th' assassination<br>Could trammel up the consequence and catch<br>With his surcease success, that but this blow<br>Might be the be-all and the end-all here,<br>But here, upon this bank and shoal of time,<br>We'd jump the life to come. But in these cases<br>We still have judgment here, that we but teach<br>Bloody instructions, which, being taught, return<br>To plague th' inventor. This even-handed justice<br>Commends th' ingredience of our poisoned chalice<br>To our own lips. He's here in double trust:<br>First, as I am his kinsman and his subject,<br>Strong both against the deed; then, as his host,<br>Who should against his murderer shut the door,<br>Not bear the knife myself. Besides, this Duncan<br>Hath borne his faculties so meek, hath been<br>So clear in his great office, that his virtues<br>Will plead like angels, trumpet-tongued, against<br>The deep damnation of his taking-off; | Our house stood within a few rods of the Chesapeake Bay, whose broad bosom was ever white with sails from every quarter of the habitable globe. Those beautiful vessels, robed in purest white, so delightful to the eye of freemen, were to me so many shrouded ghosts, to terrify and torment me with thoughts of my wretched condition. I have often, in the deep stillness of a summer's Sabbath, stood all alone upon the lofty banks of that noble bay, and traced, with saddened heart and tearful eye, the countless number of sails moving off to the mighty ocean. The sight of these always affected me powerfully. My thoughts would compel utterance; and there, with no audience but the Almighty, I would pour out my soul's complaint, in my rude way, with an apostrophe to the moving multitude of ships:—<br><br>"You are loosed from your moorings, and are free; I am fast in my chains, and am a slave! You move merrily before the gentle gale, and I |

And pity, like a naked newborn babe
Striding the blast, or heaven's cherubin horsed
Upon the sightless couriers of the air,
Shall blow the horrid deed in every eye,
That tears shall drown the wind. I have no spur
To prick the sides of my intent, but only
Vaulting ambition, which o'erleaps itself
And falls on th' other—

sadly before the bloody whip! You are freedom's swift-winged angels, that fly round the world; I am confined in bands of iron! O that I were free! O, that I were on one of your gallant decks, and under your protecting wing! Alas! betwixt me and you, the turbid waters roll. Go on, go on. O that I could also go! Could I but swim! If I could fly! O, why was I born a man, of whom to make a brute. The glad ship is gone; she hides in the dim distance. I am left in the hottest hell of unending slavery. O God, save me! God, deliver me! Let me be free! Is there any God? Why am I a slave? I will run away. I will not stand it. Get caught, or get clear, I'll try it. I had as well die with ague as the fever. I have only one life to lose. I had as well be killed running as die standing. Only think of it; one hundred miles straight north, and I am free! Try it? Yes! God helping me, I will. It cannot be that I shall live and die a slave. I will take to the water. This very bay shall yet bear me into freedom. The steamboats steered in a north-east course from North Point. I will do the same; and when I get to the head of the bay, I will turn my canoe adrift, and walk straight through Delaware into Pennsylvania. When I get there, I shall not be required to have a pass; I can travel without being disturbed. Let but the first opportunity offer, and, come what will, I am off. Meanwhile, I will try to bear up under the yoke. I am not the only slave in the world. Why should I fret? I can bear as much as any of them. Besides, I am but a boy, and all boys are bound to some one. It may be that my misery in slavery will only increase my happiness when I get free. There is a better day coming."

Thus I used to think, and thus I used to speak to myself; goaded almost to madness at one moment, and at the next reconciling myself to my wretched lot.

In class, we started with a definition of *ambition*: kids looked it up in various dictionaries. They came up with definitions like these:

- an earnest desire for some type of achievement or distinction, as power, honor, fame, or wealth, and the willingness to strive for its attainment

- the object, state, or result desired or sought after

- to seek after earnestly

- aspire to

I asked a few simple questions to start them off:

1. What is the ambition of each man? What's it driving him toward? What is he seeking?

2. What are they both wrestling against and with—morally and socially?

3. What solutions, if any, does each one reach?

A discussion developed that connected the word *ambition* with some of the other topics that they found in both texts: isolation; self-perception; moral dilemmas; questions about freedom and justice. My students came up with valuable comparisons and contrasts that I list here in no particular order:

- Both are wrestling in the mind, the imagination alive, the struggle with consequences, moral right and wrong.

- In *Macbeth*, the moral wrong is in the individual; in the Douglass story, the moral wrong is in the larger society.

- Both bring isolation, pain, and suffering; Macbeth's isolation leads to his destruction; Douglass's isolation leads him to being an orator and a major voice in the cause for the abolition of slavery.

- Macbeth's ambition has a negative outcome while Douglass's has a positive outcome.

- Both search for justice—Macbeth to avoid it and Douglass to have justice manifest.

- Macbeth has social and political power, while Douglass—a slave—is marginalized, without social and political power.

- Both are seeking freedom. Macbeth imagines freedom from consequences. Douglass imagines the consequences of freedom.

These two texts—Shakespeare's *Macbeth* and Frederick Douglass's *Narrative of the Life of Frederick Douglass: An American Slave*—are separated by time, space, culture, and geopolitics—and yet my students made wonderful connections between both texts, identifying isolation, self-perception, and moral dilemmas. They also asked big questions about freedom and justice, the function of human imagination, and ambition.

**2.** Pairing **Iago's speech in *Othello*** (3.3.367–382, he plots to use Desdemona's handkerchief to stoke Othello's jealousy) with **"Troubled with the Itch and Rubbing with Sulphur," a poem by George Moses Horton,** a contemporary of Frederick Douglass. This is a more unusual pairing, and one that is focused on language.

A note here on George Moses Horton (ca.1798–ca.1883): He was a slave in North Carolina who taught himself to read with the help of spelling books, a Bible, and a book of hymns. His master soon realized that there was money to be made sending Horton on errands to deliver produce to students and staff at the University of North Carolina in Chapel Hill. That is where Horton became a little like a celebrity; students befriended him because he created love poems that enabled them to get dates. Since Horton could not yet write, the students would write the poems down as he dictated them; they paid him in either money or books. In this way he acquired a complete works of Shakespeare, a collection of works by Lord Byron, Samuel Johnson's *Dictionary*, Homer's *Iliad*, and many more. Once paid, Horton tried to save enough to purchase his freedom, but his attempt was unsuccessful. Horton lived long enough to see the end of slavery, though, so he was freed eventually. After his first book, *Poems by a Slave* (1837), newspapers began calling him "the colored bard of Chapel Hill." In 1997, Horton was named Historic Poet Laureate of Chatham County, North Carolina.

| *Othello (3.3.367–382)* by William Shakespeare | "*Troubled with the Itch and Rubbing with Sulphur*" by George Moses Horton |
|---|---|
| IAGO<br><br>Be not acknown on 't<br>I have use for it. Go, leave me.<br>   *Emilia exits.*<br>I will in Cassio's lodging lose this napkin<br>And let him find it. Trifles light as air<br>Are to the jealous confirmations strong<br>As proofs of holy writ. This may do something.<br>The Moor already changes with my poison;<br>Dangerous conceits are in their natures poisons,<br>Which at the first are scarce found to distaste,<br>But with a little act upon the blood<br>Burn like the mines of sulfur.<br>   *Enter Othello.*<br>I did say so.<br>Look where he comes. Not poppy nor mandragora<br>Nor all the drowsy syrups of the world<br>Shall ever medicine thee to that sweet sleep<br>Which thou owedst yesterday. | 'Tis bitter, yet 'tis sweet;<br>   Scratching effects but transient ease;<br>Pleasure and pain together meet<br>   And vanish as they please.<br><br>My nails, the only balm,<br>   To every bump are oft applied,<br>And thus the rage will sweetly calm<br>   Which aggravates my hide.<br><br>It soon returns again:<br>   A frown succeeds to every smile;<br>Grinning I scratch and curse the pain<br>   But grieve to be so vile.<br><br>In fine, I know not which<br>   Can play the most deceitful game:<br>The devil, sulphur, or the itch.<br>   The three are but the same.<br><br>The devil sows the itch,<br>   And sulphur has a loathsome smell,<br>And with my clothes as black as pitch<br>   I stink where'er I dwell.<br><br>Excoriated deep,<br>   By friction played on every part,<br>It oft deprives me of my sleep<br>   And plagues me to my heart. |

In class, we read both pieces aloud first, and then I asked students to look up the word *sulfur* and its purposes. From various online sources, both medical and agricultural, they learn that, at least in the Delta, sulfur is an important substance in yielding maximum cotton crops. Yet, applied to the skin, sulfur can both cause pain *and* provide relief from itching and burning and rashes, even though as Horton points out, it stinks.

Then, I asked students to make as many connections between the two texts as possible. Where does sulfur come in? What does sulfur do?

- Sulfur can heal or burn or both.

- In both texts, it seems like the thing which is meant to heal and at first brings relief (sulfur) is also the thing which brings the pain again.

I had to do little to keep the discussion going. My students had this to say about Horton:

- Even if he's free, which means he can make his own choices and his own money, Horton is still not a citizen, not part of society, and the self is torn between two worlds—as an established reader and writer in a world that denies Blacks literacy and education.

- Horton has no way to vote or own property. In fact, he's part of a larger society where slavery exists and the laws, as well as the social practices, deny his equality with white citizens.

- For the whites, Horton's existence is problematic: he's supposed to be inferior intellectually and morally, but he has demonstrated the opposite, and it's difficult to reconcile the contradiction he creates through the racial lens. These create irrational moral dilemmas. Othello, on the other hand, is looking to solve a moral dilemma, seeking a way out of his suffering, and believing Iago is the one to heal his fears and insecurity about Desdemona's infidelity. Students saw pretty quickly that Othello thinks that Iago will bring freedom from these worries, but in reality, Iago is the cause—the sulfur that burns, and not the healing balm.

In both cases, my students have seen clearly the corrosive effects of prejudice, of racism; so with matters of prejudice, whether it's class, gender, race, or religion, there are no quick solutions, no easy balms to apply. Moreover, if we do not see the "other," we cannot see the self and cannot understand the self.

## Part Two: Pairing Various Texts with *Romeo and Juliet*

**1.** Pairing Capulet's **"God's bread, it makes me mad/Day, night, hour, tide, time, work, play"** (3.5.154–207; Capulet rages at Juliet for refusing to marry Paris) with Troy's speech, **"First you gonna get your butt down there to the A&P and get your job back,"** in August Wilson's play *Fences* (Troy rages against his son, Cory, for refusing to quit the high school football team to work at a grocery store).

As a preview, I begin by asking my students to look at Capulet's attitude about Juliet's marriage after Tybalt is killed by Romeo, and what happens after that. When Capulet insists that her marriage occur within three days (3.4.1–24), Juliet refuses her father's wish. Capulet, now enraged, asserts absolute parental authority over his daughter (3.5.154–207).

CAPULET

> How, how, how, how? Chopped logic? What is this?
> "Proud," and "I thank you," and "I thank you not,"                    155
> And yet "not proud"? Mistress minion you,
> Thank me no thankings, nor proud me no prouds,
> But fettle your fine joints 'gainst Thursday next
> To go with Paris to Saint Peter's Church,
> Or I will drag thee on a hurdle thither.                              160
> Out, you green-sickness carrion! Out, you baggage!
> You tallow face!

LADY CAPULET

> Fie, fie, what, are you mad?

JULIET, *kneeling*

> Good father, I beseech you on my knees,
> Hear me with patience but to speak a word.                            165

CAPULET

> Hang thee, young baggage, disobedient wretch!
> I tell thee what: get thee to church o' Thursday,
> Or never after look me in the face.
> Speak not; reply not; do not answer me.
> My fingers itch.—Wife, we scarce thought us blessed                   170
> That God had lent us but this only child,
> But now I see this one is one too much,
> And that we have a curse in having her.
> Out on her, hilding . . .                                             175

LADY CAPULET

> You are too hot.

CAPULET

> God's bread, it makes me mad.
> Day, night, hour, tide, time, work, play,
> Alone, in company, still my care hath been
> To have her matched. And having now provided                         190
> A gentleman of noble parentage,
> Of fair demesnes, youthful, and nobly ligned,
> Stuffed, as they say, with honorable parts,
> Proportioned as one's thought would wish a man—
> And then to have a wretched puling fool,                             195
> A whining mammet, in her fortune's tender,
> To answer "I'll not wed. I cannot love.
> I am too young. I pray you, pardon me."
> But, an you will not wed, I'll pardon you!

Graze where you will, you shall not house with me.                    200
Look to 't; think on 't. I do not use to jest.
Thursday is near. Lay hand on heart; advise.
An you be mine, I'll give you to my friend.
An you be not, hang, beg, starve, die in the streets,
For, by my soul, I'll ne'er acknowledge thee,                          205
Nor what is mine shall never do thee good.
Trust to 't; bethink you. I'll not be forsworn.

I asked my students for their thoughts about the cause for Capulet's attitude, and they responded with:

- Juliet is flouting her father's authority in having made her a suitable match, and

- It's about her father's ego and family pride.

We hang on to that and move to our next text: two scenes from August Wilson's *Fences*. The first scene is *Fences* 1.1:

ROSE: Cory done went and got recruited by a college football team.

TROY: I told that boy about that football stuff. The white man ain't gonna let him get nowhere with that football. I told him when he first come to me with it. Now you come telling me he done went and got more tied up in it. He ought to go and get recruited in how to fix cars or something where he can make a living.

ROSE: He ain't talking about making no living playing football. It's just something the boys in school do. They gonna send a recruiter by to talk to you. He'll tell you he ain't talking about making no living playing football. It's a honor to be recruited.

TROY: It ain't gonna get him nowhere. Bono'll tell you that.

BONO: If he be like you in the sports . . . he's gonna be alright. Ain't but two men ever played baseball as good as you. That's Babe Ruth and Josh Gibson. Them's the only two men ever hit more home runs than you.

TROY: What it ever get me? Ain't got a pot to piss in or a window to throw it out of.

ROSE: Times have changed since you was playing baseball, Troy. That was before the War. Times have changed a lot since then.

TROY: How in hell they done changed?

ROSE: They got lots of colored boys playing ball now. Baseball and football.

BONO:  You right about that, Rose. Times have changed, Troy. You just come along too early.

TROY:  There ought not never have been no time called too early! Now you take that fellow . . . what's that fellow they had playing right field for the Yankees back then? You know who I'm talking about, Bono. Used to play right field for the Yankees.

ROSE:  Selkirk?

TROY:  Selkirk! That's it! Man batting .269, understand? .269. What kind of sense that make? I was hitting .432 with thirty-seven home runs! Man batting .269 and playing right field for the Yankees! I saw Josh Gibson's daughter yesterday. She walking around with raggedy shoes on her feet. Now I bet you Selkirk's daughter ain't walking around with raggedy shoes on her feet! I bet you that!

ROSE:  They got a lot of colored baseball players now. Jackie Robinson was the first. Folks had to wait for Jackie Robinson.

TROY:  I done seen a hundred niggers play baseball better than Jackie Robinson. Hell, I know some teams Jackie Robinson couldn't even make! What you talking about Jackie Robinson. Jackie Robinson wasn't nobody. I'm talking about if you could play ball then they ought to have let you play. Don't care what color you were. Come telling me I come along too early. If you could play . . . then they ought to have let you play. (TROY takes a long drink from the bottle.)

I asked my students about reasons why Troy would have lost faith in social progress regarding race relations.

- They talked together about the larger society's overall disregard for African Americans in the 1930 to 1950s and provided examples.
- The disregard of professional sports—all run by white people—for Troy's athletic talents.

We then move to the scene between Troy and Cory about playing football:
*Fences* 1.3.

TROY:  First you gonna get your butt down there to the A&P and get your job back.

CORY:  Mr. Stawicki done already hired somebody else 'cause I told him I was playing football.

TROY:  You a bigger fool than I thought . . . to let somebody take away your job so you can play some football. Where you gonna get your money to take out your girlfriend and whatnot? What kind of foolishness is that to let somebody take away your job?

CORY: I'm still gonna be working weekends.

TROY: Naw . . . naw. You getting your butt out of here and finding you another job.

CORY: Come on, Pop! I got to practice. I can't work after school and play football too. The team needs me. That's what Coach Zellman say . . .

TROY: I don't care what nobody else say. I'm the boss . . . you understand? I'm the boss around here. I do the only saying what counts.

CORY: Come on, Pop!

TROY: I asked you . . . did you understand?

CORY: Yeah . . .

TROY: What?!

CORY: Yessir.

TROY: You go on down there to that A&P and see if you can get your job back. If you can't do both . . . then you quit the football team. You've got to take the crookeds with the straights.

CORY: Yessir. (*Pause.*) Can I ask you a question?

TROY: What the hell you wanna ask me? Mr. Stawicki the one you got the questions for.

CORY: How come you ain't never liked me?

TROY: Liked you? Who the hell say I got to like you? What law is there say I got to like you? Wanna stand up in my face and ask a damn fool-ass question like that. Talking about liking somebody. Come here, boy, when I talk to you. (*CORY comes over to where TROY is working. He stands slouched over and TROY shoves him on his shoulder.*) Straighten up, goddammit! I asked you a question . . . what law is there say I got to like you?

CORY: None.

TROY: Well, alright then! Don't you eat every day? (*Pause.*) Answer me when I talk to you! Don't you eat every day?

CORY: Yeah.

TROY: . . . as long as you in my house, you put that sir on the end of it when you talk to me!

CORY: Yes . . . sir.

TROY: You eat every day.

CORY: Yessir!

TROY: Got a roof over your head.

CORY: Yessir!

TROY: Got clothes on your back.

CORY: Yessir.

TROY: Why you think that is?

CORY: Cause of you.

TROY: Aw, hell I know it's 'cause of me . . . but why do you think that is?

CORY: (*Hesitant.*) Cause you like me.

TROY: Like you? I go out of here every morning . . . bust my butt . . . putting up with them crackers every day . . . cause I like you? You about the biggest fool I ever saw. (*Pause.*) It's my job. It's my responsibility! You understand that? A man got to take care of his family. You live in my house . . . sleep you behind on my bed-clothes . . . fill you belly up with my food . . . cause you my son. You my flesh and blood. Not 'cause I like you! Cause it's my duty to take care of you. I owe a responsibility to you! Let's get this straight right here . . . before it go along any further . . . I ain't got to like you. Mr. Rand don't give me my money come payday cause he likes me. He gives me cause he owe me. I done give you everything I had to give you. I gave you your life! Me and your mama worked that out between us. And liking your black ass wasn't part of the bargain. Don't you try and go through life worrying about if somebody like you or not. You best be making sure they doing right by you. You understand what I'm saying, boy?

CORY: Yessir.

TROY: Then get the hell out of my face, and get on down to that A&P.

After working through all three of these pieces, I start by asking my students a few opening questions:

What similarities exist here? They had these things to say:

- The youth in these plays (Romeo, Juliet, and Cory) speak from the heart, are passionate and optimistic about their futures.

- They seem to want to push for change.

- Juliet and Romeo are both willing to marry, despite both families' hatred for each other. And Cory is eager to seize on new possibilities of equality for Blacks through integration.

I then asked my students to get online or get into some dictionaries in class and look up the definition of *justice*.

- They came up with various definitions and discussed them. Ultimately, they settled on this one-word definition: "fairness."

- With "fairness" as the definition in mind, my students got to the fact that both Juliet and Cory suffer from injustice—both within their families and within society—and these biases and prejudices are harmful to everyone's progress.

- They identified some signs of partial social progress (Jackie Robinson breaking the color line in professional baseball in 1947, for example).

- But they also noted that laws of racial segregation were still affecting them, so the larger society hadn't made significant progress in terms of racial equality.

- Students also spoke about how in both texts, hatred and prejudice cause the youth to suffer, and that Juliet and Romeo, along with Tybalt and Mercutio, pay the ultimate price. As a result, "all are punished."

Then we take a look at these two fictional fathers—one created by a white author in 1595 or so and the other by a Black author 390 years later, in 1985.

How are they alike and not alike? They started with the similarities—in a lively conversation!

- Both Capulet and Troy are really concerned about their children's future financial security.

- It seems important to them not to challenge the established social order, and to be accepted socially.

- Both fathers speak from the heart, believing they are fulfilling their parental responsibility.

- Both fathers reject their child's desire for freedom in making a life choice.

- Both are very angry and use demeaning words to describe their children. They also refuse to listen to the children's point of view.

- Both fathers see their authority as absolute. They threaten to throw Juliet and Cory out of the house if they don't comply with their wishes.

- Past losses seem to influence both of these fathers: Capulet says that his losses have left him with nothing but Juliet, and he needs to provide for her. Troy never made it to the big leagues in baseball, and wants Cory to have a more successful life.

When I asked my students to identify how these fathers were different, they clearly saw them as being more alike than different, but spoke about these things:

- In a speech in an earlier scene, Capulet speaks with Paris, who asks him for Juliet's hand in marriage. Capulet insists that Paris abide by Juliet's choice in marriage.

He later changes his mind. Troy, however, is consistent. He is always against his son's desire to play sports—in high school or beyond—because of segregation and discrimination against African Americans living and competing in the same arenas as whites.

- They saw the worlds of *Romeo and Juliet* and *Fences* as different. In *Romeo and Juliet*, the law—the Prince—tries to right the wrong of feuding, of hatred breaking societal peace and bonds of love and friendship. He fails, though. In *Fences*, the laws of segregation make sure that racial injustice continues, and the laws are harmful across all human connections—in families, among friends, and among lovers too.

**2.** Pairing **Friar Lawrence's speech, "Holy St. Francis, what a change is here!"** (2.3.69–99)—Friar Lawrence moves from chiding Romeo for losing interest in Rosaline and quickly turning his affections to Juliet to his plan to marry Romeo and Juliet quickly in the hopes of bringing the warring Capulets and Montagues together—**with Danusha Laméris's poem** *Insha'Allah*. An Arabic phrase, *Insha'Allah* translates to "if God wills it" in English. Poet Danusha Laméris was born in Massachusetts and raised in California. She wrote "Insha'Allah" in 2014, and won the Lucille Clifton Legacy Award in 2020. We start with *Romeo and Juliet* (2.3.69–99):

---

FRIAR LAWRENCE
 Holy Saint Francis, what a change is here!
 Is Rosaline, that thou didst love so dear,   70
 So soon forsaken? Young men's love then lies
 Not truly in their hearts, but in their eyes.
 Jesu Maria, what a deal of brine
 Hath washed thy sallow cheeks for Rosaline!
 How much salt water thrown away in waste   75
 To season love, that of it doth not taste!
 The sun not yet thy sighs from heaven clears,
 Thy old groans yet ringing in mine ancient ears.
 Lo, here upon thy cheek the stain doth sit
 Of an old tear that is not washed off yet.   80
 If e'er thou wast thyself, and these woes thine,
 Thou and these woes were all for Rosaline.
 And art thou changed? Pronounce this sentence
  then:
 Women may fall when there's no strength in men.   85

ROMEO
 Thou chid'st me oft for loving Rosaline.

FRIAR LAWRENCE
 For doting, not for loving, pupil mine.

---

**ROMEO**

And bad'st me bury love.

**FRIAR LAWRENCE**  Not in a grave

To lay one in, another out to have.                                                    90

**ROMEO**

I pray thee, chide me not. Her I love now

Doth grace for grace and love for love allow.

The other did not so.

**FRIAR LAWRENCE**  O, she knew well

Thy love did read by rote, that could not spell.                           95

But come, young waverer, come, go with me.

In one respect I'll thy assistant be,

For this alliance may so happy prove

To turn your households' rancor to pure love.

To examine Friar Lawrence's words and actions throughout the play, I provide my students with a bit of context:

- As a priest and a man of the cloth, Friar Lawrence would definitely affirm his belief in God's grace—an undeserved kindness from Him. And since God's grace is mysterious, all that humans can do is prayerfully and patiently rely on God's inscrutable power.

I then asked my students:

- In this speech, what is revealed about the society and/or Friar Lawrence?

We move on to take a look at the poem "Insha'Allah" by Danusha Laméris:

## INSHA'ALLAH
### by Danusha Laméris

I don't know when it slipped into my speech
that soft word meaning, "if God wills it."
Insha'Allah I will see you next summer.
The baby will come in spring, insha'Allah.
Insha'Allah this year we will have enough rain.

So many plans I've laid have unraveled
easily as braids beneath my mother's quick fingers.

Every language must have a word for this. A word
our grandmothers uttered under their breath

as they pinned the whites, soaked in lemon,
hung them to dry in the sun, or peeled potatoes,
dropping the discarded skins into a bowl.

*Our sons will return next month, insha'Allah.*
*Insha'Allah this war will end, soon. Insha'Allah*
*the rice will be enough to last through winter.*

How lightly we learn to hold hope,
as if it were an animal that could turn around
and bite your hand. And still we carry it
the way a mother would, carefully,
from one day to the next.

I asked them to do some digging online and in dictionaries in class and come up with a definition of *hope*. One that most agreed with was "to expect the best in unlikely circumstances."

Look for the hope in both of these texts. When you think about comparing or contrasting hope in both works—Laméris's poem and *Romeo and Juliet*—what does the language reveal?

Their responses were very thoughtful:

- Both refer to a divine power at work in the world, a power greater than humans and at the center of all affairs.

- In *Romeo and Juliet*, material power, politics, and Juliet's father add up to real rigidity . . . and the absence of hope.

- At the same time, though, Friar Lawrence hopes that a marriage between Romeo and Juliet might bring about good and peace in the world, even though this hope is limited by larger social and political conditions.

- In the poem "Insha'Allah," the speaker hopes that Allah will enact the good in the world, this good which is to be acknowledged/praised by humans.

- Politics and religion should remain separate.

- Friar Lawrence views the marriage of Romeo and Juliet as means to some greater good of civil peace, and in doing this, he treats Romeo and Juliet as objects he can manipulate to an end.

- Although he might have good intentions for others, Friar Lawrence tries to control matters, and his ego gets in the way. The speaker in "Insha'Allah" understands they are not in control of events in Nature or in human affairs.

All of these texts—Shakespeare's *Romeo and Juliet*, August Wilson's *Fences*, and Danusha Laméris's "Insha'Allah"—are separated by time, space, gender, culture, and geopolitics, and yet students can make wonderful connections between these texts! The conversations that began with these pairings led to compelling discussions around big human questions that occur throughout literature and throughout life—and affect us all.

# Sources

Douglass, Frederick. *Narrative of the Life of Frederick Douglass: An American Slave.* New York: Penguin Books, 1968. Print. https://docsouth.unc.edu/neh/douglass/douglass.html.

Horton, George M. (1845). *The Poetical Works of George M. Horton, the colored bard of North-Carolina: to which is prefixed The life of the author, written by himself.* Hillsborough, North Carolina.

Wilson, August. *Fences.* New York: Penguin Books, 1986.

Danusha Laméris, "Insha'Allah," from *The Moons of August.* Copyright © 2014 by Danusha Laméris. Reprinted with the permission of The Permissions Company, LLC on behalf of Autumn House Press, www.autumnhouse.org.

# PART FOUR

# Five More Resources for You

- *Folger Teaching*—folger.edu/teach—The Folger's online universe for teachers! Search lesson plans, podcasts, videos, and other classroom resources. Connect with like-minded colleagues and experts. Access on-demand teacher workshops and participate in a range of live professional development opportunities from hour-long sessions to longer courses, all offering CEU credit. Complete access to *Folger Teaching* is one of many benefits of joining the Folger as a Teacher Member.

- *Folger Shakespeare* online—folger.edu/shakespeares-works—Shakespeare's complete works free and online, and all downloadable in various formats that are particularly useful for teachers and students. The Folger texts are the most up-to-date available online; behind the scenes, they have been encoded to make the plays easy to read, search, and index. Also available here are audio clips of selected lines performed.

- *Folger Shakespeare* in print—Shakespeare's plays and sonnets in single-volume paperbacks and ebooks. The texts are identical to those of *Folger Shakespeare* online; the books, however, are all in the format featuring the text on the right-hand page with glosses and definitions on the left. Used in many, many classrooms, the *Folger Shakespeare* in print is published by Simon & Schuster and available from booksellers everywhere.

- *The Folger Shakespeare Library*—folger.edu—The online home of the wide world of the Folger Shakespeare Library, offering all kinds of experiences and resources from the world's largest Shakespeare collection. We're waiting for you, your class, and your family! Explore the Folger collection, enjoy the magic of music and poetry, participate in a workshop, see a play! We're a great opportunity for lively and satisfying engagement with the arts and humanities.

- *Shakespeare Documented*—shakespearedocumented.folger.edu—A singular site that brings together digitized versions of hundreds of the known primary source documents pertaining to Shakespeare—the playwright, actor, and stakeholder; the poet; and the man engaged in family and legal matters. A destination for curious students! Convened by the Folger, this collection is a collaboration among the Folger and Shakespeare Birthplace Trust, the National Archives of Great Britain, the Bodleian Library at Oxford, and the British Library.

# ACKNOWLEDGMENTS

Seven or eight years ago, Mark Miazga, an exceptional high school teacher from Baltimore—and a Folger teacher—said, "We should make a series of books where we lay out for teachers key specifics about the play, and then how to teach the whole play using the Folger Method."

Ignition.

An important idea with a huge scope: five books, each focused on a single play—*Hamlet*, *Macbeth*, *Romeo and Juliet*, *Othello*, and *A Midsummer Night's Dream*. Each one a pretty revolutionary dive into basic info, scholarship, and the how of teaching each of the plays to *all* students. *Every* student. This demanded assembling an extraordinarily strong array of knowledge, expertise, and experience and moving it into action.

It is finally time to name and celebrate this crowd of people who, with generosity of all kinds, had a hand in creating the book you are reading right now:

Folger director Michael Witmore, a deep believer in the importance of learning, teaching, and the power of the Folger to support both for all and at all levels, has been a fan and a wise advisor from the start.

The generosity of the Carol and Gene Ludwig Family Foundation—and in particular our fairy godmother, Carol Ludwig—has fueled every part of the creation of this series, including making certain that every English teacher in Washington, DC, has their own set of books *gratis*. I express the gratitude of the Folger as well as that of teachers in DC and beyond.

None of these volumes would exist without Folger Education's extraordinary Katie Dvorak, who, from the first minute to the last, herded not cats but our many authors, contracts, editorial conferences, publisher meetings, the general editor, and a series of deadlines that *never ever* stopped changing. Much of this was accomplished as Covid covered all lives, work, families, everything. Katie's persistence, along with her grace, humor, empathy, and patience, kept us moving and was the glue we never did not need.

We appreciate the support and guidance of our team at Simon & Schuster: Irene Kheradi, Johanna Li, and Amanda Mulholland.

All along, the overall project benefited from the wisdom and support of these key players: Skip Nicholson, Heather Lester, Michael LoMonico, Corinne Viglietta, Maryam Trowell, Shanta Bryant, Missy Springsteen-Haupt, and Jessica Frazier . . . and from the creative genius of Mya Gosling.

Major gratitude to colleagues across the Folger who contributed to building these books in terms of content and business support. Our thanks to Erin Blake, Caroline Duroselle-Melish, Beth Emelson, Abbey Fagan, Esther French, Eric Johnson, Adrienne

Jones, Ruth Taylor Kidd, Melanie Leung, Mimi Newcastle, Rebecca Niles, Emma Poltrack, Sara Schliep, Emily Wall, and Heather Wolfe.

We are in debt to the schoolteachers and scholars who generously shared their time and wisdom as we got started, helping us to map our path and put it in motion—all along the intersections where scholarship and teaching practice inform each other. Massive gratitude to Patricia Akhimie, Bernadette Andreas, Ashley Bessicks, David Sterling Brown, Patricia Cahill, Jocelyn Chadwick, Ambereen Dadabhoy, Eric DeBarros, Donna Denizé, Ruben Espinosa, Kyle Grady, Kim Hall, Caleen Sinnette Jennings, Stefanie Jochman, Heather Lester, Catherine Loomis, Ellen MacKay, Mark Miazga, Noémie Ndiaye, Gail Kern Paster, Amber Phelps, Katie Santos, Ian Smith, Christina Torres, and Jessica Cakrasenjaya Zeiss.

It's impossible to express our thanks here without a special shout-out to Ayanna Thompson, the scholarly powerhouse who has been nudging Folger Education for the last decade. Know that nudges from Ayanna are more like rockets . . . always carrying love and a challenge. We could not be more grateful for them, or for her.

With endless admiration, I give the close-to-the-last words and thanks to the working schoolteachers who authored major portions of these books. First here, we honor our colleague Donnaye Moore, teacher at Brookwood High School in Snellville, Georgia, who started on this project teaching and writing about *Othello* but succumbed to cancer far too soon. None of us have stopped missing her or trying to emulate her brilliant practicality.

I asked working teachers to take on this challenge because I know that no one knows the "how" of teaching better than those who do it in classrooms every day. The marvels I am about to name were teaching and living through all the challenges that Covid presented in their own lives *and* thinking about you and your students too, putting together (and testing and revising) these lessons for you who will use these books. Over a really loud old- fashioned PA system, I am shouting the names of Ashley Bessicks, Noelle Cammon, Donna Denizé, Roni DiGenno, Liz Dixon, David Fulco, Deborah Gascon, Stefanie Jochman, Mark Miazga, Amber Phelps, Vidula Plante, Christina Porter, and Jessica Cakrasenjaya Zeiss! You rock in every way possible. You honor the Folger—and teachers everywhere—with your wisdom, industry, and generosity.

Finally, I wrap up this project with humility, massive gratitude to all for all, and—perhaps amazingly in the complicated days in which we are publishing—HOPE. Hamza, Nailah, and Shazia O'Brien, Soraya Margaret Banta, and gazillions of children in all parts of the world deserve all we've got. Literature—in school, even!—can get us talking to, and learning from, one another in peace.  Let's get busy.

—Peggy O'Brien,
General Editor

# ABOUT THE AUTHORS

**Amber Phelps** teaches in both the International Baccalaureate (IB) English Literature HL and AP Literature programs at Baltimore City College (BCC) in Maryland. Amber is an alum of both Teach for America (Baltimore 2010) and the Folger Shakespeare Library's 2012 Teaching Shakespeare Institute. In 2018, Amber was the recipient of the Kennedy Leadership Award for Excellence in Teaching. In addition to her instructional work at BCC, she is Assistant Director of the Speech and Debate Program and advisor of the school newspaper, *The Collegian*. When Amber is not teaching, she is traveling with her partner, Sam, and playing in the dirt along with their dog, Houston.

**Dr. Christina Porter** is a 2006 alumna of the Folger's Teaching Shakespeare Institute. She began her career as an English teacher and literacy coach for Revere Public Schools in Revere, Massachusetts. Currently, she is Director of Humanities for her school district. She is also a faculty member at Salem State University. She resides in Salem, Massachusetts, with her two precocious daughters.

**Corinne Viglietta** teaches Upper School English at The Bryn Mawr School in Baltimore, Maryland. From 2014 to 2022, Corinne was associate director of education at the Folger Shakespeare Library, where she had the honor of exploring the wonders of language with thousands of amazing teachers, students, and visitors. Corinne played a key role in Folger's national teaching community and school partnerships. Corinne is a lifelong Folger educator, having first discovered the power of this approach with her multilingual students in Washington, DC, and France. She has degrees in English from the University of Notre Dame and the University of Maryland.

**Dr. Catherine Loomis** holds a PhD in Renaissance Literature from the University of Rochester, and an MA in Shakespeare and Performance from the Shakespeare Institute. She is the author of *William Shakespeare: A Documentary Volume* (Gale, 2002) and *The Death of Elizabeth I: Remembering and Reconstructing the Virgin Queen* (Palgrave, 2010), and, with Sid Ray, the editor of *Shaping Shakespeare for Performance: The Bear Stage* (Fairleigh Dickinson, 2016). She has taught at the University of New Orleans, the University of North Carolina at Greensboro, and the Rochester Institute of Technology.

**Dr. Deborah Gascon** is a National Board–certified teacher of English and Journalism in Columbia, South Carolina. She also taught English in Romania on a Fulbright Teacher Exchange. Deborah is a 2012 Teaching Shakespeare Institute alum and a Folger Summer Academy mentor teacher. Her doctorate in Curriculum and Instruction is from the University of South Carolina; her dissertation is about the teaching of Shakespeare to increase student comprehension, empathy, and awareness of gender and race issues. When she isn't teaching, she loves to attend her weekly tap dance class, play tennis, travel to new places, and dig in the dirt.

Of Haitian American descent, **Donna Denizé** holds a BA from Stonehill College and an MA in Renaissance Drama from Howard University. She has contributed to scholarly books and journals, and she is the author of a chapbook, *The Lover's Voice* (1997), and a book, *Broken Like Job* (2005). She currently chairs the English Department at St. Albans School for boys, where she teaches Freshman English; a junior/senior elective in Shakespeare; and Crossroads in American Identity, a course she designed years ago and which affords her the opportunity to do what she most enjoys—exploring not only the cultural and intertextual crossroads of literary works but also their points of human unity.

**Dr. Ellen MacKay** is Associate Professor of English and Chair of Theatre and Performance Studies (TAPS) at the University of Chicago, where she teaches courses on Shakespeare, Renaissance Drama, Performance Historiography, and Theatre Theory. She has served as Head Scholar at the Teaching Shakespeare Institute since 2014. She has published articles in *Theatre Survey*, *Shakespeare Survey*, *Shakespeare Yearbook*, and *Theatre History Studies*, and in numerous edited volumes and disciplinary guides, including the forthcoming *Routledge Companion to Shakespeare and Religion*.

**Dr. Jocelyn A. Chadwick** is a lifelong English teacher and international scholar. She was a full-time professor at Harvard Graduate School of Education and now occasionally lectures and conducts seminars there. In addition to teaching and writing, Chadwick also consults and works with teachers and with elementary, middle, and high school students around the country. Chadwick has worked with PBS, BBC Radio, and NBC News Learn and is a past president of the National Council of Teachers of English. She has written many articles and books, including *The Jim Dilemma: Reading Race in Adventures of Huckleberry Finn* and *Teaching Literature in the Context of Literacy Instruction*. Chadwick is currently working on her next book, *Writing for Life: Using Literature to Teach Writing*.

**Michael LoMonico** has taught Shakespeare courses and workshops for teachers and students in 40 states as well as in Canada, England, and the Bahamas. He was an assistant to the editor for the curriculum section of all three volumes of the Folger's Shakespeare Set Free series. Until 2019, he was the Senior Consultant on National Education for the Folger. He is the author of *The Shakespeare Book of Lists*, *Shakespeare 101*, and a novel, *That Shakespeare Kid*. He was the co-founder and editor of *Shakespeare*, a magazine published by Cambridge University Press and Georgetown University.

**Dr. Michael Witmore** is the seventh director of the Folger Shakespeare Library, the world's largest Shakespeare collection and the ultimate resource for exploring Shakespeare and his world. He was appointed to this position in July 2011; prior to leading the Folger, he was Professor of English at the University of Wisconsin–Madison and at Carnegie Mellon University. Under his leadership and across a range of programs and policies, the Folger has begun the process of opening up to and connecting with greater and more diverse audiences nationally, internationally, and here at home in Washington, DC. He believes deeply in the importance of teachers; also under his leadership, the Library's work in service of schoolteachers continues to grow in breadth, depth, and accessibility.

**Mya Lixian Gosling** (she/her) is the artist and author of *Good Tickle Brain*, the world's foremost (and possibly only) stick-figure Shakespeare comic, which has been entertaining Shakespeare geeks around the world since 2013. Mya also draws *Keep Calm and Muslim On*, which she co-authors with Muslim American friends, and *Sketchy Beta*, an autobiographical comic documenting her misadventures as an amateur rock climber. In her so-called spare time, Mya likes to read books on random Plantagenets, play the ukulele badly, and pretend to be one of those outdoorsy people who is in touch with nature but actually isn't. You can find her work at goodticklebrain.com.

**Dr. Peggy O'Brien** founded the Folger Shakespeare Library's Education Department in 1981. She set the Library's mission for K–12 students and teachers then and began to put it in motion; among a range of other programs, she founded and directed the Library's intensive Teaching Shakespeare Institute, was instigator and general editor of the popular Shakespeare Set Free series, and expanded the Library's education work across the country. In 1994, she took a short break from the Folger—20 years—but returned to further expand the education work and to engage in the Folger's transformation under the leadership of director Michael Witmore. She is the instigator and general editor of the Folger Guides to Teaching Shakespeare series.

**Roni DiGenno** is a special education teacher at Calvin Coolidge Senior High School in Washington, DC. She earned her BA in Literature from Stockton University in Pomona, New Jersey, and her MA in English from Rutgers University in Camden, New Jersey. Her background in English and passion for special education led her to the educational mission of the Folger Shakespeare Library, participating in the Teaching Shakespeare Institute in 2016. She currently lives in Maryland with her husband, daughter, and two dogs.